# Fly Fishing
## the
# Mid-Atlantic

## A No Nonsense Guide to Top Waters

**Beau Beasley**

Illustrations by Alan Folger
Foreword by King Montgomery

*The author trying his luck on Pennsylvania's famed Penns Creek. Photo by Eric Stroup.*

NO NONSENSE

Tucson, Arizona

**Fly Fishing the Mid-Atlantic**
A No Nonsense Guide to Top Waters

ISBN-10  1-892469-24-3
ISBN-13  978-1-892469-24-3
© 2011 Beau Beasley

Published by:
No Nonsense Fly Fishing Guidebooks
P.O. Box 91858
Tucson, AZ 85752-1858
(520) 547-2462
www.nononsenseguides.com

Printed in China

Editor: Howard Fisher
Illustrations: Alan Folger,
    www.clearwatermemories.com
Maps, Knot Illustrations, and Fly Photos:
    Pete Chadwell, Dynamic Arts
Photos: by Beau Beasley, except where noted.
Design and Production: Doug Goewey
Front Cover: Rich Hiegel fishes a native trout
    pool in Virginia's Shenandoah National
    Park. Photo by Beau Beasley.
Back Cover:
    Top: An angler fishes for shad on Virginia's
        Rappahannock River. Photo by Mark
        Sargent Photography.
    Middle: Guide Karl Weixlmann stalking
        steelhead on Pennsylvania's Elk Creek.
        Photo by Jack Hanrahan.
    Bottom: The author fishes Maryland's
        Beaver Creek. Photo by Larry Coburn.

# The No Nonsense Creed

The best way to go fly fishing is to find out a little something about a water, and then just go there. Experimentation, trial and error, wrong turns, surprises, self-reliance, and new discoveries, even in familiar waters, are what make the memories. The next best way is to learn enough from a local to save you from going too far wrong. You still find the water on your own, and it still feels as if you were the first to do so.

This is the idea for our unique No Nonsense fly-fishing series. Our books reveal little hush-hush information, yet they give all you need to find what will become your own secret places.

Painstakingly pared down, our writing is elegantly simple. Each title offers a local fly-fishing expert's candid tour of his or her favorite fly-fishing waters. Nothing is oversold or out of proportion. Everything is authentic, especially the discoveries and experiences you enjoy after using our books. In his outstanding book *Jerusalem Creek,* Ted Leeson echoes our idea: "Discovering a new trout stream is a wonderful thing, and even if its whereabouts are common knowledge, to come upon the place yourself for the first time is nonetheless true discovery."

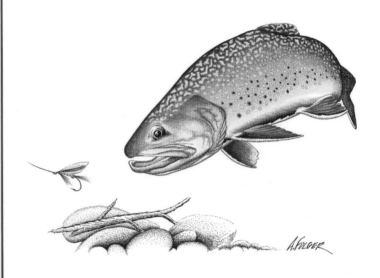

# Where No Nonsense Guides Come From

No Nonsense Guidebooks give you a quick, clear understanding of the essential information needed to fly fish a region's most outstanding waters. The authors are highly experienced and qualified local fly fishers. Maps are tidy versions of the author's sketches. These guides are produced by the fly fishers, their friends, and spouses of fly fishers, at No Nonsense Fly Fishing Guidebooks.

All who produce No Nonsense guides believe in providing top-quality products at a reasonable price. We also believe all information should be verified. We never hesitate to go out, fly rod in hand, to verify the facts and figures that appear in the pages of these guides. The staff is committed to this research. It's hard work, but we're glad to do it for you.

# Table of Contents

Photo by King Montgomery

Photo by Jon Luke.

Photo courtesy Mike Smith.

*Photo courtesy Alan Folger.*

5

*Beau Beasley with a hefty rainbow trout caught on Beaver Creek, Maryland. Photo by Larry Coburn.*

## About the Author

Beau Beasley is a frequent contributor to the *Mid-Atlantic Fly Fishing Guide,* a contributing editor for *Fly Fish America,* and the Mid-Atlantic states field editor for *Eastern Fly Fishing.* His work has appeared in *Fly Fisherman, American Angler, Fly Tyer, Virginia Wildlife, Flyfisher, Blue Ridge Outdoors,* and *Fly Rod & Reel.*

In 2005 Beau won the Talbot Denmead Award for conservation, sponsored by Bass Pro Shops, for his work on the Chesapeake Bay. His first book, *Fly Fishing Virginia: A No Nonsense Guide to Top Waters,* won the Mason-Dixon Outdoor Writers Book Award as well as the prestigious Excellence in Craft Award in 2009.

Beau is a husband and father of two, the director of the Virginia Fly Fishing Festival, a member of Gainesville Presbyterian Church, and a veteran firefighter of 26 years in Fairfax County, Virginia. He currently serves as a captain on Engine Company 427 in West Springfield.

*When not in his studio, artist Alan Folger enjoys fishing in the mountains of North Carolina. Photo courtesy Alan Folger.*

# About the Illustrator

When not chasing trout through the mountains of North Carolina, angling artist and illustrator Alan Folger is usually found in his studio, Clearwater Memories, working on his next big catch. Born to an avid family of fly fishers, Folger spent many days as a toddler playing on a blanket streamside or along the banks of a river as his parents fished.

With time, Folger's fishing travels have taken him to the Ozarks, to the Rockies, and to his favorite haunts in the beautiful Blue Ridge Mountains. Folger enjoys creating his piscatorial artistry for those who share his passion for clear waters, rising trout, and God's creation. You can see more of Folger's work on the Web at www.clearwatermemories.com.

Alan Folger lives with his wife, Shirley, in Hendersonville, North Carolina.

# Dedication

This book is dedicated to the memory of hazardous materials technician John Loss, a fireman's fireman who served with honor on Fairfax County's Rescue 1 in McLean, Virginia. John's love of the fire service and his commitment to duty were exceeded only by his love for his coworkers and especially for his family. John was an angler and an avid reader, and it was my privilege to serve with him for a number of years at Fire Station 1, where I often saw him reading. One morning while standing in front of the station, he told me that he thought I'd be an author before I left the department—an encouragement that I'll never forget.

I remember John most of all for three things: He was neither impressed nor intimidated by rank, he had a great sense of humor, and he continually encouraged others. John never failed to respectfully confront an officer he believed to be wrong—and he never stopped ribbing me either, even after I made captain. He also tirelessly encouraged me in my writing, which always meant a lot to me. I only hope that I've created a book that John would have enjoyed reading.

# Acknowledgments

This book would not have been possible without the strong support of several fly-shop owners and guides who took time out of their busy lives to help me on the water and whose advice and constructive criticism were invaluable. I'm also grateful for the beautiful artwork rendered by Alan Folger, as talented an artist as any I know. He was a joy and a pleasure to work with. I also wish to extend my thanks to my publisher, Howard

Fisher, and his colleague Anthony Taylor, who kept me excited about the project on days when I was dragging. I'd be remiss in not thanking my wife, Leila, who edits everything I write, acts as a check to my pride, and generally makes my life worth living. Finally, I thank the God who made this world and filled it with such breathtaking beauty and magnificent creatures. By His grace I can see His hand behind every bend in the river.

# Foreword

## By King Montgomery

*King Montgomery is the past president of the Mason-Dixon Outdoor Writers Association and an avid fly angler. Photo courtesy King Montgomery.*

The finest fly-fishing guidebook I've ever seen is Beau Beasley's *Fly Fishing Virginia: A No Nonsense Guide to Top Waters.* I believe this new work will be even better. That's saying a lot since the Virginia book recently was awarded top honors at a Mason-Dixon Outdoor Writers Association (M-DOWA) Awards Banquet. And Beau took the highest prize for excellence-in-craft for his effort.

The Eastern Seaboard states from New Jersey to North Carolina (including West Virginia) have some of the finest fly-fishing waters in the country. The bountiful coastal waters and estuaries are legend for a variety of species including false albacore, redfish, sea trouts, bluefish, striped bass, and many more tippet busters.

Tidal rivers see runs of anadromous fishes such as hickory and American shad, white and yellow perch, and striped bass that seasonally augment endemic species such as largemouth and smallmouth bass, various sunfishes, and others. Interior rivers, reservoirs, and lakes boast several kinds of black bass and sunfishes, and other game fishes willing to rise to a popper or attack a well-presented streamer.

Colder waters of some rivers and mountain streams, both limestone and freestone, are home to the trouts: native Eastern brook trout, and introduced rainbow and brown trout. Yes, trout do live in beautiful places, and our Mid-Atlantic trout haunts often are stunning in their natural splendor.

I don't believe there is another geographic region on the continent that is as diverse in its fisheries as the Mid-Atlantic. We can fish the many waters with everything from a 1-weight to a 15-weight and every size in between. Bluegill, bluefish, or blue marlin—you name it and it's nearby.

Beau Beasley knows these waters and has fished every destination in this fine book. As a fishing-tackle representative for a number of years, Beau traveled throughout the region, always with fishing gear at the ready. In this guide to some of the area's top waters, he shares his experience with his fellow fly anglers. Where to go, how to get there, what tackle and flies to use, and so on—it's all here replete with excellent maps, guide and outfitter listings, and more.

A Beau Beasley guide is special because he doesn't just give information, he shares it, emotionally at times, and often with good humor. You see, Beau truly believes that fly fishing is not just about fish, it's about people as well. I suspect this guidebook will win the best book award for Beau again from M-DOWA. And, like before, he will have earned his honor.

King Montgomery
Outdoor Writer & Photographer
Mid-Atlantic Regional Editor,
*Fly Fish America* magazine

# Fly Fishing the Mid-Atlantic

When I decided to write a book about the best waters of the Mid-Atlantic, I little realized what a daunting task I'd set for myself. How exactly does one choose the top waters in a region that is so blessed? Who is to say whether, for example, a Keystone State limestoner trumps a wild brook-trout water in Shenandoah National Park? Is the blistering run of a false albacore more exhilarating than that of a Lake Erie steelhead? Does a massive Sandy Hook striper inhaling your popper beat the dogged determination of a Greenbrier River smallie? I enjoyed landing my first American shad in the Brandywine River just as much as I did chasing cutthroat trout on the North Branch of the Potomac. How does one choose?

When all is said and done, my river choices may not—most probably, *will* not—be yours. Nevertheless I've endeavored to present the best waters of the Mid-Atlantic. If I didn't mention your favorite water, then you have a few choices to make: You can write your own book that includes your top pick, you can invite me to join you in your neck of the woods for a little on-the-water research, or you can keep that honey hole of yours a secret that only you and your kids and closest friends enjoy. I'll respect your decision no matter which you choose.

## Maps

If you purchased this book, chances are you're looking for a place to fish. I've tried to make these maps as reliable as possible, but mistakes do happen. So if a callout on a river doesn't seem exactly right, look around—it should be close by. This book is not intended to be the last word in maps: Do yourself a favor and pick up a DeLorme Gazetteer and a state road map. County and local maps generally provide excellent details that state maps simply cannot.

Maps have come a long, long way thanks in large part to advances in technology. North Carolina mapmaker and guide Chris Gibbs (www.csgibbs.com), for instance, has a whole host of excellent maps at his disposal covering dozens of waters. Prefer steelhead? Then I unreservedly refer you to Ron Guttu (www.sgcmaps.com), who has detailed maps of most of the better steelhead waters in Pennsylvania and Ohio. Both of these gentlemen assisted me with my own mapmaking efforts. The map of the Brandywine River was especially tough downtown, and I appreciate the assistance of Chris Madden with the city of Wilmington. As always, Pete Chadwell has done a magnificent job of pulling together all my source information to make the best possible maps for this book.

*A view of historic Harpers Ferry, West Virginia, where the Shenandoah River (left) and the Potomac River (right) meet. Photo by Steve Probasco.*

*The author enjoys fly fishing for warmwater fish as often as he can. Photo by King Montgomery.*

On the road, a good GPS is invaluable. Remember, though, that in many cases your GPS simply can't get you to some very desirable waters—a lesson I learned the hard way doing field work in the mountains of North Carolina and West Virginia. Yes, GPS technology is fantastic, but you'll still need a good old-fashioned map to get to more remote streams. Your local fly shop can often suggest little-known access roads to local waters as well as the best places to park.

## Flies

The fly patterns I've mentioned are just a sampling of the flies you can fish successfully in the Mid-Atlantic. Some of the patterns I've featured are made by well-known companies such as Umpqua Feather Merchants, Orvis, and Montana Fly Company. But wherever possible, I've tried to shine a spotlight on lesser-known but wildly successful local patterns that might be new to you. Those local and regional patterns may break out nationally. For

*Lady fly anglers such as Lisa Wissmath compose a growing segment of the fly-fishing community. She often fishes the trout waters of the Shenandoah National Park. Photo by Dusty Wissmath.*

example, Solitude Flies was inking a contract to produce the regionally famous Walt's Poppers while this book was being written. Often, however, you'll come across absolute gems that never reach a broader market than your local fly shop—or even your fishing buddy's well-loved vise. Give them a try.

The discussion of each river includes a sidebar that highlights patterns that reflect a certain local hatch or a locally tied fly that has performed well for me. Your experience may be different. If you don't see your favorite local pattern listed, just assume that I probably haven't fished it successfully—yet. Drop me a line and let me know what works for you in your neck of the woods. I'm always looking for a great fly.

## Game Laws

While I've tried to identify delayed-harvest waters or fly-fishing-only waters or waters that a fly angler might be especially interested in, I've steered clear of specific harvesting regulations for two reasons: First, game laws

*Bluegill can be great sport on a fly rod and usually fall hard for poppers. Photo by Beau Beasley.*

*An angler takes a break streamside in New Jersey's Raritan River to pick out just the right fly. Photo by Beau Beasley.*

change every year, and I'd hate to think that one of my readers might accidentally harvest fish illegally because I've passed along dated information. Second, I strongly encourage catch-and-release fishing. While there is no shame in taking a few fish home from time to time, just because you can keep a fish doesn't necessarily mean that you *should*. As my friend Boyd Pfeiffer once told me, "If you want a bunch of fish to eat, go fishing at Safeway or Giant." Please consult the current game laws before going home with fish.

## Pass It On

In writing this book, many guides shared with me the secrets of their waters. Many shop owners pointed out to me the best patterns to use and the easiest ways to reach local rivers. The combined wisdom of these angling

*Trout should be held facing upstream while recovering. They'll swim off on their own when they're ready. Photo by Dusty Wissmath.*

veterans is breathtaking—and their generosity in sharing the fruits of their labors of love is, in my experience, unmatched. After all, their insights can mean the difference between a great day of fishing and a long and disappointing day of wading and casting. Why, one wonders, do they give this kind of information away for free?

They share what they've learned because they love the quiet sport. Their passion for fly fishing compels them to take as many willing acolytes under their wings as they can. Will you do the same? Nearly all of those who excel in our sport have had a special someone come alongside and mentor them. No matter how new you are to fly fishing, you know more about it than *someone* does. Will you invite that someone to fish with you one day? Someone brought you into the sport. Will you pass it on?

My father took me fishing, and those days on the water with him are among the most precious memories of my childhood. Bob Guess, the namesake of the now-legendary Mr. Bob's Lucky Day Lures popping bugs, taught me how to fly fish. My good friend and angling mentor Steve Vlasak of Pennsylvania once mailed me a hip-length fishing vest. When I called to thank him for it, he told me that it wasn't for fishing—rather, it was to keep my notebook, camera, and other writing paraphernalia in while doing research streamside. Steve died of cancer not long after he gave me the vest, and I wear it now whenever I write. I wore it while writing most of this book, and I'm wearing it right now as I write these words. Steve, Mr. Bob, my daddy: You needn't be Lefty Kreh to instill a love for the outdoors in someone you care about. Start by taking your kids out to the local farm pond—those memories

*Values and passions are often caught as much as taught. Here the author's son comes to visit the station in his own uniform. Note the Dalmatian-colored boots. Photo by Beau Beasley.*

*Upper Penns Creek can be quite small near the head-waters, but it still holds large trout. Photo by King Montgomery.*

will last a lifetime. Values are caught, not taught, and nothing beats spending time with your kids.

### Now It's Your Turn

I began writing this book in Cabin #3 at Harman's North Fork Cottages in Cabins, West Virginia—a perfect setting, following a great day on the water. I had no idea how many thousands of miles I would have to travel—or how

many gallons of coffee I'd have to drink—to finish the book. (In truth, it's always better not to know or one might never begin.) Now I'm finished, and I might just sit back here for a while with Steve's vest on and put my feet up, sip a glass of wine, or take my kids fishing—not necessarily in that order.

I got lost all over the Mid-Atlantic so you don't have to. Please enjoy the book.

*Guide Patrick Fulkrod floats his pattern under a tree limb hoping to catch wary trout in the Virginia section of the South Holston. Photo by Beau Beasley.*

# Flies to Use in the Mid-Atlantic—Drys & Terrestrials

Adams Parachute

Adult Midge

Black Foam Flying Ant

Blue-Winged Olive Comparadun

Blue-Winged Olive

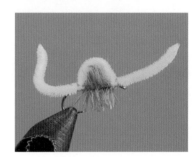

Coburn's Inch Worm

Dave's Cricket

Dave's Hopper

Dusty's Deviant

Elk Hair Caddis

Braided Butt Damsel

Gelso's Little Black Stonefly

Green Weenie

Griffith's Gnat

Hickey's Condor

Light Cahill

Light Hendrickson

March Brown

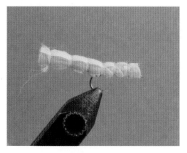

Mann's Inchworm

Mike's Magic Beetle

Murray's Mr. Rapidan

Pale Morning Dun

Quill Gordon

Royal Wulff

Steeves's Attract Ant

Steeves's Bark Beetle

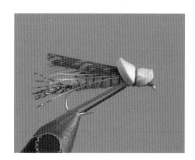

Steeves's Crystal Butt Hopper

Steeves's Disco Beetle

Stimulator

Yellow Sally

15

# Nymphs

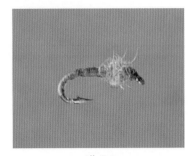

Al's Rat

Anderson's Bird of Prey

CDC Emerger

Copper John

Harold's Indestructible

JC's Electric Caddis

McAuliffe's Horror Business

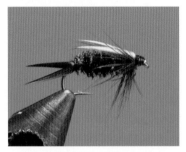

Prince Nymph

Rainbow Warrior

Shuler's Carolina Midge

Soft Hackle Pheasant Tail

Stroup's Sulphur Nymph

WD-40

Zebra Midge

Zug Bug, Beadhead

# Streamers and Wet Flies

Brandywine Ugly Bug

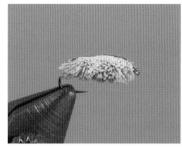

Coburn's Cress Bug

Egg-Sucking Leech

George's Killer

Howell's Big Nasty

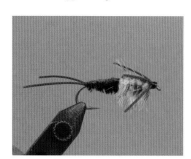

Kevin's RL Stonefly

Mike's Simple Shrimp

Muddler Minnow

Pink Lady

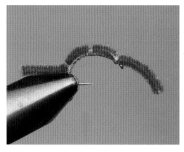

San Juan Worm

Scott's Golden Retriever

Scud

Walt's Worm

Woolly Bugger

Zonker, Olive

# Warmwater Flies

Chocklett's Disc Slider

Chocklett's Gummy Minnow

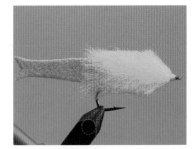

CK Baitfish, Chartreuse

Clouser Minnow

Forage Fly

Murray's Lead Eye Hellgrammite

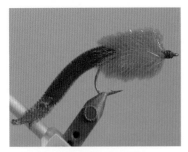

Cramer's Jail Bait Minnow

Kraft's Claw-Dad

Kreelex

Skilton's Hellgrammite

Smith's Creature

Walt's Frog Slider

Walt's Popper

Whitlock's Crayfish

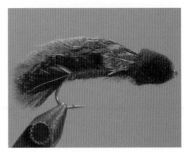

Woolhead Sculpin

# Saltwater and Striper Flies

Blados's Crease Fly

Bob's Banger

Bruce's Bay Anchovy

Bruce's Crystal Shrimp

Cowen's Baitfish

Dubiel's Finesse Fly

Dubiel's Red-Ducer, Chartreuse

Dubiel's Lil'Haden

Lefty's Deceiver

Lefty's Half & Half

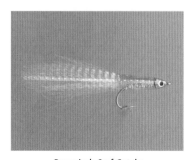
Popovics's Surf Candy

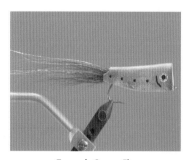
Tommy's Crease Fly

Tommy's Torpedo

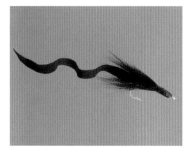
Tommy's Eel

Walt's Saltwater Popper, Chartreuse

# Top Mid-Atlantic Fly-Fishing Waters

Photo by Mark Sargent Photography.

Photo courtesy Dan Pribanic.

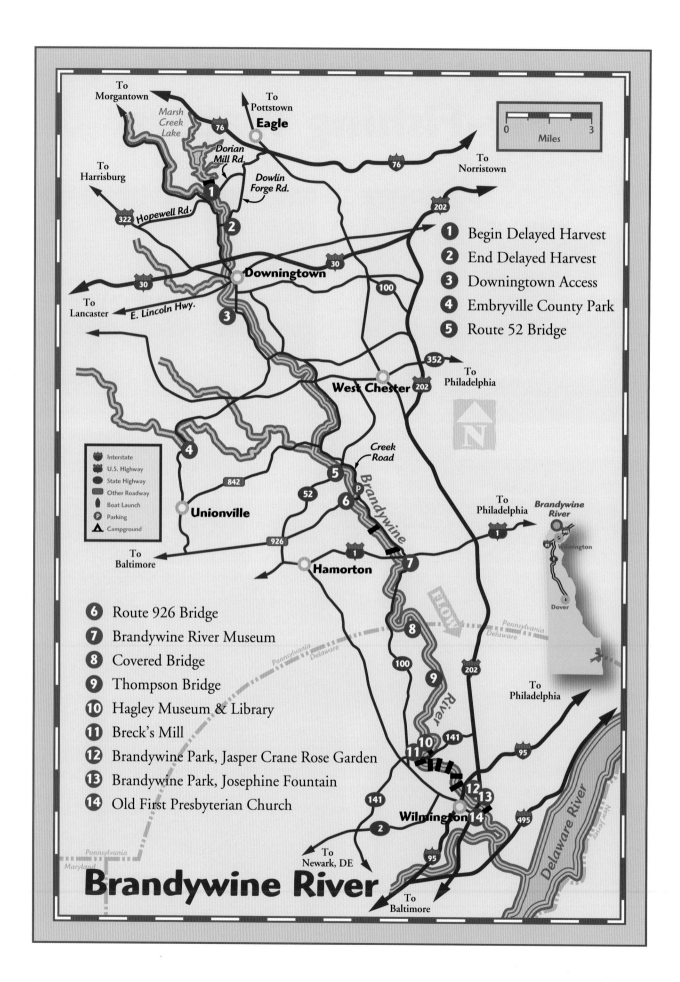

To Morgantown
To Pottstown
Eagle
Marsh Creek Lake
76
Dorian Mill Rd.
To Harrisburg
Dowlin Forge Rd.
322 Hopewell Rd.
**1**
**2**
76
To Norristown
202

**1** Begin Delayed Harvest
**2** End Delayed Harvest
**3** Downingtown Access
**4** Embryville County Park
**5** Route 52 Bridge

Downingtown
30
100
30
To Lancaster
E. Lincoln Hwy.
**3**

352
West Chester
202
To Philadelphia

N

Creek Road

**4**
842
**5**
Brandywine
**52**
**6**
P
Unionville

To Philadelphia
1
Brandywine River
Wilmington

926
1
To Baltimore
Hamorton
**7**

FLOW

**8**
Pennsylvania
Delaware

Dover

**6** Route 926 Bridge
**7** Brandywine River Museum
**8** Covered Bridge
**9** Thompson Bridge
**10** Hagley Museum & Library
**11** Breck's Mill
**12** Brandywine Park, Jasper Crane Rose Garden
**13** Brandywine Park, Josephine Fountain
**14** Old First Presbyterian Church

100
**9**
202
River
**141**
**10**
95
**11**
To Philadelphia

141
**12**
**13**
Wilmington **14**
495
Delaware River

2

Interstate
U.S. Highway
State Highway
Other Roadway
Boat Launch
P Parking
Campground

Pennsylvania
Delaware

Pennsylvania
Maryland

To Newark, DE
95
To Baltimore

# Brandywine River

# Brandywine River

### Types of Fish
Smallmouth bass are the primary target here, although you can also catch largemouth bass, fallfish, schoolie stripers as well as hickory and American shad.

### Known Hatches
There are a variety of mayfly hatches as well as a *Hexagenia* and a damselfly hatch. Crayfish are an important food source here so patterns that mimic this profile will work also.

### Equipment to Use
*Rods:* 5- to 8-weight, 7 to 9 feet in length.
*Spey rods:* 5- to 8-weight, 11 to 13½ feet.
*Reels:* Standard trout reel.
*Lines:* Weight-forward floating, matched to rod.
*Leaders:* 0X-4X leaders, 7½ to 9 feet in length.
*Wading:* Chest waders are useful here as well as a wading staff. Once it warms up you can wet wade.

### Flies to Use
*For Bass:* Brandywine Rubber Leg, sizes 4-6; Chocklett's Gummie Minnow, 2-6; Clouser Minnow, 1/0-6; Howell's Big Nasty, 6-10; Muddler Minnow, 6-10; Scott's Golden Retriever, 6-10; Wooly Bugger, 4-10; Walt's Popper, 4-10; Woolhead Sculpin, 4-6.

*For Shad:* Simmons's Shad Fly, sizes 6-10; Tommy's Torpedo, 6-10.

*Continued*

Delaware's Brandywine River may be one of the more underappreciated fisheries on the East Coast. The Brandywine begins in Pennsylvania, passes through the bucolic Delaware countryside, and visits busy Wilmington before picking up significant speed and making a mad dash to the Delaware River and, finally, the Chesapeake Bay. What many of the good people of Wilmington—and many Mid-Atlantic fly anglers—don't know is that fishing opportunities abound right in Wilmington's backyard.

I am forever indebted to Terry Peach for introducing me to this great metropolitan fishery. I met Terry at A Marblehead Flyfisher, his well-stocked fly shop just off Kennett Pike in Delaware, and 15 minutes later we were on the banks of the Brandywine. Much to my surprise we went fishing in downtown Wilmington. "You know, there are still a few American shad in the river," Terry said as we got out of his car. "Perhaps we'll get lucky." Sure enough, within minutes we'd located the shad, which were headed upstream, and 30 minutes after that Terry had me hooked up to my first-ever American shad. Rather than blind-casting, Terry knew just how to drift the right patterns to these fish—and that made all the difference. His enthusiasm for the Brandywine fishery is infectious, and as I landed my first American, it was hard to tell who was prouder. Shortly afterward, Terry began catching shad

*Terry Peach, owner of A Marblehead Fly Fisher in Wilmington, Delaware, often guides on the Brandywine River. Photo by Jim Graham Photography.*

*The lack of canopy cover allows room for plenty of long casts on the Brandywine. Photo by Jim Graham Photography.*

Brandywine Ugly Bug

on his Spey rod, which is the perfect tool for casting near the dams.

Anglers fishing in the downtown section of the Brandywine will do so by fishing below or slightly above some of the low-water dams that are strung along the river. Dam #1 is located just off West Street, adjacent to Old First Presbyterian Church (circa 1740). Several old locks still run alongside the river and support Wilmington's water supply. Another good location downtown is opposite the Jasper Crane Rose Gardens below Dam #2. This spot is popular with tourists because of the lovely rose garden. Take a few minutes to enjoy the gorgeous view while you stretch your legs before reentering the river. Breck's Mill, located downriver, also has a small dam and is a great location to throw poppers at dusk or dredge a few streamers. This old mill offers the admirer a chance to step back in time: You can still see where the river had once been redirected to support the millworks. You should also consider visiting the Hagley Museum just up the road from Breck's Mill if the fishing is slow.

If you do fish the Brandywine in Wilmington, remember that you're not in Kansas anymore: Park your car in a well-lighted spot and lock up, or take your valuables with you.

If you venture still farther upstream on the Brandywine, you'll watch the urban landscape give way to meandering rural Pennsylvania. Gone are the sights and sounds of the city and large concrete structures. In their place you'll find rolling hills and barns and farms and even the occasional cow. Ramsey's Road provides easy access to the river and several pullouts are available.

The upper section of the river is much easier to wade, as the river widens and the current slows. This is the place to stalk large smallies and the occasional carp. You can fish many warmwater patterns here, but my choice is the Brandywine Ugly Bug. The ever-modest Terry Peach created this pattern, and he's quick to point out that it's little more than a variation of numerous other patterns—which is why he refuses to put his name on it. "All I know is that it works like crazy," insists Terry. "And I don't think the fish care much about the name."

*Smallmouth bass are often a target of fly anglers on the lower Brandywine, while excellent trout water exists in the upper portion of the river in Pennsylvania. Photo by Jim Graham Photography.*

*Fly anglers can land American shad near the dams in downtown Wilmington, Delaware. Photo by Stewart Maloney.*

## When to Fish
Open all year.

## Season & Limits
For a complete listing of rules and regulations for Delaware go to www.dnrec.delaware.gov, and for Pennsylvania go to www.fish.state.pa.us.

## Nearby Fly Fishing
Anglers fishing here might consider a trip to the Delaware River or White Clay Creek. Though the Brandywine River terminates near Wilmington, Delaware, the upper section of the river in Pennsylvania goes on for quite a while and is well worth exploring.

## Accommodations & Family Activities
The city of Wilmington can provide you with all the hotels and types of restaurants you'd ever want. One activity that some families might like is a visit to Winterthur, Henry Francis du Pont's 18th-century-style estate built in the early 20th century.

## Fly Shops & Guides
A Marblehead Flyfisher
Wilmington, Delaware
www.amarbleheadflyfisher.com
(302) 654-6515

The Evening Rise
Lancaster, Pennsylvania
www.theeveningrise.com
(717) 509-3636

Orvis
Downingtown, Pennsylvania
www.orvis.com/downingtown
(610) 873-8400

Orvis
Plymouth Meeting, Pennsylvania
www.orvis.com/plymouthmeeting
(610) 825-1010

Sporting Gentleman
Media, Pennsylvania
www.sportinggentleman.com
(610) 565- 6140

TCO Fly Shop
Bryn Mawr, Pennsylvania
www.tcoflyfishing.com
(610) 527-3388

White Clay Outfitters
Newark, Delaware
www.flyfishingdelaware.com
(302) 369-9730

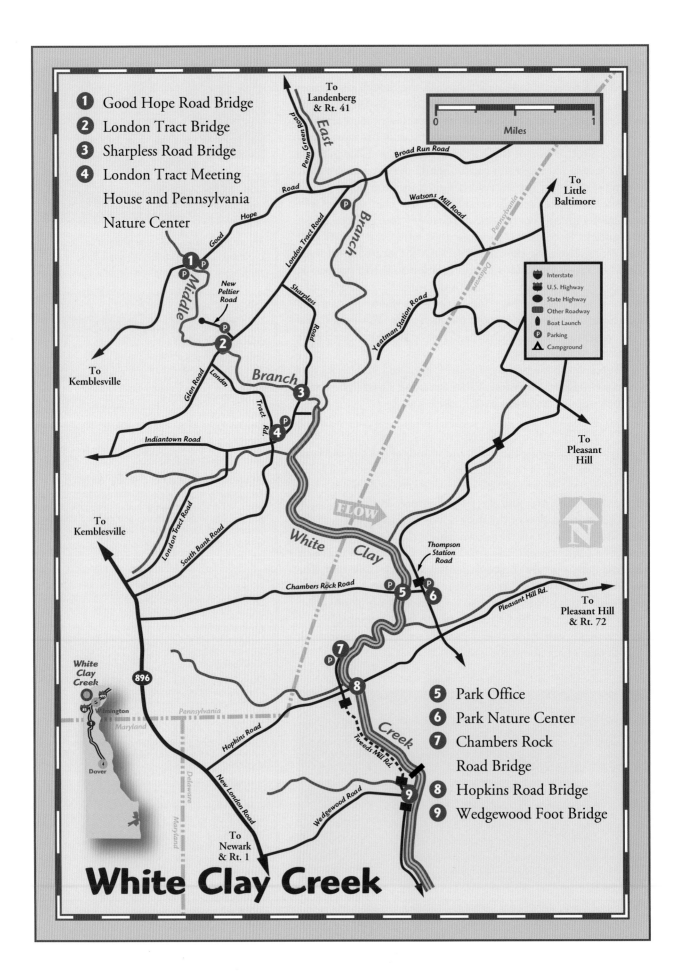

1 Good Hope Road Bridge
2 London Tract Bridge
3 Sharpless Road Bridge
4 London Tract Meeting House and Pennsylvania Nature Center

5 Park Office
6 Park Nature Center
7 Chambers Rock Road Bridge
8 Hopkins Road Bridge
9 Wedgewood Foot Bridge

To Landenberg & Rt. 41
To Little Baltimore
Broad Run Road
Watsons Mill Road
Penn Green Road
East
Branch
Good Hope Road
London Tract Road
Sharpless Road
New Peltier Road
Middle
To Kemblesville
Glen Road
London Tract Rd.
Indiantown Road
Branch
Yeatman Station Road
Pennsylvania
Delaware
To Pleasant Hill
London Tract Road
South Bank Road
To Kemblesville
White Clay
FLOW
Chambers Rock Road
Thompson Station Road
Pleasant Hill Rd.
To Pleasant Hill & Rt. 72
N
White Clay Creek
Wilmington
Pennsylvania
Maryland
Dover
896
Delaware
Maryland
Hopkins Road
New London Road
Creek
Tweeds Mill Rd.
Wedgewood Road
To Newark & Rt. 1

Miles
0                    1

Interstate
U.S. Highway
State Highway
Other Roadway
Boat Launch
P  Parking
△  Campground

# White Clay Creek

## DELAWARE & PENNSYLVANIA
# White Clay Creek

**H**iding in the wide open. That's the best way to describe White Clay Creek, a great little gem of a trout stream shared by Delaware and Pennsylvania. Despite its relative proximity to urban development, the creek still feels wild, surrounded as it is by state-park land that prevents development along its banks. In fact, back in 2000 White Clay Creek was listed as a National Wild and Scenic River, a designation that affords it a great deal of protection. White Clay Creek Preserve—the only such preserve in the Keystone State—surrounds the Middle and East Branches of the creek, so the land must remain in its original state. The acreage around the preserve was part of a much larger tract of land purchased from the Lenape Indians in 1683 by the estimable William Penn.

Anglers often begin their day on White Clay Creek fishing the Middle Branch just off of Good Hope Road near North Creek Road. Ken Prager, owner of White Clay Outfitters in Newark, Delaware, introduced me to this section of the river one June morning. He and I immediately found rising fish and enjoyed working our way downstream. "I sometimes hit this section of the river before I go into work or whenever I need a quick fishing fix," Prager said. "There's posted land 500 yards above this bridge, so I remind my

*White Clay Creek offers lots of easy wading. Photo by Beau Beasley.*

*Fishing near structure, such as downed trees, and in shady places often proves successful for trout anglers. Photo by Beau Beasley.*

*Ken Prager knows White Clay Creek inside and out, and fishes the river as often as he can. He often fishes for an hour or so in the morning before opening his fly shop, White Clay Outfitters. Photo by Beau Beasley.*

Scott's Golden Retriever

customers that if they see posted property, please respect the landowner's rights. The good news," he continued, " is that if anglers exit the river and walk up North Creek Road until they get to the next bridge, only about a quarter of a mile, they can fish upstream to their heart's content."

White Clay Creek is rarely over 20 feet wide and has a general depth of about two feet or thereabouts; so keep those casts small. This is great nymphing water, though, and some of the larger pools are quite deep. Casting streamers in the larger pools, especially around dead and blown-down trees, is the perfect way to connect with larger trout. Most of the trout here run under 16 inches, though larger fish exist. Members of White Clay Fly Fishers, a local fly-angling club, take great pride in their local stream and help with stockings each spring and fall. The group has also been instrumental in building stream improvements.

Eventually Prager and I made our way to the London Tract Baptist Meeting House, which was built in 1729 from local stone, some of which no doubt came from the creek. Today the White Clay Fly Fishers meet here to teach fly tying and conservation classes to local students. Imagine this history buff's delight when Prager produced a key to the old meeting house and kindly showed me some of the area's local historical pieces and artwork. I highly recommend that history-loving anglers check out the meeting house when they next find themselves fishing White Clay Creek.

The terrain is easy and the access is plentiful—which of course means that White Clay Creek does get crowded at times. Avoid other folks by fishing near the Wedgewood Road section of the river in Delaware. This area has good parking, and Creek Road, which shadows the river, is open only to pedestrian traffic. The cover is much tighter here, so be prepared to pull on those waders and whip out your best roll cast.

Finally, leaving your vehicle in a state parking area in Delaware will set you back $3 if you're a resident and $6 if you're from out of state. When you consider how inexpensive a Delaware fishing license is, the parking's a pretty good deal.

*London Tract Baptist Meeting House near White Clay Creek. Photo by Beau Beasley.*

## Types of Fish
Trout, smallmouth bass, red-eyed rockfish, and fallfish are species sought after by anglers on White Clay Creek.

## Known Hatches
Hatches here include but are not limited to little black stoneflies, brown stoneflies, blue-winged olives, March browns, Hendricksons, sulfurs, caddisflies, light Cahills, midges, tricos, inchworms, and terrestrials.

## Equipment to Use
*Rods:* 2- to 5-weight, 7 to 9 feet in length.
*Reels:* Standard trout reel.
*Lines:* Weight-forward floating lines, matched to rod.
*Leaders:* 4X to 7X leaders, 9 to 12 feet in length.
*Wading:* Hip boots are fine during summer months, but waders are especially useful in the spring.

## Flies to Use
*Drys:* Adams, sizes 14-20; Blue-winged Olives, 14-20; Crane Flies 8-12; Dave's Hopper, 10-14; Elk-Hair Caddis, 14-20; Flying Ant, 10-18; Little Black or Brown Stonefly, 16-20; Light Cahill, 14-20; Yellow Sally, 14-20; March Brown, 10-16; Pale Morning Dun, 14-20; Quill Gordon, 12-22; Stimulator, 12-20; Sulfurs, 14-18; Trico, 16-18.

*Nymphs & Streamers:* Black Ghost, sizes 2-12; Green Weenie, 10; Copper John, 14-20; Chironomid (olive), 16-22; Crane Fly Larvae, 6-16; Hendrickson Wet, 12-16; Midge Pupa, 18-22; Picket Pin, 10-14; Pheasant Tail Nymph, 14-20; Scott's Golden Retriever, 6-10; Zebra Midge, 18-24; Conehead Zonkers, 8-12.

## When to Fish
Fishing is the best in spring and fall, but the trout often bite right through the summer months.

## Season & Limits
There's a delayed-harvest section on the Middle Branch from Good Hope Road to the confluence with the East Branch at Sharpless Road. The entire East Branch of White Clay Creek in Pennsylvania is an all-tackle stream. A fly-fishing-only section exists in Delaware from Chambers Rock Road upstream to the Pennsylvania state line. The all-tackle section also begins at Chambers Rock Road but runs downstream. For a complete listing of rules and regulations for Delaware go to www.dnrec. delaware.gov, for Pennsylvania go to www.fish.state.pa.us.

## Nearby Fly Fishing
Anglers fishing here might consider a trip to the Delaware or the Brandywine, which is a great alternative if the weather is warm.

## Accommodations & Family Activities
If you need to start your day off right, the Dunkin Donuts adjacent to White Clay Outfitters in Newark serves a mean cup of coffee. Bringing one to Ken Prager while he's slaving away in the fly shop might earn you some good inside skinny.

## Fly Shops & Guides
A Marblehead Flyfisher
Wilmington, Delaware
www.amarbleheadflyfisher.com
(302) 654-6515

Sporting Gentleman
Media, Pennsylvania
www.sportinggentleman.com
(610) 565- 6140

White Clay Outfitters
Newark, Delaware
www.flyfishingdelaware.com
(302) 369-9730

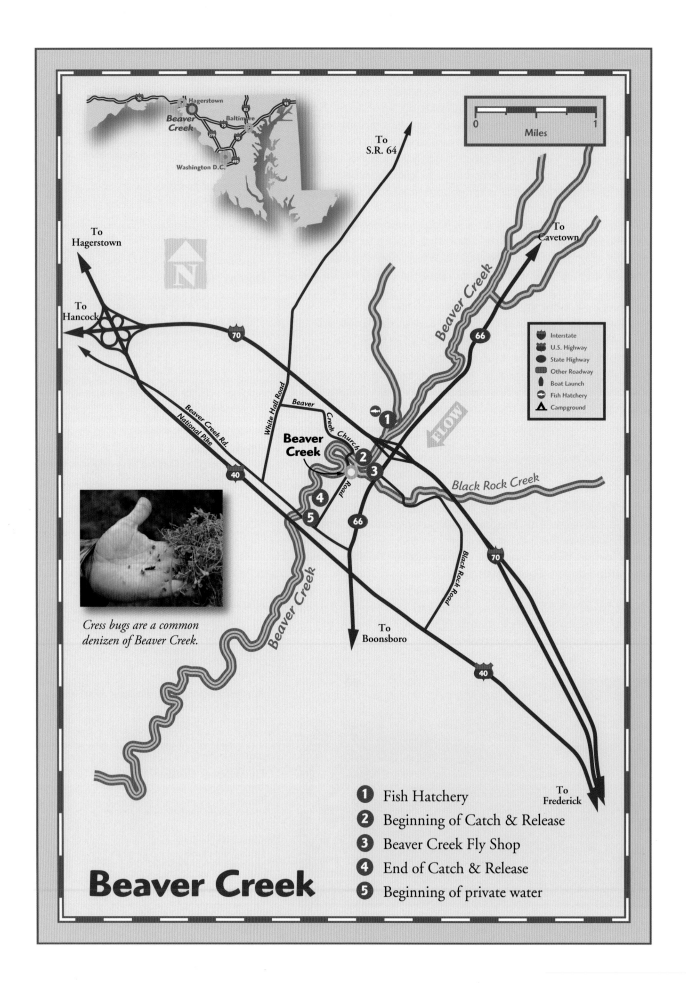

To S.R. 64

To Cavetown

0     Miles     1

To Hagerstown

To Hancock

Beaver Creek

FLOW

70

66

Beaver Creek Rd.
National Pike

White Hall Road

Beaver
Creek Church
Road

Beaver Creek

40

66

Black Rock Creek

Black Rock Road

70

40

To Boonsboro

To Frederick

Interstate
U.S. Highway
State Highway
Other Roadway
Boat Launch
Fish Hatchery
Campground

*Cress bugs are a common denizen of Beaver Creek.*

**1** Fish Hatchery
**2** Beginning of Catch & Release
**3** Beaver Creek Fly Shop
**4** End of Catch & Release
**5** Beginning of private water

# Beaver Creek

# Beaver Creek

I n Washington County just a few miles from busy Hagerstown, Maryland, sits the surprisingly good trout fishery known as Beaver Creek. Just like Virginia's Mossy Creek, much of Beaver Creek runs through private land that's easily accessible to the general public. The catch-and-release section is fly-fishing-only and extends for about a mile and a half, and it rarely exceeds 50 feet in width. Despite its diminutive size, it's a great little stream and easy to fish when the trout are in the right mood. This river was a favorite of outdoor writer Joe Brooks, whose protégé Lefty Kreh caught his first brown trout longer than 18 inches here.

Beaver Creek is unique among Free State trout waters. It's the sole limestone stream in the state. Other streams are influenced by limestone springs, but none are as large as Beaver Creek. This limestone influence pays big dividends all year long as underground springs warm trout in the winter and, more important, cool them throughout the dog days of summer. This limestone spring's head

*This trout fell for a Coburn's Cress Bug. Photo by Beau Beasley.*

*Beaver Creek offers anglers the chance to fish in a pastoral setting. Photo by Larry Coburn.*

*The author shows why anglers take the time to seek out Beaver Creek. Photo by Larry Coburn.*

Coburn's Cress Bug

is adjacent to the Albert Powell Hatchery and produces nearly 3,500 gallons of cool fresh water every day, making Beaver Creek fishable 12 months a year. Though fishing is available directly below the hatchery, the catch-and-release section begins near Country Store Lane.

Beaver Creek is home to nice brown trout as well as fairly large rainbows. Anglers who carefully walk the banks with polarized glasses may well see some of these brutes lying in wait for an easy meal. Outdoor writer Larry Coburn, co-author of the *Guide to Maryland Trout Fishing: The Catch and Release Streams* and a fish-catching machine if ever I've seen one, walked with me along the banks of Beaver Creek and pointed out the prime trout hangouts. I would fish my way through a section pretty thoroughly, and then Coburn would come behind me after I struck out and land one trout after another. Initially I was pretty impressed with his fishing acumen, but I'll admit that after a while I was tempted to drown him. Fortunately, I eventually got the hang of Beaver Creek myself and landed a few nice trout. Still, I admit with no hard feelings that the pattern that did the trick was a Coburn's Cress Bug, a pattern he created to mimic the insects that live in the stream's watercress vegetation. And this same pattern has proven successful in other trout streams, even when I didn't have Coburn around as a guide.

The catch-and-release section on Beaver Creek continues all the way to Beaver Creek Road. The anglers' parking lot is just a few hundred yards from the stream and is an easy walk, even in waders. A private section of stream directly below the catch-and-release section is home to huge rainbows. The good news is that the fish don't know where the private water ends and the public water begins, and if you have one of Coburn's Cress Bugs on you, you might just get lucky enough to catch one.

*Larry Coburn provides evidence that rainbows as well as browns inhabit Beaver Creek. Photo by Beau Beasley.*

## Types of Fish
The average trout here is 9 to 14 inches. Anglers typically find browns and rainbows. Both types of trout can be large here, but they don't get that way from being pushovers.

## Known Hatches
There are a lot of cress bugs here as well as sculpins and crayfish and other baitfish. Winter stonefly, Hendrickson, March brown, and caddis in many colors hatch here. Inchworms and terrestrials, especially hoppers, can work here.

## Equipment to Use
*Rods:* 4- to 6-weight, 7 to 9 feet in length.
*Reels:* Standard trout reel.
*Lines:* Weight-forward floating lines matched to rod.
*Leaders:* 4X to 6X, 9 to 12 feet in length.
*Wading:* You can get by with hip boots here.

## Flies to Use
*Drys:* Adams, sizes 14-20; Blue-winged Olive, 14-20; Coburn's Inchworm, 12-14; Elk-Hair Caddis, 14-20; Flying Ant, 10-18; Gelso's Little Black Stonefly, 16-20; Mann's Inchworm, 10-16; March Brown, 10-14; Stimulator, 12-20; as well as various terrestrials.

*Nymphs & Streamers:* BH Hare's Ear, sizes 14-20; BH Prince Nymph, 14-20; Coburn's Cress Bug, 14-20; Dover's Peach Fly, 6-10; Green Weenie, 14-16; Harold's Indestructible, 12-16; Muddler Minnow, 6-10; Patuxent Special, 6-10; Scud, 10-18; Sculpin, 4-8; Woolly Bugger, 6-10.

## When to Fish
Open all year.

## Season & Limits
The section of Beaver Creek focused on here is strictly a catch-and-release fishery. For a complete list of rules and regulations contact the Maryland Department of Natural Resources at 1-877-620-8367, or go to www.dnr.state.md.us.

## Nearby Fly Fishing
Other locations to fish in Maryland include Gunpowder Falls and Big Hunting Creek.

## Accommodations & Family Activities
Beaver Creek is a real success story because much of it flows on private land but is open to the public. The river has had a serious problem with erosion and its banks were worn down from cattle. Anglers can thank Doug Hutzell as well as Potomac–Patuxent and the Seneca Valley Chapters of Trout Unlimited for their hard work in rebuilding the stream. Thanks should also be passed on to the Maryland Department of Natural Resources as well as the Antietam Fly Anglers and, of course, the Beaver Creek Watershed Association. There are plenty of things for families to see and do in nearby Hagerstown, Maryland. Civil War sites, golf courses, and museums are just the beginning. For a full listing of activities go to www.marylandmemories.org.

## Fly Shops & Guides
Beaver Creek Fly Shop
Hagerstown, Maryland
www.beavercreekflyshop.com
(301) 393-9090

Hunting Creek Outfitters
Frederick, Maryland
www.huntingcreekoutfitters.com
(301) 668-4333

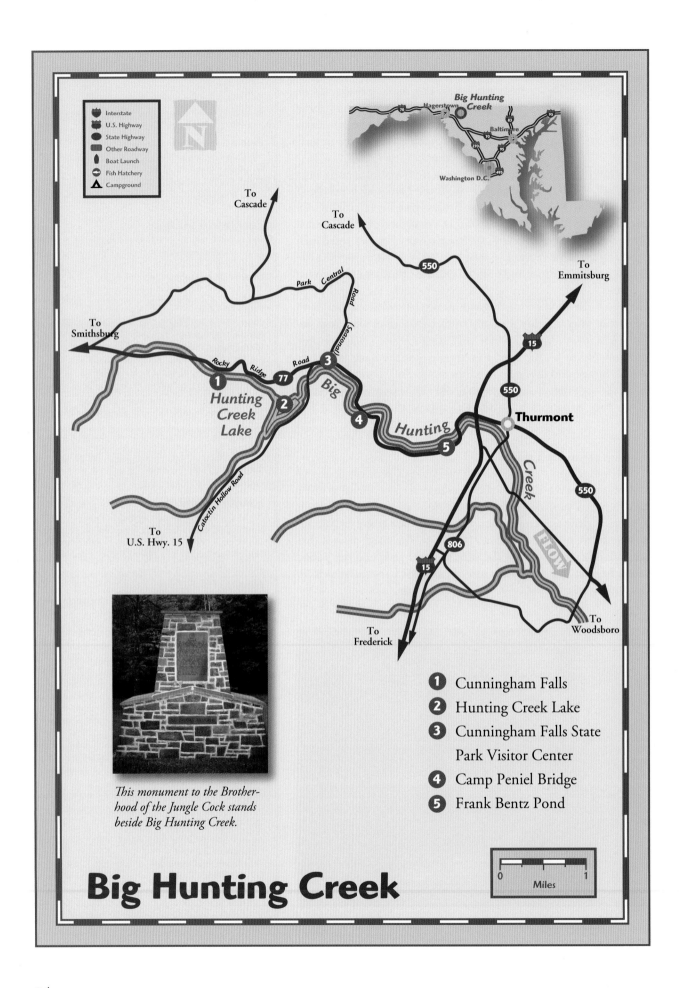

Legend:
- Interstate
- U.S. Highway
- State Highway
- Other Roadway
- Boat Launch
- Fish Hatchery
- Campground

N

To Cascade

To Cascade

550

To Emmitsburg

Park Central

Road

Seasonal

15

To Smithsburg

Rocky Ridge Road

77

550

1

2

3

4

5

Hunting Creek Lake

Big Hunting Creek

Thurmont

Creek

FLOW

Catoctin Hollow Road

To U.S. Hwy. 15

806

15

550

To Frederick

To Woodsboro

Big Hunting Creek

Hagerstown

70

Baltimore

70

270

95

495

Washington D.C.

This monument to the Brother-hood of the Jungle Cock stands beside Big Hunting Creek.

1 Cunningham Falls
2 Hunting Creek Lake
3 Cunningham Falls State Park Visitor Center
4 Camp Peniel Bridge
5 Frank Bentz Pond

# Big Hunting Creek

0    Miles    1

# Big Hunting Creek

I met Big Hunting Creek thanks to Murray Friedman, owner of Hunting Creek Outfitters in Frederick, Maryland. "This is a great little river, and there are still lots of folks who don't know about it," said Friedman as we strung up our rods. "Once folks fish it, though, they generally come back." This was Maryland's very first catch-and-release stream, and it has been the training ground for a host of outdoor enthusiasts. It was on the banks of Big Hunting Creek that outdoor-writing legend Joe Brooks and a few of his friends founded the Brotherhood of the Jungle Cock, an organization dedicated to teaching youngsters how to fly fish and the importance of conservation. The Brotherhood of the Jungle Cock is still alive and well and operates in multiple states across the country. Visitors to Big Hunting Creek will find a stone monument dedicated to Brooks and the organization just across the street from Camp Peniel Bridge.

Modern fly anglers owe Brooks a great deal, though few realize it. He is considered by many to be the father of modern saltwater fly fishing and was the first person to catch a permit on a fly. His talent for the written word eventually landed him a spot as the fishing editor for *Outdoor Life,* where he was the first to promote

*Big Hunting Creek is one of Maryland's more famous trout streams. President Carter fished here often when staying at Camp David. Photo by Beau Beasley.*

*Murray Friedman knows Big Hunting Creek well and guides here often. Photo by Beau Beasley.*

Blue-Winged Olive

destination fly fishing. Before Joe Brooks, most fly anglers thought fly fishing was limited to local trout streams (as many folks suppose to this day). Brooks traveled widely, however, and wrote about his experiences everywhere he went. Brooks also frequently took others under his wing and shared his knowledge of the sport. One young man he took a shine to was an aspiring outdoor writer from Frederick, Maryland, named Lefty Kreh.

Located just outside Thurmont, we can easily split Big Hunting Creek into upper and lower sections with Camp Peniel Bridge as the dividing point. The lower section of the stream begins near Frank Bentz Pond and is on your right-hand side as you're driving west on Route 77. The lower section, often called the canyon section, is quite beautiful and is surrounded by imposing trees that cast their shadows across the stream. Lush green ferns and pale green moss seem to create a lime-colored carpet that extends through the forest onto the lichen-covered rocks. Hidden among these rocks and shadows are beautiful trout that excel at peek-a-boo with any fly angler willing to test his skills here. Also hidden in the forest is the entrance to Camp David, the famed presidential retreat. President Jimmy Carter in particular liked fishing Big Hunting Creek whenever he visited Camp David.

The upper portion of the river changes to the left-hand side of the road once it passes under Camp Peniel Bridge and continues all the way to Big Hunting Creek Lake, also called Cunningham Falls Lake. In the upper section, the river, which has a rock bottom, takes on a less imposing look, but is no less beautiful. Just upstream from the parking area there is a small bluff that anglers can walk to easily, and from there, they can look down on the river. At this point the river seems undecided about which way to go. The riverbed seems to have changed courses several times over the years, and no doubt its banks swell during spring rains.

Anglers might want to visit Cunningham Falls Park. There's a fee to enter the park but once there you can hike to the falls or fish in the lake as well.

*The pristine trout waters near Big Hunting Creek were popular with moonshiners long before fly anglers discovered it. Photo by Beau Beasley.*

### Types of Fish
Anglers typically find rainbow trout, brown trout, and some brookies here.

### Known Hatches
Winter stonefly, blue quills, Hendrickson, March brown, little yellow sallies, caddisfly, Cahill, inchworm, and various terrestrials.

### Equipment to Use
*Rods:* 3- to 5-weight, 7 to 8½ feet in length.
*Reels:* Standard trout reel.
*Lines:* Weight-forward floating lines matched to rod.
*Leaders:* 4X to 7X, 9 to 12 feet in length.
*Wading:* You can get by with hip boots, but chest waders can be useful here.

### Flies to Use
*Drys:* Adams, sizes 14-20; Dusty's Deviant, 12-16; Elk-Hair Caddis, 14-20; Flying Ant, 10-18; Gelso's Little Black Stonefly, 16-20; Light Cahill, sizes 14-20; Little Yellow Sally, 14-20; March Brown, 10-14; Murray's Mr. Rapidan, 14-20; Quill Gordon, 12-22; Royal Coachman, 14-20; Royal Wulff, 14-16; Stimulator, 12-20; Steeves's Attract Ant, 16-20; Steeves's Bark Beetle, 12-16.

*Nymphs & Streamers:* BH Goldilox, sizes 6-10; BH Hare's Ear, 14-20; BH Prince Nymph, 14-20; Coburn's Inchworm, 12-14; Copper John, 16-22; Green Weenie, 14-16; Muddler Minnow, 6-10; Pheasant Tail, 14-20; Woolly Bugger, 6-10.

### When to Fish
Spring is often the best time to go.

### Season & Limits
A catch-and-release section for this river begins above Cunningham Falls and runs nearly the length of the river to just above Frank Bentz Pond. For a complete list of rules and regulations contact the Maryland Department of Natural Resources at 1-877-620-8367, or go to www.dnr.state.md.us.

### Nearby Fly Fishing
Anglers here could check out Cunningham Falls Lake.

### Accommodations & Family Activities
It would be nice to visit Camp David which is nearby, but as the Secret Service isn't likely to give you a tour, you're better off visiting Old Town in Frederick, Maryland. Incidentally one of the feeder creeks on the upper section to Big Hunting Creek is Blue Blazes Creek. This site was the location of the largest illegal whiskey-still operation ever captured by law enforcement agents in Maryland. Moonshiners, who operated at night so as to avoid detection, found it was easiest to work during full moon periods, thus the name. During prohibition, most stills produced a few dozen gallons for personal use. This operation was no small potatoes. When agents arrived they were shocked to find 18 vats, which held 500 gallons of whiskey each! There is a small museum and walking tour of Blue Blazes Creek adjacent to the river.

### Fly Shops & Guides
Beaver Creek Fly Shop
Hagerstown, Maryland
www.beavercreekflyshop.com
(301) 393-9090

Hunting Creek Outfitters
Frederick, Maryland
www.huntingcreekoutfitters.com
(301) 668-4333

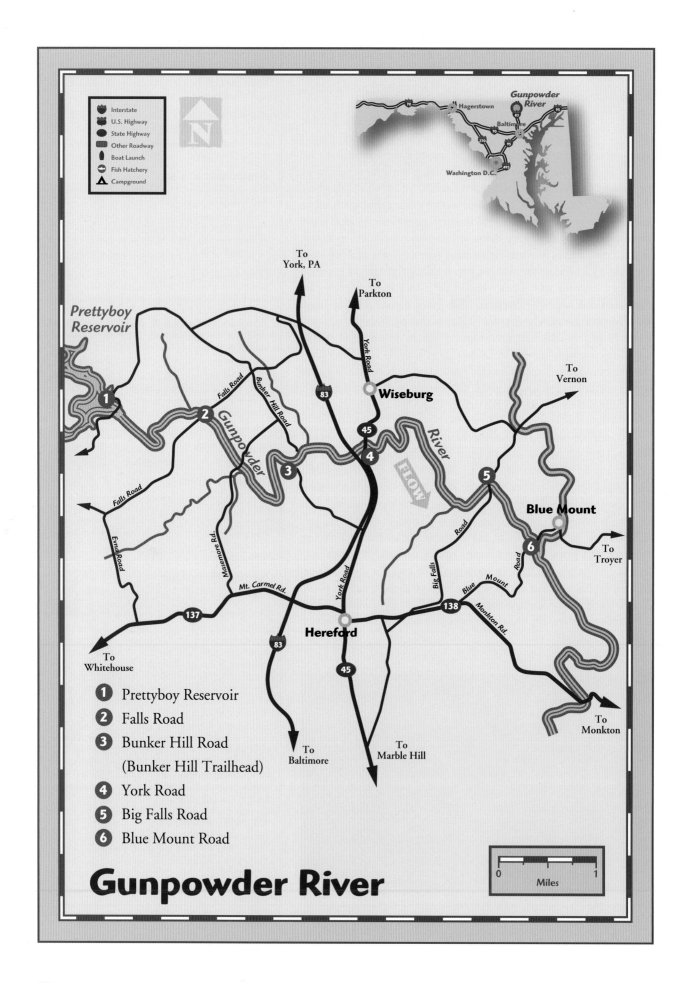

**Legend:**
- Interstate
- U.S. Highway
- State Highway
- Other Roadway
- Boat Launch
- Fish Hatchery
- Campground

N

Gunpowder River

Hagerstown
Baltimore
Washington D.C.

To York, PA

To Parkton

Prettyboy Reservoir

Falls Road

Bunker Hill Road

York Road

Wiseburg

To Vernon

Gunpowder

River

FLOW

Blue Mount

To Troyer

Falls Road

Evna Road

Masemore Rd.

Mt. Carmel Rd.

Big Falls Road

Blue Mount Road

Monkton Rd.

137

To Whitehouse

83

Hereford

York Road

45

138

To Monkton

To Baltimore

To Marble Hill

① Prettyboy Reservoir
② Falls Road
③ Bunker Hill Road
   (Bunker Hill Trailhead)
④ York Road
⑤ Big Falls Road
⑥ Blue Mount Road

# Gunpowder River

0 — Miles — 1

# Gunpowder River

**B**ig Gunpowder Falls has no falls at all and most likely got its name from a nearby foundry that produced guns during the Revolutionary War. The river was also the site of a copper foundry. In fact, the copper used on the Capitol Dome after the War of 1812 was extracted from here. The river has an interesting fish history as well. "The Gunpowder Falls tailwater is by far the best wild-trout fishery in Central Maryland," argues Charlie Gougeon, fisheries biologist for the Maryland Department of Natural Resources and a man who has watched over the Gunpowder for decades. "It is also," he continues, "one of just a few wild-trout streams in the entire state of Maryland."

Although the Gunpowder is nearly 53 miles long, most fly anglers concentrate on three sections covering about 17 miles. Each of the three sections is distinctive and has its own character and charm. The first section, stretching from Prettyboy Dam to Falls Road, is entirely catch-and-release and may be fished by traditional anglers as well as fly rodders. Blown-down trees are

### Types of Fish
Anglers typically find brown trout, rainbow trout, the occasional brook trout, and farther down river, bluegill and smallmouth bass.

### Known Hatches
Winter stonefly, Hendrickson, March brown, little yellow stonefly, sulfur, caddisfly, Cahill, inchworm, terrestrial, and slate drake.

### Equipment to Use
*Rods:* 3- to 5-weight, 7 to 9½ feet in length.
*Reels:* Standard trout reel.
*Lines:* Weight-forward floating lines matched to rod.
*Leaders:* 3X to 6X, 9 to 12 feet in length.
*Wading:* You can get by with hip boots, but chest waders can be useful here.

### Flies to Use
*Drys:* Adams, sizes 16-20; Blue-winged Olive, 16-24; Elk-Hair Caddis, 14-20; Flying Ant, 10-22; Gelso's Little Black Stonefly, 16-20; Griffith's Gnat, 18-20; Hendrickson, 14-16; March Brown, 10-14; Midges, 24-28; Pale Morning Dun, 14-20; Quill Gordon, 14-18; Rusty Spinner, 12; Tricos, 22-24.

*Continued*

*An angler sizes up Gunpowder Falls with his trusty companion. Photo by Beau Beasley.*

*Gunpowder Falls has excellent canopy cover, which helps keep the water cold. In the summer, higher air temperatures make the water look like it is smoking. Photo by Beau Beasley.*

Copper John

plentiful here, and pocket water is abundant. Anglers need to pay strict attention to their patterns, as strikes will not only come fast, but the trout seem to know that running below the limbs of submerged trees provides a sure release from careless anglers. Another word to the wise: Hiking into and around the river here is a must. Despite the nearby parking lot, this section's grading is best left to people with good knees who take their time making their way to the water. If you like being able to see where you are putting each step, you might want to fish farther down as the fern cover is so thick here that you often can't see your own wading shoes while standing on the bank.

The second section of the river, which runs from Falls Road to York Road, is classic trout water of which purists dream—runs, riffles, the occasional long pool—and yet one needn't be part billy goat to move around. Yes, the walking is easier—but there is also a bit less cover, which means that the fish can be easily spooked. You'll still find plentiful undergrowth and ferns, so take your time and watch your step. You can enter at Bunker Hill Trail if you like, and fish upstream or downstream.

The third frequently fished section of the river, which is deeper and much slower than the other two, stretches from York Road to Blue Mount Road. The last two sections of the river are popular with canoeists, though you'll probably only spot canoes on weekends.

No matter which section you fish, the Gunpowder is simply lovely—elves and gnomes would feel right at home in this foggy fairy glen. If you're a big fan of brown trout, then the Gunpowder is your river. Though you may catch rainbows and brookies, the overwhelming majority (about 95 percent) of the Gunpowder's fish are browns. The Gunpowder boasts an unbelievable population of wild trout ranging from 3,500 to 5,000 trout per mile, rivaling even the best Western rivers for fish per mile. Although the typical trout here is 9 to 10 inches, 18-inchers are not unheard of. Remember that these are *wild* fish and they don't suffer rookie anglers lightly. For this reason, I suggest hiring a guide for your first Gunpowder trip.

*Gunpowder Falls offers an excellent fishery very close to both Baltimore and Washington, D.C. Photo by Beau Beasley.*

### Flies to Use (continued)
*Nymphs & Streamers:* BH Hare's Ear, sizes 14-22; BH Prince Nymph, 14-22; Coburn's Inchworm, 12-14; Clouser Minnow, 6-10; Copper John, 16-24; Scotts Golden Retriever, 6-10; Red Ass, 16-20; Green Weenie, 14-16; Harold's Indestructible, 12-16; Mann's Inchworm, 12-14; Matuka, 4-10; Sculpin, 4-8; Woolly Bugger, 6-10; Zonker, size 8.

### When to Fish
Open all year.

### Season & Limits
There are 17 miles of trout river here, including 7 miles of catch-and-release-only water.

### Nearby Fly Fishing
Anglers fishing here might consider a trip to Yellow Breeches or the Susquehanna in nearby Pennsylvania.

### Accommodations & Family Services
The tiny town of Monkton, Maryland, is the hub for the Gunpowder River, but there isn't much here for anglers in the way of lodging that isn't high-end. Visiting anglers would be better off staying in Hunt Valley or Timonium, Maryland, or perhaps going in to Pennsylvania, which is very close by and also offers good water. Keep in mind there are quite a few folks who float the lower end of the river so you might want to avoid that section, unless of course that doesn't bother you. The only good thing is that you can pick up nice smallies that way, occasionally.

### Guides & Fly Shops
Backwater Angler
Monkton, Maryland
www.backwaterangler.com
(410) 357-9557

The Evening Rise
Lancaster, Pennsylvania
www.theeveningrise.com
(717) 509-3636

Great Feathers
Sparks, Maryland
www.greatfeathers.com
1-888-777-0838

Orvis
Bethesda, Maryland
www.orvis.com/bethesda
(301) 652-3562

Tochterman's
Baltimore, Maryland
(410) 327-6942

Trout & About Guide Service
Monkton, Maryland
www.troutandabout.com
(410) 472-0740

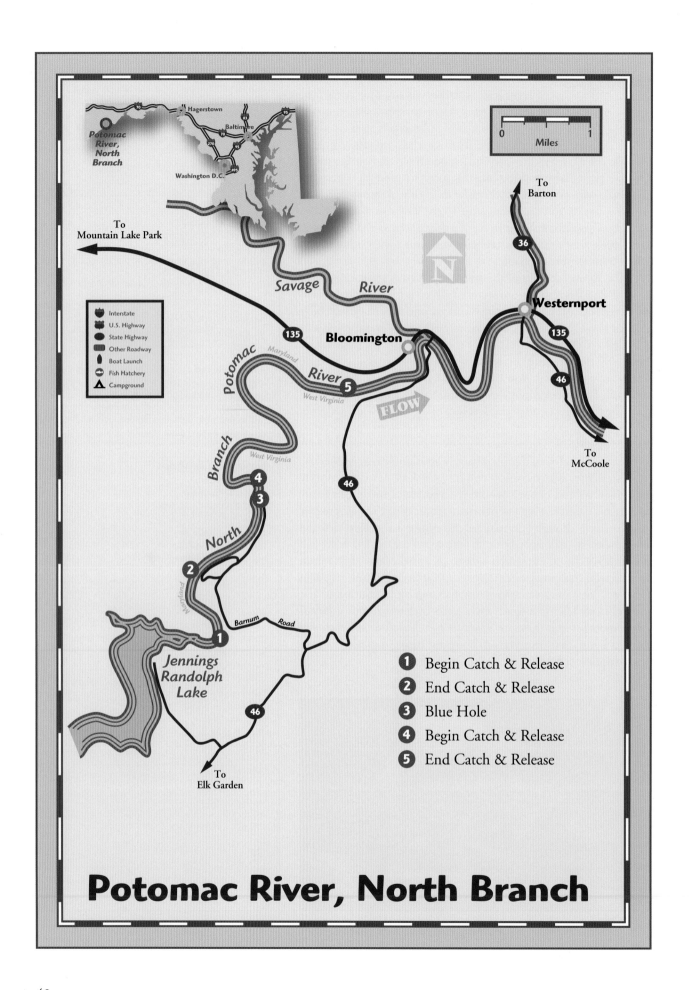

# Potomac River, North Branch

# Potomac River, North Branch

Two things come to mind when I reflect on Western Maryland's Garrett County, the wilder side of the Free State. First, I think of my close friend Lee Livengood, who is like a brother to me. Second, I think of great trout fishing. I met Lee more than 20 years ago, and he's the very essence of an outdoorsman. He can hunt, track, shoot, field dress, and then cook nearly anything with four feet. I like to tease him that his house looks like the inside of a Cabela's catalog, complete with lamps made out of antlers. Once, when I was visiting him and his family, we went for a hike and Lee directed me to pull up what looked like a few weeds and take them back to the house. Seemed like a strange notion to me, but I've learned not to question Lee when we're walking through the woods. Imagine my surprise when, ten minutes after our return, he presented me with a steaming cup of sassafras tea that he'd made from the "weeds."

As a matter of fact, it was Lee who took me fishing for trout for the first time. We fished just below the lovely and popular

### Types of Fish
Anglers can find big rainbows, bigger brown trout, and even cutthroat trout. Hefty smallmouth bass and the occasional muskie are also landed here.

### Known Hatches & Baitfish
Hendrickson, March brown, little yellow stonefly, sulfur, caddisfly, Cahill, inchworm, terrestrials, as well as frogs, damselflies, and all manner of creek chubs and minnows.

### Equipment to Use
*Rods:* 5- to 8-weight, 8 to 9½ feet in length.
*Reels:* Disc-drag reel, possible large-arbor applications.
*Lines:* Weight-forward floating lines matched to rod.
*Leaders:* 3X to 6X, 9 to 12 feet in length.
*Wading:* Chest waders are a must here.

### Flies to Use
*Drys:* Adams, sizes 14-20; Blue-winged Olive, 14-20; Elk-Hair Caddis, 14-20; Flying Ant, 10-18; Gelso's Little Black Stonefly, 16-20; Light Cahill, 14-20; Little Yellow Sally, 14-20; March Brown, 10-14; Pale Morning Dun, 14-20; Stimulator, 12-20; and terrestrials.

*Continued*

*Western Maryland's Garrett County has thousands of miles of trout water to explore. Photo by Harold Harsh.*

*Anglers face many challenges on the North Branch of the Potomac, but finding room to cast isn't one of them. Photo by Beau Beasley.*

Muddler Minnow

Swallow Falls, and by the end of the afternoon I'd managed to land my first rainbow—caught, I'm not ashamed to admit, on a kernel of canned corn compliments of the local grocery store.

The North Branch of the Potomac is arguably Maryland's best known trout stream, and its sheer size affords anglers the luxury of floating this expansive and beautiful river. It's so large, in fact, that you might be forgiven for thinking that you'd died and gone to Wyoming or Montana. Diversity is the watchword here. The North Branch plays host to a variety of game fish, including rainbows, browns, and even the occasional muskie. Prefer cutthroats or feisty, bronze-backed smallies? No problem, they're here, too. In terms of its fishery, the North Branch can boast both quality and quantity—but the key to success is being at the right place at the right time with the right pattern.

The North Branch of the Potomac was essentially dead for nearly a century thanks to acid runoff from local coal mines. Fortunately the river has bounced back to become the pride of Maryland's fly anglers and the delight of hundreds of fishing guests each season. This river fishes best when you're floating it, but it does offer some good access for wading anglers below the dam at Jennings-Randolph Lake. The river's expansive size allows anglers to fish for hours if not days at a time without scratching the surface of one particular section. It goes without saying that watching your backcast isn't an issue here as there is so much room.

Because this section of the river is a tailrace fishery, it enjoys the benefits of the coldwater releases, which can have a dramatic effect on the river's current. As a result you need to wade carefully, and it is also a good idea to take along a wading staff. There are two clearly marked catch-and-release-only sections here that run for about a mile each. The first begins below the dam and stretches down to just above an old bridge abutment near the parking area on Barnum Road. The second area is just below Blue Hole, and runs to Piney Swamp Run. The section between the two areas is all-tackle and heavily stocked.

I'll be forever indebted to Lee Livengood for introducing me to the great trout waters of Western Maryland. If you haven't tried these waters yet you should. If you refer to the "Flies to Use" and the "Fly Shops & Guides" sections, you might even be able to leave the canned corn at home.

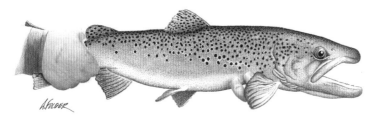
*Brown in Hand by Alan Folger.*

## Flies to Use (continued)

*Nymphs & Streamers:* BH Goldilox, sizes 6-10; BH Hare's Ear, 14-20; BH Prince Nymph, 14-20; Double Bunny, 1/0-2; CK Baitfish, 1/0-6; Clouser Minnow, 2-8; Dover's Peach Fly, 6-10; Forage Fly, 4-6; Green Weenie, 14-16; Harold's Indestructible Nymph, 12-16; Howell's Big Nasty, 4-6; Kreelex, 2-6; Muddler Minnow, 4-10; Patuxent Special, 4-10; Sculpin, 4-8; Super Patuxent Special, 4-10; Skilton's Hellgrammite, 4-6; Woolly Bugger, 2-10; and Zonkers, 2-8.

## When to Fish

Winters in this section of Maryland can be downright brutal. Don't even think of fishing here before the end of April.

## Season & Limits

There are all-tackle sections on this river mixed with delayed-harvest sections. For a complete list of rules and regulations contact the Maryland Department of Natural Resources go to www.dnr.state.md.us.

## Nearby Fly Fishing

Anglers fishing here can easily fish the Savage River, Casselman River, Youghiogheny River, and of course Deep Creek Lake.

## Accommodations & Family Activities

If you get past taking in the scenery you can go hiking, biking, skiing, whitewater rafting, golfing, play paint ball, and take pontoon and kayak tours of nearby Deep Creek Lake.

Savage River Lodge
Frostburg, Maryland
www.savageriverlodge.com
(301) 689-3200

## Fly Shops & Guides

Big Frog Fly Shop
Oakland, Maryland
www.springcreekoutfitter.com
(301) 387-6587

Eastern Trophies Fly Fishing
Swanton, Maryland
www.easterntrophies.com
(571) 213-2570

Kelly's White Fly Shoppe
Shepherdstown, West Virginia
www.kellyswhitefly.net
(304) 876-8030

Native Trout Fly Fishing
Warrenton, Virginia
www.nativetroutva.com
(540) 878-1638

Savage River Outfitters
Swanton, Maryland
www.savageriveroutfitters.com
(703) 517-1040

Spring Creek Outfitters
Oakland, Maryland
www.springcreekoutfitter.com
(301) 387-6587

Wisp Resort Fly Shop
McHenry, Maryland
www.wispresort.com
(301) 387-4911

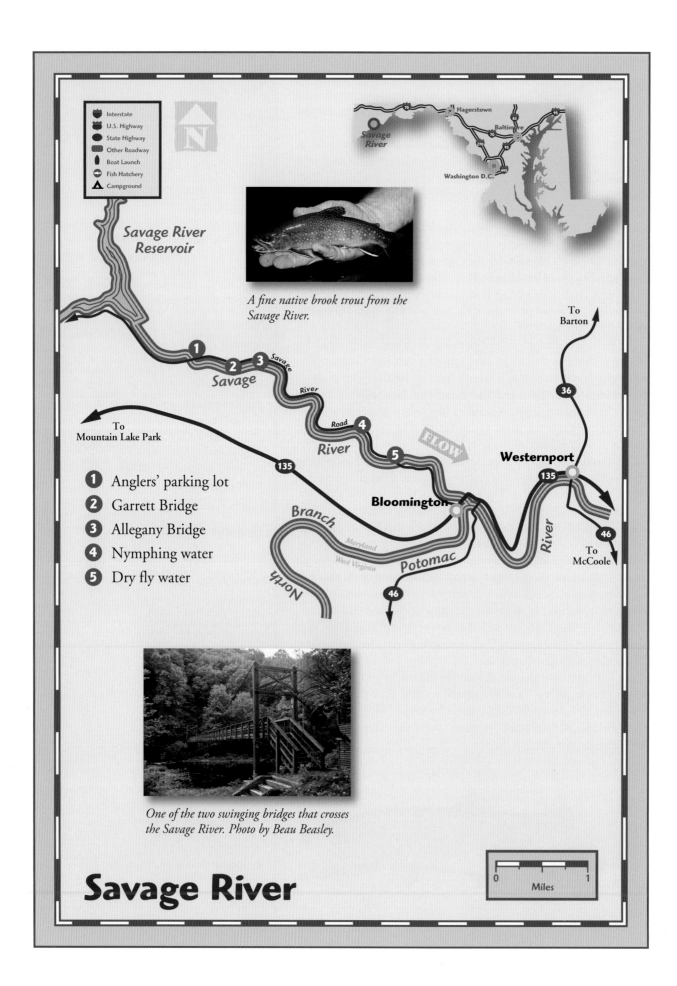

Legend:
- Interstate
- U.S. Highway
- State Highway
- Other Roadway
- Boat Launch
- Fish Hatchery
- Campground

Savage River Reservoir

Savage River

Savage River Road

To Mountain Lake Park

FLOW

135

Westernport

To Barton

36

Bloomington

North Branch Potomac River

Maryland
West Virginia

46

46

To McCoole

Hagerstown
Baltimore
Washington D.C.
Savage River

1 Anglers' parking lot
2 Garrett Bridge
3 Allegany Bridge
4 Nymphing water
5 Dry fly water

*A fine native brook trout from the Savage River.*

*One of the two swinging bridges that crosses the Savage River. Photo by Beau Beasley.*

0 Miles 1

# Savage River

# Savage River

T ucked in the far western corner of Maryland, the Savage River has long been a favorite water among those hardy souls who like nothing better than to match wits with wary native brook trout. This picturesque river flows from Savage River Reservoir and winds its way back and forth, tumbling over mountainous rocks for nearly four miles before it empties into the North Branch of the Potomac. What lies in between is a brook-trout-lover's nirvana, perfect for those who specialize in lightweight gear. Access points abound along the road, and pulling off at any of these locations and walking a few yards will put anglers into position on the river.

"This is a great trout stream—but if I have relatively new clients, it's not my first choice," confides Harold Harsh, owner of Spring Creek Outfitters, the oldest fly-fishing guide service in Garrett County, Maryland. "There are plenty of fish here, but at times they can be unforgiving." Harsh was casting a beautiful bamboo rod on the day that we fished together. "This is just the right river for guys who want to fish bamboo," he says. "There's tight cover here at times, but also enough room to make some long casts if you take your time and pay attention." As if on cue, a

## Types of Fish
Visitors to this river will land browns primarily and, of course, beautiful native brookies. On rare occasion, a rainbow or cutthroat enters the lower edge of the river from the nearby North Branch of the Potomac.

## Known Hatches
The hatches here are pretty typical of a mountain trout stream and consist of winter stonefly, Hendrickson, March brown, little yellow stonefly, sulfur, caddisfly, Cahill, inchworm, and of course, terrestrials.

## Equipment to Use
*Rods:* 3- to 5-weight, 7½ to 8 feet in length.
*Reels:* Standard trout reel.
*Lines:* Weight-forward floating lines matched to rod.
*Leaders:* 5X to 7X, 9 to 14 feet in length.
*Wading:* You can get by with hip boots here, but of course, chest waders give you a few more wading options.

## Flies to Use
*Drys:* Blue-winged Olive, sizes 14-24; Elk-Hair Caddis, 12-16; Flying Ant, 12-18; Green Drake, 8-10; Gelso's Little Black Stonefly, 16-20; Light Cahill, 14-20; Little Yellow Sally, 14-20; March Brown, 10-14; Red Quill, 14-20; Quill Gordon, 12-22; Stimulator, 16-20.

*Continued*

*Though the Savage River is trophy trout water, small native brookies can bring a smile to an angler's face as well. Photo by Beau Beasley.*

*When given the chance, guide Harold Harsh fishes the Savage River with vintage bamboo rods. Photo by Beau Beasley.*

Harold's Indestructible

spunky native brookie crashed Harold's pattern, and he quickly brought the beauty to hand.

Access to the Savage is easy, as Savage River Road runs along most of the stream and allows for multiple pull-offs. Also, two steady footbridges—the Garrett and the Allegany—traverse this river, both of which are great spotting platforms for anglers. Above the Garrett Bridge is "7x Pool," which should indicate how tough it is to fish this still water. This pool is as wide as the river and seems to be a few hundred yards long. Trout often cruise around here and love to lazily sip insects. I say lazily because there is so little current here that the fish simply aren't in a hurry—and consequently, catching the fish here can be really tough. You may try to spot a particular fish from the bridge and then try to position yourself for a good cast. Be careful, though, as you're not likely to get a second chance. An artificial-flies-only section runs from the reservoir to the Allegany Bridge. On the downstream side of the bridge and for the remainder of the river's length, anglers can use flies and lures only.

The Savage also provides options for anglers who wish to cast drys along the broken sections of the river, and nymphing can be excellent here. Rocks ranging in size from softball to wheelbarrow provide plenty of stair-step pools for anglers who want to fish the river methodically. A fly fisherman who can afford to take his time and thoroughly fish the river could easily spend two days on the Savage and not fish the same place twice.

The picturesque mountain laurel stands out beautifully against the dark rock riverbanks, strangely magnifying the solitude an angler feels on the aptly named Savage. Despite the wild setting and wily trout, the Savage River is a great place for the whole family to spend the day. You'll find picnic tables and open areas where families can enjoy the river together—and yet alone.

Anglers who prefer a little bushwhack with their bamboo can fish the single mile of the Savage above the reservoir. The fishing can be good, but the river is smaller with much tighter cover. It is also rumored to harbor a healthy population of rattlesnakes. Consider yourself warned: They don't call it the Savage for nothing.

*Phil Gay, a well-known guide and casting instructor, wet wades on the Savage River. Photo by King Montgomery.*

### Flies to Use (continued)

*Nymphs & Streamers:* BH Goldilox, sizes 6-10; BH Hare's Ear, 14-20; BH Prince Nymph, 14-20; Coburn's Inchworm, 12-14; Copper John, 16-22; Harold's Indestructible Nymph, 12-16; Patuxent Special, 6-10; Super Patuxent Special, 6-10; Woolly Bugger, 6-12.

### When to Fish

Fishing is best when the flow is between 50 to 70 cubic feet per second. For the latest info on releases and flows, call the Water Resources Section of the Baltimore Corps of Engineers at (410) 962-7687.

### Season & Limits

The Savage can be fished only with artificial flies. For a complete list of rules and regulations contact the Maryland Department of Natural Resources at 1-877-620-8367 or go to www.dnr.state.md.us.

### Nearby Fly Fishing

Anglers fishing here also have plenty of opportunity to fish the North Branch of the Potomac, the Casselman, and Youghiogheny rivers.

### Accommodations & Family Activities

If you're fishing the Savage River there's no finer place to stay than Savage River Lodge. This well-appointed lodge is the perfect place for a family getaway or a small group gathering. In 2009 they were honored by being named the Maryland Chamber of Commerce Small Business of the Year. Anglers who wish to prepare their own food can stay at Savage River Outfitters.

Savage River Lodge
Frostburg, Maryland
www.savageriverlodge.com
(301) 689-3200

### Fly Shops & Guides

Big Frog Fly Shop
Oakland, Maryland
www.springcreekoutfitter.com
(301) 387-6587

Eastern Trophies Fly Fishing
Swanton, Maryland
www.easterntrophies.com
(571) 213-2570

Savage River Outfitters
Swanton, Maryland
www.savageriveroutfitters.com
(703) 517-1040

Spring Creek Outfitters
Oakland, Maryland
www.springcreekoutfitter.com
(301) 387-6587

Wisp Resort Fly Shop
McHenry, Maryland
www.wispresort.com
(301) 387-4911

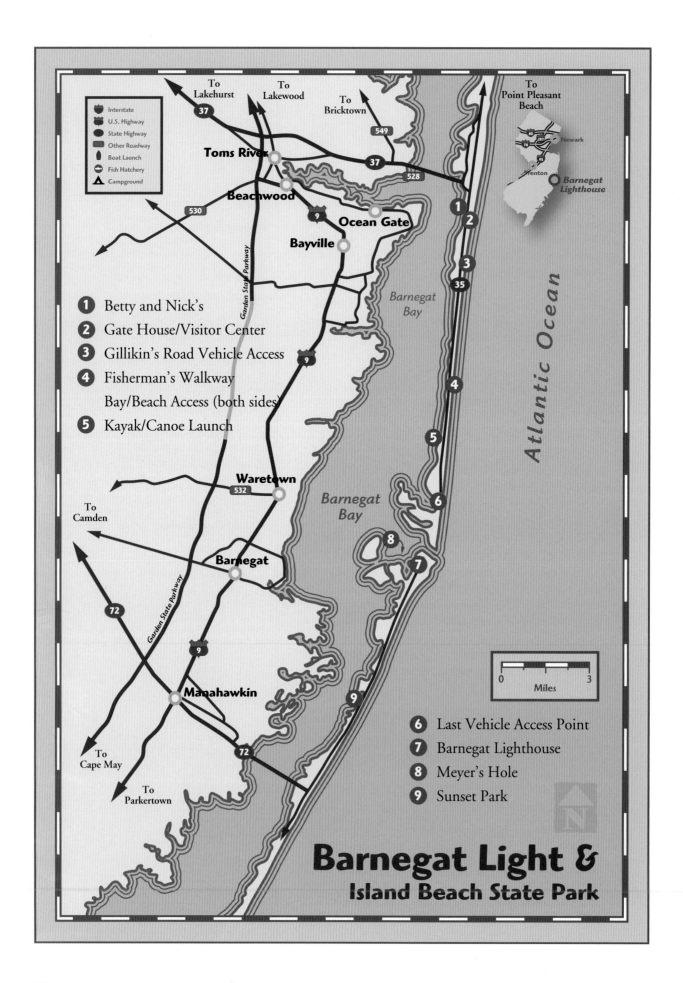

Legend:
- Interstate
- U.S. Highway
- State Highway
- Other Roadway
- Boat Launch
- Fish Hatchery
- Campground

**1** Betty and Nick's
**2** Gate House/Visitor Center
**3** Gillikin's Road Vehicle Access
**4** Fisherman's Walkway
   Bay/Beach Access (both sides)
**5** Kayak/Canoe Launch

**6** Last Vehicle Access Point
**7** Barnegat Lighthouse
**8** Meyer's Hole
**9** Sunset Park

To Lakehurst
To Lakewood
To Bricktown
To Point Pleasant Beach

Toms River
Beachwood
Ocean Gate
Bayville
Waretown
Barnegat
Manahawkin

Barnegat Bay
Atlantic Ocean

Newark
Trenton
Barnegat Lighthouse

To Camden
To Cape May
To Parkertown

Garden State Parkway

0    Miles    3

# Barnegat Light &
## Island Beach State Park

# Barnegat Light, Island Beach State Park

After all these years, I've still got my southern Virginia accent—so you can imagine how popular I am in the Garden State. My introduction to Jersey saltwater angling came in the form of Bob Atticks, king of all things fishing at the Sportsmen's Center in Bordentown, New Jersey. I've known Bob for many years now, and although he never tires of poking fun at my drawl, I must grudgingly admit that here is a man who cares deeply about the New Jersey fishery. "Most people from out of state don't have any idea how good the fishing is here," he insists. "All they think about when you say 'New Jersey' is the Turnpike, and most just drive through the state on their way somewhere else." This might well be true. But I've got to go with Bob on this one: Traveling anglers would do well to stop and sample this fishery, and at the top of the list of hotspots sits Barnegat Light and Island Beach State Park.

There are hard-core saltwater fly anglers—and then there are Jersey anglers who have taken saltwater fly fishing to a whole new level. Take, for example, Bob Popovics, whose amazing

## Types of Fish
Fly anglers fishing Barnegat Light and Island Beach State Park can expect to land stripers, bluefish, and the occasional weakfish. Anglers can also score with flounder, false albacore, and bonita.

## Baitfish
Menhaden, eels, spearing, glass minnows, shrimp, squid, and crabs.

## Equipment to Use
*Rods:* 8- to 11-weight rods, 9 to 10 feet in length.
*Reels:* Large-arbor reels with a good drag system.
*Lines:* Fast-intermediate matched to rod, as well as 200- to 400-grain sinking lines.
*Leaders:* 10- to 30-pound-test leaders, 3 to 5 feet in length (wire leaders should be used if fishing for blues).
*Wading:* Can be done in a variety of locations around Barnegat Light and especially at Island Beach State Park.

## Flies to Use
Bob's Banger, sizes 4/0-2/0; Clouser Minnow, 2/0-4; Cowen's Baitfish, 1/0; Cowen's Magnum Baitfish, 4/0; Dubiel's Red-Ducer, 1/0 and 2; Lefty's Deceiver, 3/0-2; Lefty's Half and Half, 3/0-2; Popovics's Candy Eel, 1/0; Popovics's Deep Candy, 1; Popovics's Surf Candy, 3/0-2.

## When to Fish
This area fishes well April through December.

*Continued*

*Stand-up stripping baskets, such as this one used by Capt. Al Zlata, keep anglers from stepping on their fly lines. The basket also keeps the line from tangling and allows the line to play out easily. Photo by Beau Beasley.*

*Anglers fishing the rocky shoreline near Old Barney enjoy good fishing and a great view. Be very careful when fishing off any jetty, as the rocks are often slippery. Photo by Beau Beasley.*

Popovics's Surf Candy

patterns have played an enormous part in defining saltwater fly fishing. His books, complete with careful step-by-step tying instructions, were often "researched" on the beaches of Island Beach State Park. Another big name in New Jersey fly angling is Gene Quigley, owner of Shore Catch Guide Service. His innovative patterns work quite well in and around the waters of Barnegat Light. "Old Barney" still works. If you feel up to checking out the beautiful view from the top of the light, you can scout the contour of the surrounding area very well from Old Barney.

Anglers will find plenty of places to cast a line just below the lighthouse, but beware: This area is very slippery, so watch your step. Kayakers will find plenty of places to launch their kayaks as well. Anglers who wish to fish in the surf at Island Beach State Park will pay an entrance fee of between $5 and $10 per vehicle. Those with 4x4 vehicles may pay $195 for a beach permit, which is good from January 1 through December 31. You may also opt for a three-consecutive-day pass for $50. The areas marked for fishing and beach access are easy to find. Anglers and swimmers don't mingle here: You can do one or the other, but not both in the same place. Anglers may pick up last-minute information at local fixture Betty and Nicks Bait and Tackle before they hit the beach or park. The guys at the shop are really in touch with what goes on here.

I recently fished the Barnegat Light area of New Jersey with Capt. Al Zlata of A-2-Z Fishing. Captain Al's specialty is working the shorelines carefully for stripers and weakfish. "I don't do anything but fly fish," he says. "It's not that I'm against bait. I just like the added challenge of fly fishing." At low tide, the verdant shorelines near the lighthouse resemble miniature putting greens; the grassy islands that dot the area provide excellent cover for a variety of fish. "Fish like hanging off these ledges," Captain Al told me. "They produce excellent ambush points, but you really have to pay attention to be successful."

If you're just passing through New Jersey, you're making a big mistake. Take the time to explore this area, and you'll find the fishing great and people pleasant—despite their funny accents.

*Working the shoreline with baitfish patterns often proves very effective. Photo by Beau Beasley.*

### Season & Limits
For the latest information on fishing near Barnegat Light or Island State Park contact New Jersey Division of Fish, Game, and Wildlife at (609) 292-2965 or www.state.nj.us/dep/fgw.

### Nearby Fly Fishing
There are all sorts of places along the Jersey Coast, including Sandy Hook and, of course, the New York Bight. A terrific source of information for fly anglers can be found by contacting the Atlantic Saltwater Fly Rodders (www.aswf.info).

### Accommodations & Services
While fishing at Barnegat Light, I stayed at the White Whale Motel, which is conveniently located within walking distance of the lighthouse and a marina. For great food be sure to visit Shady Rest in Bayville, New Jersey. This restaurant is owned by saltwater fly-tying icon Bob Popovics. If you're lucky Bob will be in, and perhaps he'll give you some tying pointers. If not, the food is still great.

White Whale Motel
Barnegat Light, New Jersey
www.whitewhalemotel.com
(609) 494-3020

### Shops & Guides
A-2-Z Fish
Barnegat Light, New Jersey
www.a2zfish.com
(609) 660-0956

Betty and Nicks
Seaside Park, New Jersey
www.bettyandnicks.com
(732) 793-2708

Island Beach State Park
Seaside Park, New Jersey
www.njparksandforests.org
(732) 793-0506

L.L. Bean
Marlton, New Jersey
www.llbean.com/marlton
(856) 810-5560

Orvis
Marlton, New Jersey
www.orvis.com/marlton
(856) 983-0960

Ramsey Outdoor
Paramus, New Jersey
www.ramseyoutdoor.com
(201) 261-5000

Shore Catch Guide Service
Manasquan, New Jersey
www.shorecatch.com
(732) 528-1861

Sportsmen's Center
Bordentown, New Jersey
www.sportsmenscenter.com
(609) 298-5300

Streams of Dreams
Upper Saddle River, New Jersey
www.streamsofdreams.com
(201) 934-1138

Tackle Direct
Somers Point, New Jersey
www.tackledirect.com
1-888-354-7335

Tight Lines Fly Fishing
Pine Brook, New Jersey
www.tightlinesflyfishing.com
(973) 244-5990

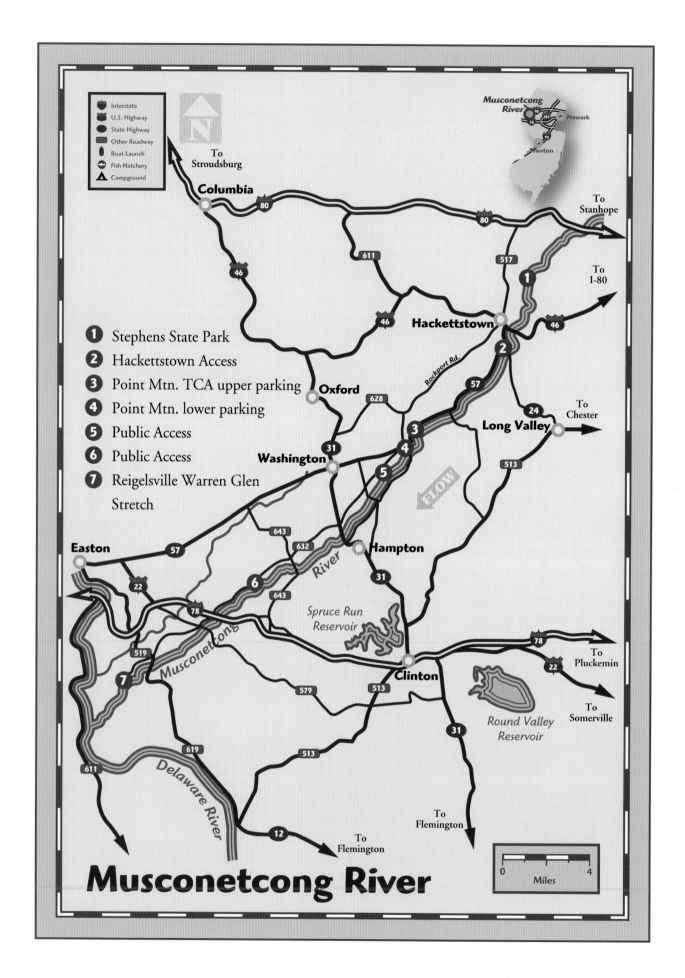

Legend:
- Interstate
- U.S. Highway
- State Highway
- Other Roadway
- Boat Launch
- Fish Hatchery
- Campground

N

1 Stephens State Park
2 Hackettstown Access
3 Point Mtn. TCA upper parking
4 Point Mtn. lower parking
5 Public Access
6 Public Access
7 Reigelsville Warren Glen
  Stretch

Musconetcong River
Newark
Trenton

To Stroudsburg

Columbia

To Stanhope

To I-80

80
80
611
517
46
46
46
1
Hackettstown
2
Rockport Rd.
57
24
To Chester
Long Valley
513
Oxford
628
3
4
31
5
Washington
FLOW

643
632
River
Hampton
31
Easton
57
22
6
643
Spruce Run Reservoir
78
78
To Pluckemin
22
519
Musconetcong
7
Clinton
579
513
To Somerville
Round Valley Reservoir
31
To Flemington
619
611
Delaware River
12
To Flemington

0    Miles    4

# Musconetcong River

# Musconetcong River

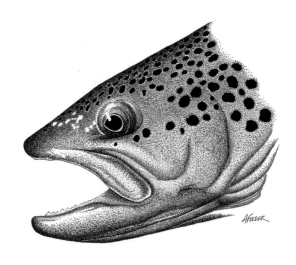

**T**he Musconetcong River—better known as the "Musky" by those who fish it—rises out of Lake Hepatcong and eventually flows into the Delaware River. What lies in between is some of the best trout fishing in the northeastern Mid-Atlantic. The Musky is a broad river with significant current unlike its sister streams, the nearby Pequest and Raritan. This river can and does carry a great deal of water, for which wading anglers should remain mindful. The quirky Musky also gets colder rather than warmer as it leaves its headwaters because feeder creeks and underground streams feed the Musky on its rush to the Delaware. It picks up flow and gets colder as it goes.

If you've got the time, the Musky's got the fish. Because of its size, many anglers opt to start upstream near Hackettstown

*Due to good flows, the Musky holds plenty of water and a strong trout population. Joey Scarangello with fish on. Photo by Beau Beasley.*

*Guide Mike McAuliffe works at Ramsey Outdoor and often guides on the Musky. He is surprised by how many trout anglers don't know about this fishery. Photo by Beau Beasley.*

JC's Electric Caddis

where the flow is smaller. This area does afford good access, and the river runs very close to Routes 46 and 57. Entering the river here may allow you to get a few trout under your belt before you move on to larger portions of the river. A Trout Conservation Area (TCA) exists near Penwell, and because Route 57 borders the river here for a few miles before heading inland, anglers use this road as a good jumping-off point. I fished this section of the river with well-known guide Mike McAuliffe and was duly impressed. "Most people have no idea how great the trout fishing is here," he said as he landed one trout after another. "They really don't know what they're missing."

Farther down the river not far from the town of Bloomsbury and the tiny hamlet of Alpha near Route 519 is good water for anglers willing to walk a bit. Because it's so far from the TCA, this section is less well known—but it holds plenty of fish. I've listed several river access points on the map, but this is by no means an exhaustive list. If you see a place on the side of the road that affords access to the river, by all means park and explore that section of water. Unless there's a sign that prevents you from parking along the road, chances are you can make a quick entry to the river. You'll find private clubs along the Musky that will deny you access, but even they have their upsides: First, these clubs often make improvements to their sections of the river, including structures that improve habitat and prevent erosion. Second, the club sections are often routinely stocked with large trout that don't know they're supposed to stay put.

The Musky is not the most famous trout stream in New Jersey—that honor is held by the famed Raritan—but I think that perhaps it should be. When I fished the Musky, I realized at last why New Jersey is called the Garden State. The river and its surroundings are lush and verdant, and the water itself is teeming with rainbows, browns, and the occasional brookie. If you find yourself in Jersey, do yourself a favor and fish the Musky. You'll never think of New Jersey the same way again.

*One look at this photo and you can see why any trout angler would want to come here. Who would believe that New Jersey could hold such beautiful trout water? Photo by Beau Beasley.*

## Types of Fish

Anglers typically find rainbow trout here as well as wild browns and native brook trout. Small- and largemouth bass are caught here along with carp, pickerel, and walleye in the upper reaches where the river is slower and warmer.

## Known Hatches

Blue-winged olive, Hendrickson, stonefly, sulfur, Iso, light Cahill, trico, terrestrials, and midges.

## Equipment to Use

*Rods:* Medium-action 4- to 5-weight, 9 feet in length.
*Reels:* Disc-drag reel, some large-arbor applications.
*Lines:* Weight-forward floating lines matched to rod.
*Leaders:* George Harvey–style slack leader 4X to 5X, 9 to 12 feet in length.
*Wading:* Chest waders will give you the most options.

## Flies to Use

*Drys:* Adams, sizes 14-20; Blue-winged Olive, 14-20; Elk-Hair Caddis, 14-20; Griffith's Gnat, 18-26; Light Cahill, 14-20; Sulfur Parachute, 14-18; Sulfur Emerger, 14-18; Parachute Iso, 10-14; Patriot, 18-22.

*Nymphs & Streamers:* BH Hare's Ear, sizes 14-20; BH Prince Nymph, 14-20; Blood Dot, 16; Gray Scud, 14-16; Lafontaine's Emergent Sparkle Pupa, 14-16; McAuliffe's Horror Business, 18-24; Midge Pupa and Larvae, 18-26; Muddler Minnow, 6-10; Pheasant Tail Nymph, 14-20; Red Brassie, 18-24; San Juan Worm, 14; Stroup's Sulphur Nymph, 12-18; Sculpin, 4-8; Walt's Worm, 12; Woolly Bugger, 6-10; RS2, 18-26.

## When to Fish

Open all year.

## Season & Limits

For the latest information on fishing the Musconetcong, contact the New Jersey Division of Fish, Game, and Wildlife at (609) 292-2965 or www.state.nj.us/dep/fgw.

## Nearby Fly Fishing

Anglers fishing here can also hit the Pequest and the Raritan. Anglers might also consider fishing the Flatbrook.

## Accommodations & Family Activities

The town of Stanhope, New Jersey, is centrally located to good trout water. I stayed at the Whistling Swan and found it to be a great place to stay. There are several events held near Stanhope each year. If you're looking for some interesting food and like microbreweries, be sure to check out Long Valley Brew Pub.

The Whistling Swan Inn
Stanhope, New Jersey
www.whistlingswaninn.com
1-888-507-2337

Long Valley Brew Pub
Long Valley, New Jersey
(908) 876-1122

## Fly Shops & Guides

Mike McAuliffe
Ledgewood, New Jersey
www.riseformstudio.tv
(973) 668-5026

Ramsey Outdoor
www.ramseyoutdoor.com
Succasunna, New Jersey
(973) 584-7798
Paramus, New Jersey
(201) 261-5000

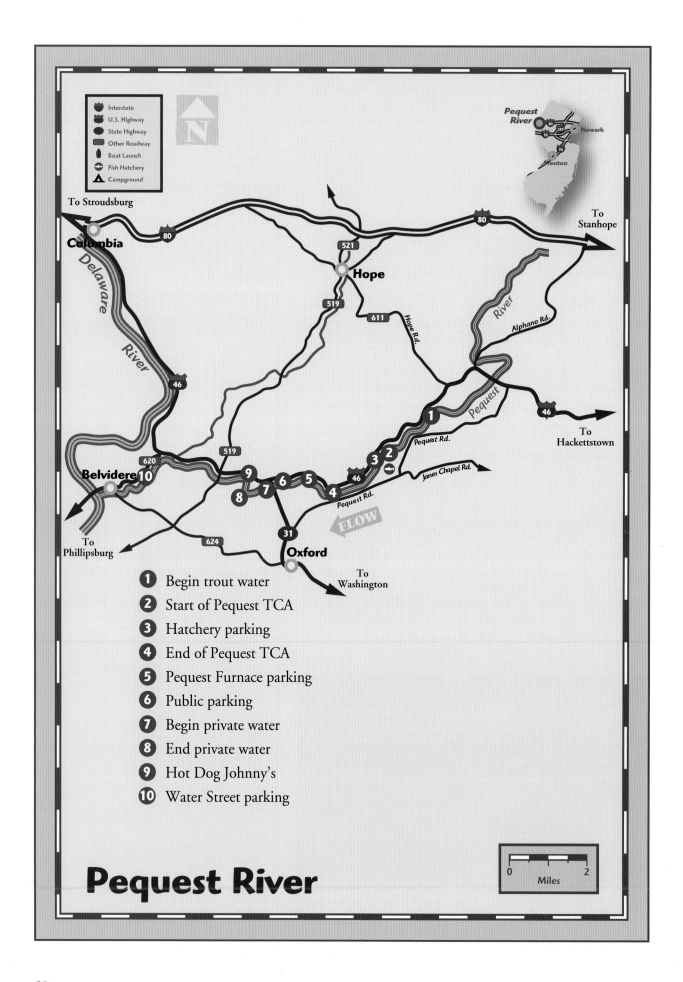

Legend:
- Interstate
- U.S. Highway
- State Highway
- Other Roadway
- Boat Launch
- Fish Hatchery
- Campground

N

Pequest River

To Stroudsburg

Columbia

Delaware River

80

521

Hope

519

611

Hope Rd.

80

To Stanhope

Alphano Rd.

Pequest River

46

Pequest Rd.

To Hackettstown

46

**1**

**3** **2**

Janes Chapel Rd.

519

620

Belvidere

**10**

**9**

**6** **5**

**8** **7** **4**

46

Pequest Rd.

FLOW

To Phillipsburg

624

31

Oxford

To Washington

**1** Begin trout water

**2** Start of Pequest TCA

**3** Hatchery parking

**4** End of Pequest TCA

**5** Pequest Furnace parking

**6** Public parking

**7** Begin private water

**8** End private water

**9** Hot Dog Johnny's

**10** Water Street parking

0 Miles 2

# Pequest River

# Pequest River

The Pequest is not the type of river that will impress you with its sheer size. As a matter of fact, if this body of water were in Virginia or Pennsylvania it would no doubt be called Pequest Creek. The Pequest River, however, lies in the great state of New Jersey and it holds sizeable trout all year, so it should certainly be on your list of places to fish regardless of its diminutive nature. The old adage, "Great things often come in small packages," is rightly applied here. The Pequest, located near the town of Stanhope, offers easy access off of Route 46, and the fact that fly anglers here can get a trout fix without having to leave the state is noteworthy to say the least.

The best-known part of the Pequest is commonly referred to as the hatchery section, which lies within the Trout Conservation Area. As the name implies, a state-run hatchery lies just off its banks and occasionally some trout no doubt "escape" from the hatchery. The coldwater discharge from the hatchery travels downstream and actually helps keep this section of the river from becoming overheated, which in turn keeps the trout content to stay nearby. There's a large parking area near the hatchery section, so unless you

## Types of Fish

Anglers may catch browns, rainbows, and brook trout here. The bottom end of the river can also produce smallies.

## Known Hatches

Winter stonefly, blue-winged olive, Hendrickson, March brown, sulfur, caddisfly, Cahill, midges, and terrestrials.

## Equipment to Use

*Rods:* 4- to 5-weight, 9 feet in length.
*Reels:* Standard trout reel.
*Lines:* Weight-forward floating lines.
*Leaders* George Harvey–style slack leaders in 4X or 5X, tapered from 9 to 12 feet in length.
*Wading:* Chest waders work best here.

## Flies to Use

*Drys:* Adams, sizes 14-26; Blue-winged Olive, 14-26; Patriot, 12-18; Elk-Hair Caddis, 14-20; Flying Ant, 10-18; Light Cahill, 14-20; March Brown, 10-14; Midge, 18-26; Stimulator, 16-20; Steeves's Attract Ant, 16-20, Steeves's Bark Beetle, 16-20.

*Nymphs & Streamers:* BH Hare's Ear, sizes 14-20; BH Prince Nymph, 14-20; Blood Midge, 18-26; Brassie, 18-26; Copper John, 18-22; Green Weenie, 14-16; JC's Electric Caddis Larva, 12-18; LaFontaine's Emergent Sparkle Pupa, 14-16; McAuliffe's Horror Business, 18-24, Pheasant Tail Nymph, 14-20; Woolly Bugger, 6-10; RS2, 18-26; San Juan Worm, 14-18; Stroup's Sulphur Nymph, 12-18.

*Continued*

*The Pequest is not a big river but its trout pack a punch. Photo by Beau Beasley.*

*Though the hatchery section on the Pequest can be crowded at times, it doesn't seem to bother the fish. Photo by Beau Beasley.*

Soft Hackle
Pheasant Tail

arrive in the wee hours of the morning, don't be surprised to see multiple vehicles already parked there. If this is the case, simply walk up- or downstream to find open water, as few anglers take the time or effort to do this. That being said, there is a lot of pressure on this section of the stream, because trout often stack up here in small pods. The locals often call this section of the river the Kiddie Pool, as finding and catching fish here is not considered difficult. Be forewarned that some of the older local fly anglers consider the Pequest *their* river and will have no problem walking within easy casting distance of you. One older gentleman told me he was going to go in just above me but give me plenty of room to fish. He stopped all of 15 feet upstream of me. Oddly enough, it really didn't affect the fishing.

Fishing the Pequest is hardly limited to the well-known hatchery section. Anglers can find multiple pull-offs all along Route 46, some of which are easily spotted while others are barely able to accommodate two cars—but they are there. One likely looking spot is right behind Hot Dog Johnny's, a New Jersey institution. Fishing the Pequest is best done between April and November, and landing a half dozen rainbows and browns in the 14- to 18-inch class in a single afternoon is not uncommon.

Beyond the Trout Conservation Area, less pressured but productive water flows all the way to the town of Belvidere before the river empties into the Delaware River. Much of this section of the river is overlooked because it's not quite as scenic. Don't bother telling the trout, because they don't seem to know that they shouldn't be there. Smallies often inhabit this section of the river, too. The Pequest is the perfect place for trout bums from New York and New Jersey to get a quick trout fix without heading for a two-day road trip to some place like the Catskills. Do yourself a favor and visit the Pequest. It will be well worth the trip.

*The parking lot near the hatchery section of the Pequest affords easy access—and added fishing pressure. Photo by Beau Beasley.*

*Brook trout are very popular in New Jersey. Photo by Beau Beasley.*

### When to Fish

The best times to fish here are early spring and late fall, though the hatchery section holds fish all year.

### Season & Limits

For the latest information on fishing the Pequest, contact the New Jersey Division of Fish, Game, and Wildlife (609-292-2965 or www.state.nj.us/dep/fgw).

### Nearby Fly Fishing

Good fishing can also be found on the Raritan and the Musconetcong.

### Accommodations & Services

While I fished the Pequest I had the pleasure of staying at the Whistling Swan Inn. This fine B&B is a great jumping-off point for lots of good trout streams in northern New Jersey. While fishing the Pequest, don't miss the opportunity to eat at Hot Dog Johnny's. This 1950s-style restaurant is a local institution and sells excellent birch beer in frosted mugs and hot dogs with every condiment imaginable so long as it's ketchup, mustard, or onion. This is a serious place for anglers to consider stopping because the river runs directly behind the restaurant and has good water. Besides, you can always stop and have lunch or sip some birch beer while thinking of where you want to fish next.

The Whistling Swan Inn
Stanhope, New Jersey
www.whistlingswaninn.com
1-888-507-2337

Hot Dog Johnny's
Buttzville, New Jersey
www.hotdogjohnny.com
(908) 453-2882

### Guides & Shops

Mike McAuliffe
Ledgewood, New Jersey
www.riseformstudio.tv
(973) 668-5026

Ramsey Outdoor
www.ramseyoutdoor.com
Succasunna, New Jersey
(973) 584-7798
Paramus, New Jersey
(201) 261-5000

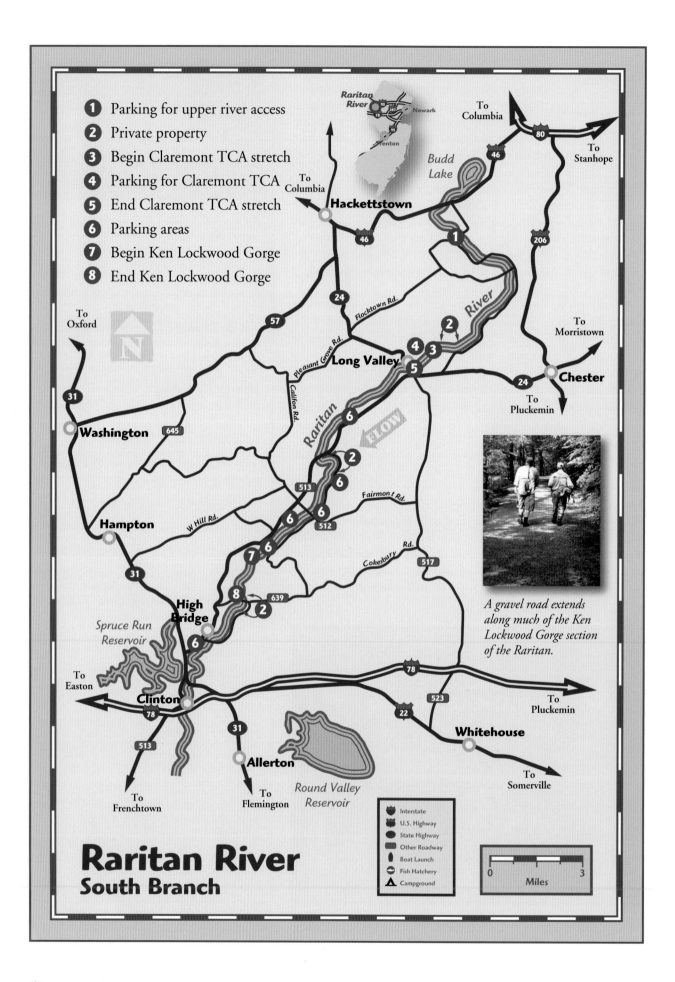

1 Parking for upper river access
2 Private property
3 Begin Claremont TCA stretch
4 Parking for Claremont TCA
5 End Claremont TCA stretch
6 Parking areas
7 Begin Ken Lockwood Gorge
8 End Ken Lockwood Gorge

Raritan River

To Columbia

To Stanhope

80

46

206

Budd Lake

To Columbia

Hackettstown

46

1

To Morristown

River

2

24

Flocktown Rd.

4 3

57

Long Valley

5

24

Chester

Pleasant Grove Rd.

To Pluckemin

To Oxford

N

Raritan

6

FLOW

31

Califon Rd.

Washington

645

6

2

Fairmont Rd.

513

6

W. Hill Rd.

Hampton

6

512

6

Rd.

7

Cokesbury

517

31

8

639

2

High Bridge

6

Spruce Run Reservoir

78

523

To Pluckemin

To Easton

Clinton

78

22

Whitehouse

513

31

To Frenchtown

Allerton

To Flemington

Round Valley Reservoir

To Somerville

A gravel road extends along much of the Ken Lockwood Gorge section of the Raritan.

Interstate
U.S. Highway
State Highway
Other Roadway
Boat Launch
Fish Hatchery
Campground

0        Miles        3

# Raritan River
## South Branch

# Raritan River, South Branch

T hough New Jersey trout fishing remains largely unsung, the South Branch of the Raritan seems to garner the most respect. Though her northern sister is no pushover and deserves recognition in her own right, the South Branch draws more anglers because she carries a significant amount of water and holds trout all year long. While it's true that the river is stocked in several places, most anglers from outside the state are shocked to learn that the South Branch of the Raritan has a healthy population of wild fish.

Bud Lake is the source of the South Branch of the Raritan, and although this section of river is small, it does support a population of native brookies. The river picks up volume—and the occasional brown trout—as it rushes toward the Trout Conservation Area (TCA) just north of Long Valley. The TCA near Claremont runs for about a mile; if you see signs that indicate private club water, just move on. Two more private stretches of club water are also marked, so keep your eyes open for the posted areas. The good news is that private clubs often provide riparian structure

*Wild browns are common in the Raritan. Photo by Beau Beasley.*

*Veteran fly angler Joey Scarangello uses the river's current to float his patterns beneath overhanging streamside vegetation. Photo by Beau Beasley.*

*The Ken Lockwood Gorge section of the river is the most famous, but other sections of the Raritan also hold plenty of trout. Photo by Beau Beasley.*

McAuliffe's Horror Business

and cover that help the whole river. And remember that the monster fish cruising through these private sections don't actually know where the private water ends and the public water begins, so you still have a shot at catching them when they move during high- and low-water events.

Near the first private stretch anglers can park and walk across the field to the Gillette Trail, which is a fairly long though easy walk to the river. You should find a good population of native brook trout as well as wild browns. As the river continues to twist and turn through the bucolic pastures of New Jersey, it eventually enters Ken Lockwood Gorge Wildlife Management Area, spoken about in hushed tones as the Gorge by those familiar with this section of the South Branch. When I fished here, I was struck by how much it reminded me of the Rapidan River in the Shenandoah National Park in Virginia.

Mike McAuliffe, who fished the river with me along with his friend Joey Scarangello, notes that this picturesque gorge section of the South Branch is the ideal classroom for aspiring anglers: "I often have clients who really want to hone their nymphing skills, and this is the perfect place to teach them." McAuliffe punctuated this statement by summarily landing one brown trout after another. I even managed to land a few myself.

The Ken Lockwood Gorge may be the best known part of this river—but it's far from the only place to find good trout water. Anglers driving along Route 513 will find all sorts of places to stop and wet a line, but take care not to park on private property or trespass while fishing the Raritan. Anglers fishing toward the lower end of the river, below the towns of High Bridge and Clinton, will start to see less trout action but could just as easily be rewarded with a hefty smallmouth.

It's true that some Garden State anglers think the beautiful bountiful South Branch is akin to holy water—and it turns out that they might be on to something. Old Stone Union Church, built in Washington Township in 1774, was the pastorate of Dr. Henry Muhlenberg, known as the father of Lutheranism in America. You'll find the ruins of the old church in Long Valley.

*Local patterns such as McAuliffe's Horror Business are very effective on tight-lipped trout. Photo by Beau Beasley.*

## Types of Fish

Anglers typically find rainbow trout as well as a wild brown and native brook trout in the upper reaches of the South Branch. Anglers can also catch smallmouth bass, pike, and other warmwater fish below Clinton, New Jersey.

## Known Hatches

Blue-winged olive, caddisflies, Hendrickson, March brown, slate drake, sulfur, light Cahill, white fly, terrestrials, and midges.

## Equipment to Use

*Rods:* Medium-action 4- to 5-weight, 9 feet in length.
*Reels:* Standard trout reel.
*Lines:* Weight-forward floating lines matched to rod.
*Leaders:* George Harvey–style slack leader, 4X to 5X, 9 to 12 feet in length.
*Wading:* Chest waders will give you the most options.

## Flies to Use

*Drys:* Adams, sizes 12-22; Ant, 14-20; Blue-winged Olive, 14-24; Elk-Hair Caddis, 14-28; Griffith's Gnat, 18-26; Light Cahill, 14-18; March Brown Parachute, 10-14; Parachute Iso, 10-14; Sulfur Parachute, 14-18; Sulfur Emerger, 14-18.

*Nymphs & Streamers:* Blood Dot, size 16; BH Hare's Ear, 12-20; BH Prince Nymph, 14-20; Gray Scud, 14-18; LaFontaine's Emergent Sparkle Pupa, 18-20; McAuliffe's Horror Business, 18-24; Midge Pupa and Larva, 18-26; Pheasant Tail Nymph, 12-20; Sculpin, 4-8; Woolly Bugger, 6-10; RS2, 18-26; JC's Electric Caddis Larva, 12-16; San Juan Worm, 14, Stroup's Sulphur Nymph, 14-18; Walt's Worm, 12.

## When to Fish

Spring is good on the Raritan, but don't overlook winter fishing here, because it can be great.

## Season & Limits

For the latest information on fishing the Raritan, contact the New Jersey Division of Fish, Game, and Wildlife (609-292-2965 or www.state.nj.us/dep/fgw).

## Nearby Fly Fishing

Anglers fishing here can also hit the Pequest or the Musconetcong rivers, of course you can also fish the North Branch of the Raritan.

## Accommodations & Family Activities

The town of Stanhope, New Jersey, is centrally located to good trout water. I stayed at The Whistling Swan and found it to be a great place. If you're looking for some interesting food, check the Long Valley Brew Pub.

Long Valley Brew Pub
Long Valley, New Jersey
(908) 876-1122

The Whistling Swan Inn
Stanhope, New Jersey
www.whistlingswaninn.com
1-888-507-2337

## Fly Shops & Guides

Mike McAuliffe
Ledgewood, New Jersey
www.riseformstudio.tv
(973) 668-5026

Ramsey Outdoor
www.ramseyoutdoor.com
Succasunna, New Jersey
(973) 584-7798
Paramus, New Jersey
(201) 261-5000

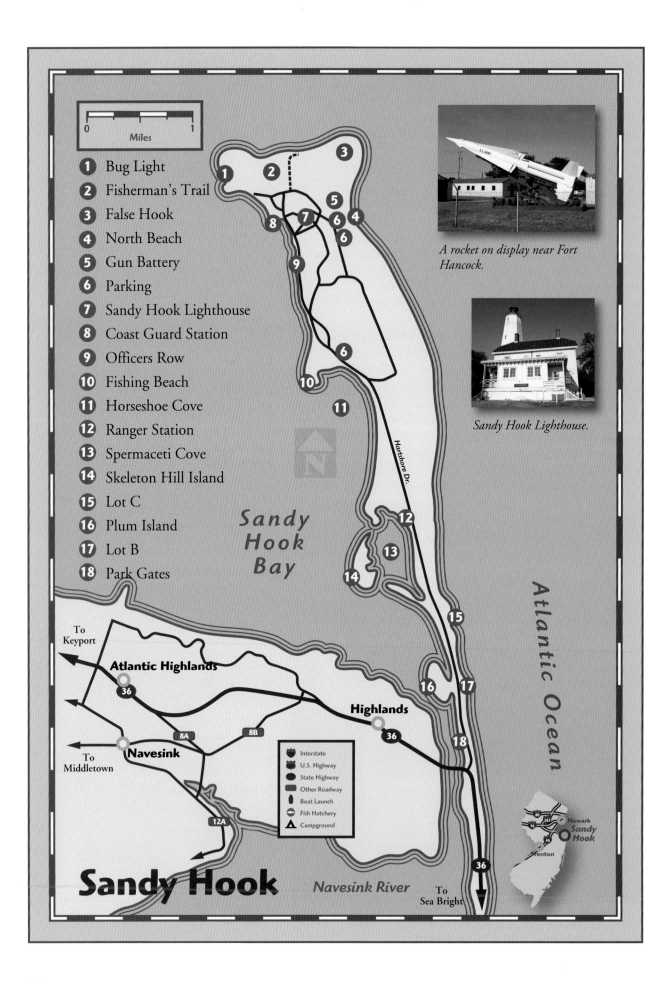

1. Bug Light
2. Fisherman's Trail
3. False Hook
4. North Beach
5. Gun Battery
6. Parking
7. Sandy Hook Lighthouse
8. Coast Guard Station
9. Officers Row
10. Fishing Beach
11. Horseshoe Cove
12. Ranger Station
13. Spermaceti Cove
14. Skeleton Hill Island
15. Lot C
16. Plum Island
17. Lot B
18. Park Gates

A rocket on display near Fort Hancock.

Sandy Hook Lighthouse.

Sandy Hook Bay

Hartshore Dr.

Atlantic Ocean

To Keyport

Atlantic Highlands

To Middletown

Navesink

Highlands

To Sea Bright

Navesink River

Sandy Hook

Interstate
U.S. Highway
State Highway
Other Roadway
Boat Launch
Fish Hatchery
Campground

Newark
Sandy Hook
Trenton

# Sandy Hook

The Mid-Atlantic is replete with top-notch saltwater fly-fishing destinations, but few offer the excitement and allure of New Jersey's famed Sandy Hook, which is the go-to spot for countless traditional and fly anglers for all manner of saltwater species. The Hook is essentially an island off the Jersey coast that offers a commanding view of New York City's skyline. Its view of New York is precisely why Fort Hancock was built here in 1874. The fort was very active for decades and was quite busy during World War II protecting the harbor from German naval vessels. The fort served as a citadel complete with secret weapons ranging from hidden cannons and concrete machine-gun nests to launching sites for Nike missiles, then the cutting edge in rocket technology. You can still check out the remnants of Fort Hancock's history today, along with old gun emplacements and lookout stations. Directly beside the anglers' parking area you can still see vestiges of the old gun emplacements. Though the guns were taken out of service long ago, they still have an eerily stalwart look about them. The fort was decommissioned in 1974, however the U.S. Coast Guard still has an active station there.

The energetic and enthusiastic James Jindal of Tight Lines Fly Fishing, in nearby Pine Brook, is a committed Sandy Hook fan and fishes there anytime he gets a chance. "This is a great fishery,

### Types of Fish
Depending on the time of year, fly anglers fishing off the Hook can expect to land stripers, bluefish, weakfish, flounder, croaker, false albacore, and bonita.

### Baitfish
Menhaden, eels, spearing, glass minnows, shrimp, squid, and crabs.

### Equipment to Use
*Rods:* 8- to 10-weight rods, 9 to 10 feet in length.
*Reels:* Mechanical and disc-drag large-arbor reels.
*Lines:* Fast-intermediate lines matched to rod, as well as 200- to 400-grain sinking lines.
*Leaders:* 10- to 30-pound test leaders 3 to 5 feet in length. Wire leaders should be used if fishing for blues.
*Wading:* Can be done in a variety of locations.

### Flies to Use
Blados's Crease Fly, sizes 3/0-4; Bob's Banger, 4/0-2/0; Cowen's Baitfish, 1/0; Clouser Minnow, 2/0-4; Dubiel's Red-Ducer, 1/0-2; Lefty's Deceiver, 3/0-2; Lefty's Half and Half, 3/0-2; Popovics's Surf Candy, 1.

### When to Fish
Fishing Sandy Hook offers so many opportunities that it's hard to know when to go. Ultimately it's a question of what you are fishing for. Keep in mind that flounder can be a great alternative when larger fish aren't biting.

*Continued*

*Capt. Joe Mattioli of On the Bite Charters holds a schoolie striper. Photo by Beau Beasley.*

*Fly angler James Jindal with a nice fly-caught flounder he landed near Sandy Hook, New Jersey. Photo by Beau Beasley.*

Cowen's Baitfish

and it's not hard at all to succeed here once you get the basics down," he insists. Jindal and fly-shop owner Andrew Moy, who has made a name for himself as a Spey-casting instructor, introduce dozens of anglers to the Sandy Hook fishery each year.

New Jersey lays claim to Sandy Hook, but plenty of New Yorkers love the place, too. Bryan Kaczkin of Urban Angler in Manhattan sends his customers to the Hook as well. "It's pretty easy to hop on the ferry and hit Sandy Hook," he says. "Guys like it because it gets them out of the city and fishing without much hassle." Capt. Joe Mattioli of On the Bite Charters operates out of Staten Island, but he often picks up clients in New Jersey and fishes the Hook. In fact, I spent a lovely June day chasing schoolie stripers off the Hook with Captain Joe. He really knows his stuff and can get clients into all sorts of surrounding waters like the Raritan Bay and Jamaica Bay.

Wading anglers have choices galore: Spermaceti Cove and Horseshoe Cove are easily accessible and known for weakfish. Or simply drive to the end of the island, and walk out to the point. A 300- to 400-yard walk will bring you to the beach, and once there you can scout where to fish. Jindal and I spent an afternoon on the point, and he easily landed a handful of flounder and a sea robin—all on the fly—in about 90 minutes. "I know folks come here for stripers," laughs Jindal, "but I have to admit that when I need a quick fix, I'll often come here and catch flounder all evening. The funny thing is that the striper fishing is so good here that many anglers often overlook other species that are literally only a few feet away from them." You'll find so much accessible water at Sandy Hook that you could easily stay for a week.

Between surf fishing and exploring the Hook's many coves, your options are almost endless. Sandy Hook is a great place to kayak as well because the island offers protection from the wind and cross currents. Finally, history buffs simply must make time to explore the fort and local lighthouse before snapping up all those stripers.

*Remnants of the gun emplacements at Fort Hancock still seem daunting. The only battles that occur there currently are between anglers and the local fish. Photo by Beau Beasley.*

*Crab patterns can be very effective when fishing off Sandy Hook.*

### Season & Limits

For the latest information on fishing near Sandy Hook contact New Jersey Division of Fish, Game, and Wildlife (609-292-2965 or www.state.nj.us/dep/fgw).

### Nearby Fly Fishing

There are all sorts of places along the Jersey Coast including Island Beach State Park and Barnegat Light.

### Accommodations & Family Activities

While fishing at Sandy Hook I stayed at the Laingdon Hotel B&B. Its 17 Victorian-styled rooms have the latest conveniences and offer tourists the chance to relax in a quiet setting or stroll along the seaside boardwalk. For great seafood check out Bahr's Seafood in Atlantic Highlands, New Jersey, and for the latest offerings in Monmouth County check out www.tourism. visitmonmouth.com.

Laingdon Hotel Bed & Breakfast
Ocean Grove, New Jersey
www.laingdonhotel.com
(732) 774-7974

### Shops & Guides

There are too many guides to list who service this area. One of the finest is Capt. Joe Mattioli of On the Bite Charters, which operates out of Staten Island, New York. Fishing with him gives you the option of fishing the Hook or going to other waters in and around New York. You can meet him at Staten Island or some New Jersey locations. Kayak fishing is an option with Reel Therapy.

On the Bite Charters
Staten Island, New York
www.flyfishnyc.com
(908) 612-2575

Ramsey Outdoor
Paramus, New Jersey
www.ramseyoutdoor.com
(201) 261-5000

Reel Therapy
Sandy Hook, New Jersey
www.reeltherapy.com
(732) 922-4077

Tight Lines Fly Fishing
Pine Brook, New Jersey
www.tightlinesflyfishing.com
(973) 244-5990

Urban Angler
New York, New York
www.urbanangler.com
1-800-255-5488

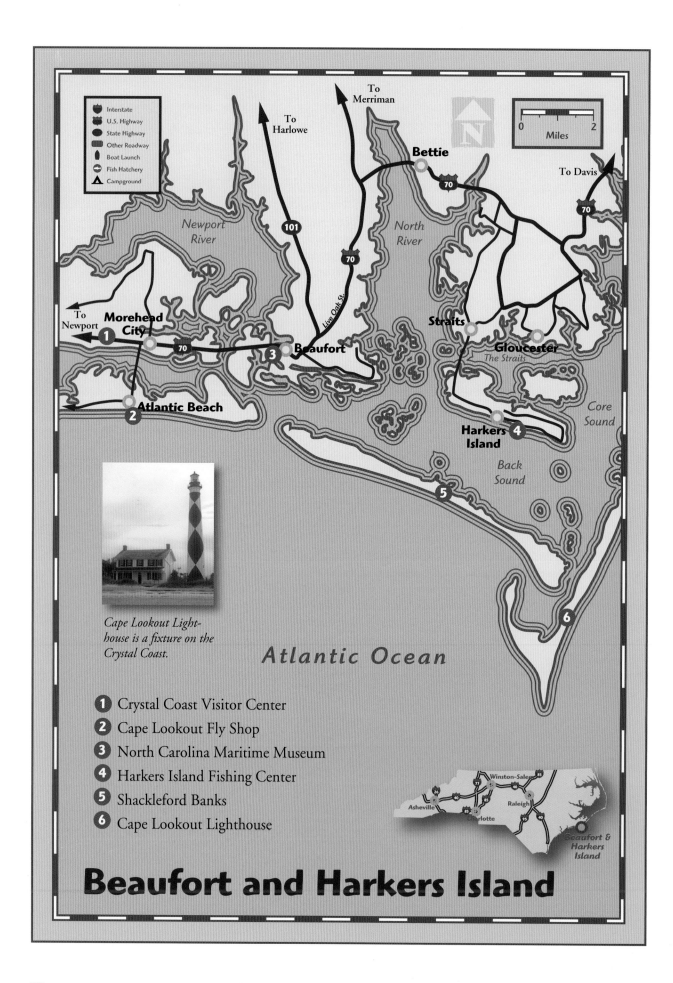

## Legend

- Interstate
- U.S. Highway
- State Highway
- Other Roadway
- Boat Launch
- Fish Hatchery
- Campground

N

0    Miles    2

To Harlowe

To Merriman

Bettie

To Davis

70

70

Newport River

North River

101

70

Live Oak St.

To Newport

Morehead City

Beaufort

Straits

Gloucester

The Straits

1

70

3

Atlantic Beach

2

Harkers Island

4

Core Sound

Back Sound

5

6

*Cape Lookout Light-house is a fixture on the Crystal Coast.*

Atlantic Ocean

1 Crystal Coast Visitor Center
2 Cape Lookout Fly Shop
3 North Carolina Maritime Museum
4 Harkers Island Fishing Center
5 Shackleford Banks
6 Cape Lookout Lighthouse

Winston-Salem

Asheville

Raleigh

Charlotte

Beaufort & Harkers Island

# Beaufort and Harkers Island

# Beaufort and Harkers Island

L anding your first false albacore is an experience you never forget. It seems like yesterday when I caught my first. I was fishing off North Carolina's Crystal Coast when an albie hit like a ton of bricks and nearly jerked the rod right out of my hand. As the fight ensued, I distinctly remember feeling that I might as well have been trying to land a tractor trailer with my 9-weight rod. That crazy little tunny just kept going and going. I hadn't seen so little backing on my reel since it was spooled up on the day I bought it. Eventually he tired, and I brought him to hand. As I sat on the edge of the boat after throwing him back into the water like a spear, I felt like I really needed a cigarette—which is surprising, because I don't smoke. After a short breather I was at it again, and by the end of the day I knew I'd be back in Beaufort and fishing off Harkers Island again soon.

### Types of Fish
Most anglers headed to Beaufort and Harkers Island in the fall are after false albacore. Other fish that can be landed here include bluefish, cobia, flounder, drum, and Spanish mackerel.

### Baitfish
Menhaden, eels, spearing, glass minnows, shrimp, squid, and crabs.

### Equipment to Use
*Rods:* 9- to 11-weight rods, 9 to 10 feet in length.
*Reels:* Strong anti-reverse saltwater reels with a minimum of 150 yards of 30-pound backing.
*Lines:* Fast-intermediate matched to rod, some sinking lines in the 200- to 400-grain range.
*Leaders:* 10- to 30-pound-test leaders, 3- to 5-foot leaders for intermediate lines, and wire bite tippets for bluefish.
*Wading:* Anglers can wade off the point near Cape Lookout Lighthouse.

### Flies to Use
Blados's Crease Fly, sizes 1/0-2; Bob's Banger, 4/0-2/0; Bruce's Crystal Shrimp, 1/0; Clouser Minnow, 2/0-4; Cowen's Baitfish, 1/0; Dubiel's Lil' Haden, 1/0-2; Dubiel's Red-Ducer, 1/0-2; Lefty's Deceiver, 3/0-2; Lefty's Half and Half, 3/0-2. Popovics's Surf Candy, 1.

*Continued*

Capt. Gary Dubiel of Spec Fever Guide Service holds a hefty false albacore. Though many fishermen think the fall season is over by Thanksgiving, anglers can often land these speed demons as late as December 25.

*While it's true most anglers come to Beaufort and Harkers Island to fish for false albacore, other saltwater species such as flounder can be caught here as well. Photo by Beau Beasley.*

Dubiel's Lil' Haden

Each fall, countless fly anglers and guides descend on the southeastern coast of North Carolina to battle these salty speed demons. False albacore are worthless in the kitchen, so commercial anglers want nothing to do with them. As a result they generally show up in huge numbers in the fall and crash bait to their hearts' content. They're tremendously strong and will readily take flies presented in the proper manner. Accuracy is key, and more important than distance. Don't waste your time false casting, instead, consistently make thirty-five foot casts directly to the side of the school. This often produces excellent results. Once the fish strikes, strip strike him one time and then keep your line tight without delivering too much pressure. These fish can break you off in no time flat, so let them run. On my last fishing trip to Beaufort, with Capt. Gary Dubiel of Spec Fever Guide Service, I broke off six flies and two fly lines before I got into the swing of things. I'm lucky Captain Gary didn't push me overboard.

One common misconception about fishing near Harkers Island is that you need a boat to be successful. This is pure bunk. Yes, boating keeps your options open and allows to you try—and I do emphasize *try*—to follow the schools of fish. But even in this case, shore-bound anglers can be successful if they plan well. Several year-round ferries service the Cape Lookout area and Shackleford Banks. Generally speaking, these ferries provide a great service to anglers—and for relatively peanuts. For a mere $15 each, they'll ferry anglers to any number of areas, drop them off with all their gear, and pick them up later in the day.

Once on Cape Lookout you can connect with Cape Lookout Conch Tours. They'll ferry you by vehicle to various fishing spots including the tip of the Cape near the lighthouse. This prime spot has a deep drop-off and reaches well into the Atlantic Ocean, making it a great place to cast a line. The drawback is that you'll need to carry everything out with you for the day. Anglers are best served by stocking up at their local fly shop or visiting Cape Lookout Fly Shop in nearby Atlantic Beach. Talking to Capt. Joe Shute, a longtime guide and committed angler who has forgotten more about albie fishing than most anglers will ever know, is also a good idea.

Be forewarned, landing a false albacore is not just exhausting—it's addictive.

*False albacore will readily take flies but often break off unsuspecting anglers.*

### When to Fish
The season lasts from early April until mid- to late December, sometimes the false albacore will stay until early January.

### Season & Limits
Open all year. Limits and sizes will depend on species.

### Nearby Fly Fishing
Anglers fishing the Beaufort and Harkers Island area need to be aware that wind is a real factor. During a harsh blow, stick close to the small islands and inlets that provide some relief from the wind. This may allow you to pick up flounder and drum while taking a break from the wind.

### Accommodations & Family Activities
While staying at Beaufort you can't do much better than spending the night at The Inlet Inn. They have a great view of the harbor and are close enough that you can walk into the historic district of Beaufort. There are some great restaurants here such as Clawson's or one of my personal favorites, the Ruddy Duck. If you have kids, be sure to visit the North Carolina Maritime Museum in Beaufort. For a full listing of activities on the Crystal Coast go to www.crystalcoastnc.org or call 1-800-786-6962.

The Inlet Inn
Beaufort, North Carolina
www.inlet-inn.com
1-800-554-5466

Cape Lookout Conch Tours
Harkers Island, North Carolina
(252) 732-4578

Outer Banks Ferry
Beaufort, North Carolina
www.outerbanksferry.com
(252) 728-4129

### Fly Shops & Guides
Cape Lookout Fly Shop
Atlantic Beach, North Carolina
www.capelookoutflyshop.com
www.captjoes.com
(252) 240-1427

Harkers Island Fishing Center
Harkers Island, North Carolina
www.harkersmarina.com
(252) 728-3907

Outer Banks Fly Fishing
Nags Head, North Carolina
www.outerbanksflyfishing.com
(252) 449-0562

Spec Fever Guide Service
Oriental, North Carolina
www.specfever.com
(252) 249-1520

*The author in a tug of war with a fat Albert that doesn't want to give up. Photo by Capt. Gary Dubiel.*

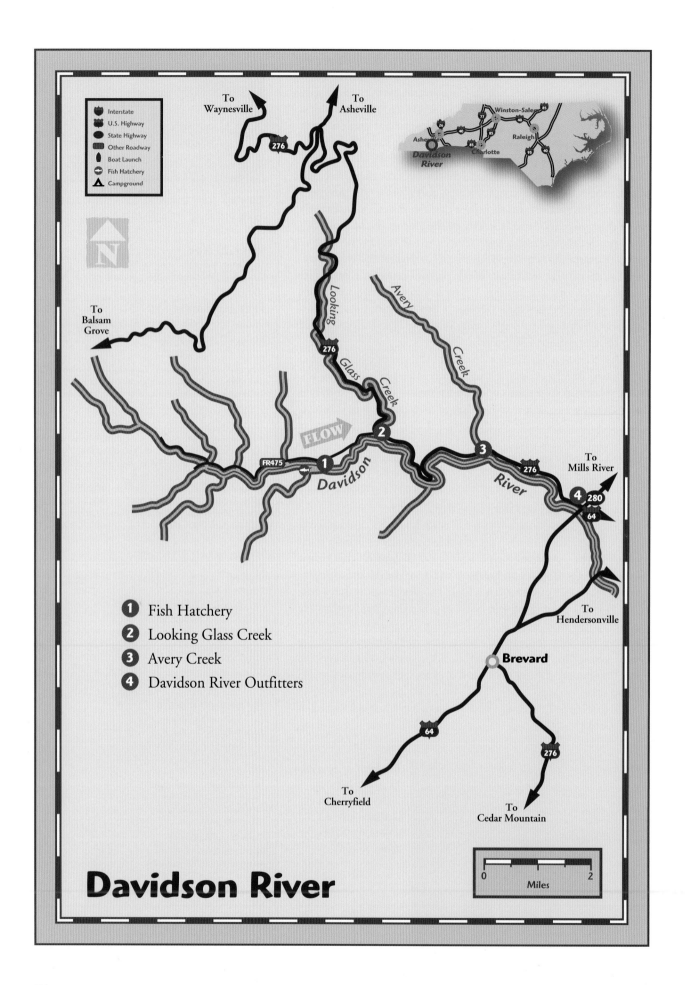

**Legend:**
- Interstate
- U.S. Highway
- State Highway
- Other Roadway
- Boat Launch
- Fish Hatchery
- Campground

N

To Waynesville
To Asheville
276

Winston-Salem
Asheville
Raleigh
Charlotte
Davidson River

To Balsam Grove

Looking
Glass
Creek

Avery
Creek

276

FLOW

FR475
1
Davidson

2

3

River
276

To Mills River
4 280
64

To Hendersonville

1 Fish Hatchery
2 Looking Glass Creek
3 Avery Creek
4 Davidson River Outfitters

Brevard

64

276

To Cherryfield

To Cedar Mountain

# Davidson River

0     Miles     2

# Davidson River

If anglers could fish only one North Carolina trout water, chances are they'd choose the Davidson, better known as the Big D. The Davidson, with its quiet pools, rock walls, and rhododendron-covered banks, is as close to trout heaven as you can get. Flowing alongside Pisgah National Forest, the river draws thousands of visitors each year and is popular with campers and anglers alike. This area is sometimes referred to as the cradle of forestry: The Biltmore Forest School was established here in 1898 by Carl Schenck, who worked as the forest manager on the Biltmore Estate in nearby Asheville.

The lower reaches of the Davidson, from the French Broad to Avery Creek, are quite deep and hold most of the river's water—and that's good news: The state stocks heavily here, and general tackle rules apply. The bad news is that occasionally you'll have to contend with tubers and spin anglers. In this area, fly anglers might want to try throwing big streamers early in the morning, especially if the water is off-color or high as a result of recent rains.

Most fly anglers fish the catch-and-release section from Avery Creek upstream to the headwaters of the river. The fish hatchery that operates on the Davidson has abundant parking, but don't go looking for solitude. The browns that call this section of the river

## Types of Fish
Anglers typically come here searching for big browns. They often see them, catching them however, is another matter entirely.

## Known Hatches
Blue-winged olive, quill Gordons, giant brown stonefly, green drakes, yellow drakes, Hendrickson, March brown, little yellow stonefly, sulfur, caddisfly, Cahill, inchworm, stonefly, and terrestrials.

## Equipment to Use
*Rods:* 3- to 6-weight, 7 to 9 feet in length.
*Reels:* Standard trout reel.
*Lines:* Weight-forward floating lines matched to rod.
*Leaders:* 5X to 8X, 9-15 feet in length.
*Wading:* Chest waders can give you a lot more options here.

## Flies to Use
*Drys:* Adams, sizes 14-20; Adams Variant, 12-18; Blue-winged Olive, 14-20; Elk-Hair Caddis, 14-20; Fat Albert, 6-14; Flying Ant, 10-18; Light Cahill 14-20; Kevin's Caterpillar, 10; Little Yellow Sally, 14-20; March Brown, 10-14; Pale Morning Dun, 14-20; Quill Gordon, 12-22; Stimulator, 12-20; Texas Piss Ant, 12-18.

*Continued*

*Simons Welter hooked up with a trout at the annual Pisgah Fly Masters Tournament. Photo by Jennifer Rowe, courtesy of North Carolina Wildlife Resources Commission.*

*Looking Glass Falls is only a stone's throw from the Davidson River and is a popular tourist attraction. Photo by Jennifer Rowe.*

Kevin's RL Stonefly

home look like miniature submarines and prefer to lie along the banks, occasionally surfacing to take in a midge. A word of warning to the uninitiated: Davidson River fishing can be nerve-wracking, especially when you watch a 26-inch brown trout charge your pattern at full speed and then at the last second decide to just watch it float by.

The upper reaches of the Davidson are quite small; anglers can actually hike up to the point at which the river is nearly small enough to jump across, though they'll have to do some bushwhacking. You'll find tight cover up here; prepare to roll cast. The good news is that this part of the river sees much less pressure. If quarters are too tight, then move back downstream. The river will widen as it picks up more water, and the canopy cover will begin to abate. Numerous access points exist along Route 475 for those whose eyes are peeled. And don't be afraid to check out Looking Glass and Avery Creeks.

Two anglers who know the Davidson intimately are Kevin Howell, owner of Davidson River Outfitters, and Walker Parrot, the shop manager. They both fish this river hundreds of times a year, and they're both experts at reading the water and stalking big fish. This fly-fishing duo teamed up to win the Fly Fishing Masters in 2006, in large part because of what they had learned the hard way on the Davidson: "You need to make your first cast count on the Davidson because these are not forgiving fish," says Kevin. "I also recommend that you pay strict attention to your wading." Kevin points out that inattentive anglers who are careless in how they enter the river often fail before they make their first move. "Poor wading on the Davidson," he jokes, "has saved more trout than catch-and-release ever has."

*The Davidson is one of the most popular trout rivers in the East. The scenery alone makes a trip here worthwhile. Photo by Jennifer Rowe.*

## Flies to Use (continued)

*Nymphs & Streamers:* Disco Midges, 14-20; Hare's Ear, 14-20; Prince Nymph, 14-20; Clouser Foxee Minnow, 6-10; Coburn's Inchworm, 12-14; Howell's The Bug, 8-12; Hot Creek Special, 10-12; Kevin's RL Stonefly, 6-12; Midges, 18-22; Pheasant-Tail Nymph, 14-20; RSII'2's, 16-20 San Juan Worm, 14-18; Sculpin, 4-8; WD 40s, 14-20; Wooly Bugger, 6-10.

## When to Fish

The Davidson fishes well nearly all year. July and August can be tough if there's been no rain.

## Season & Limits

For the latest information contact the North Carolina Wildlife Resources Commission (www.ncwildlife.org, 919-707-0010).

## Nearby Fly Fishing

There are 400 miles of public trout water located in Transylvania County in addition to the Davidson. Other favorites are the East Fork of the French Broad River, Looking Glass Creek, and Avery Creek.

## Accommodations & Family Activities

In 2008, Davidson River Outfitters teamed up with the North Carolina Wildlife Resources Commission to create the Pisgah Fly Masters Tournament. The event is held each March on the Davidson River and proceeds go toward wildlife education.

When I fished the Davidson I had the privilege of staying at Ash Grove Cabins in the wonderful town of Brevard. The cabins are exceedingly clean and well decorated. The only downside was once I checked in I really didn't want to leave.

Ash Grove Cabins
Brevard, North Carolina
www.ash-grove.com
(828) 885-7216

Pisgah Fly Masters
Pisgah Forest, North Carolina
www.ncwildlife.org/pisgahflymasters
(828) 877-4423

## Fly Shops & Guides

Curtis Wright Outfitters
Asheville, North Carolina
www.curtiswrightoutfitters.com
(828) 274-3471

Davidson River Outfitters
Pisgah Forest, North Carolina
www.davidsonflyfishing.com
1-888-861-0111

Hunter Banks
Asheville, North Carolina
www.hunterbanks.com
1-800-227-6732\

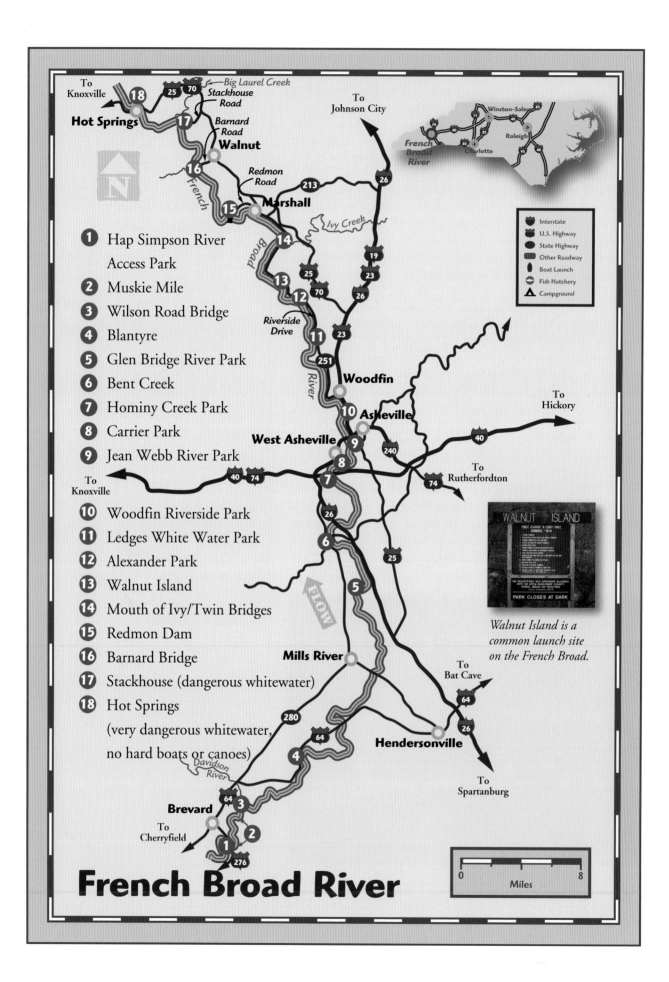

1 Hap Simpson River Access Park

2 Muskie Mile

3 Wilson Road Bridge

4 Blantyre

5 Glen Bridge River Park

6 Bent Creek

7 Hominy Creek Park

8 Carrier Park

9 Jean Webb River Park

10 Woodfin Riverside Park

11 Ledges White Water Park

12 Alexander Park

13 Walnut Island

14 Mouth of Ivy/Twin Bridges

15 Redmon Dam

16 Barnard Bridge

17 Stackhouse (dangerous whitewater)

18 Hot Springs
(very dangerous whitewater,
no hard boats or canoes)

Walnut Island is a
common launch site
on the French Broad.

# French Broad River

Interstate
U.S. Highway
State Highway
Other Roadway
Boat Launch
Fish Hatchery
Campground

Miles
0          8

# French Broad River

The French Broad—so named to distinguish it from the English Broad, which is now known simply as the Broad River—was one of two major rivers recognized by North Carolina's early settlers. European powers often named important New World land features after their sovereigns or their kingdom itself in order to maintain a foothold in an area. Its sheer size meant that the French Broad was integral to local trade among the early settlers. As the country grew, the river eventually supported various industries. In 1881, the French Broad Steamboat Company operated the *Mountain Lily*, a 90-foot-long two-decker with room for 100 passengers. The idea behind the steamboat was to connect goods and passengers between Hendersonville, Asheville, and Brevard. Unfortunately the concept never really caught on, and in 1885 she was sold off as scrap wood after the ship was damaged in a flash flood. The planks from the ship were used to build Horseshoe Baptist Church, and the ship's bell was hung in the church's belfry.

## Types of Fish

This river is known for its world-class smallies and also produces hefty muskies. Don't be surprised if you hook into an aggressive carp here as well.

## Known Hatches

Food sources here are crayfish and minnows, so consider throwing plenty of streamer patterns. There is also a sizeable mayfly hatch here.

## Equipment to Use

**Rods:** 6- to 8-weight, 8 to 9½ feet in length.
**Reels:** Disc-drag reel, unless you are fishing for muskie, for which you will need a large-arbor disc-drag reel and plenty of 30-pound-test backing.
**Lines:** Weight-forward floating, matched to rod; sinking-tip lines work as well.
**Leaders:** 1X-3X leaders, 9 feet in length, wire leaders will be needed for muskie fishing.

*Continued*

*Anglers fishing the French Broad can enjoy seeing landmarks such as the Biltmore Estate when not battling occasional muskie and resident smallmouth. Used with permission from The Biltmore Company, Asheville, North Carolina.*

*Reba Brinkman, who works with Biltmore Estate in Asheville, North Carolina, shows why anglers seek out this river. Photo courtesy Reba Brinkman.*

Howell's Big Nasty

The French Broad has east, west, and north forks, but the main body of the river is what smallie anglers rave about. Smallies aren't the only worthy opponents here. Muskie fishing has caught on lately, despite the fact that landing one of these behemoths can be tricky. Muskies prefer to lie in heavy cover, so the successful angler will repeatedly be casting very large patterns, which can be tiresome. Combine this with a fish that has the temperament of an alligator, and you can easily see why muskies are so tough to land. River conditions also play a significant part in a successful muskie fishing trip, as local river guides will tell you. The best strip of muskie fishing on the French Broad lies between Route 276, just outside of Brevard, and the Hap Simpson access. This area is known as "the muskie mile."

"Water clarity is the real issue here," said Forrest Marshall as we worked large streamers along the banks from his drift boat. "When it first rains, the fish feed like crazy. Unfortunately once it rains, the river can be muddy for more than a week because of all the construction that goes on here nearly year-round." Forrest works as head guide for Hunter Banks Fly Shop in Asheville and spends up to 200 days a year on the water, much of it on the French Broad. "Two problems I see here again and again: Guys who fish patterns that are just too small, and guys who fish too fast in the early spring. Also, if you aren't getting hung up on the bottom once in a while, you're fishing too high in the water column. These fish will move up to feed, you just have to give them a good reason." Local guide Chris Gibbs agrees: "The French Broad can fish very well, but you have to pay your dues to see what works where. That takes time."

A word of caution: What passes as a boat ramp on this river is sometimes laughable. I recommended that you check things out in person before you show up with your boat in tow.

You'll find plenty to look at on the French Broad. Floating past Asheville and viewing the Biltmore Estate from the water can be particularly memorable. Steamboats no longer ply these waters, but rafts and drift boats certainly do. Avail yourself of one to enjoy the full French Broad experience.

*Forrest Marshall loves fishing the French Broad but admits launching his drift boat can be a bit of a challenge. Once in the river, however, the smallies can make it all worthwhile. Photo by Beau Beasley.*

## Equipment to Use (continued)

*Wading:* For anglers who don't have access to a drift boat, there are multiple access and wading points along Riverside Road (Route 251) between Asheville and Marshall. You should wet wade here as deep holes are not a good match for waders.

## Flies to Use

Bunny Leeches, sizes 4-6; Claw-Dad, 2-6; Clouser Minnow, 1/0-6; Cone Head Kiwi Muddler, 4-6; Kraft's Kreelex, 2-6; Dahlberg's Diver, 4; Forage Fly, 6; Hickey's Condor, 6-10; Howell's Big Nasty, 6; Todd's Wiggle Minnow, 2-6; Walker's Wiggler, 1/0-4; Zonkers, 1/0-4.

## When to Fish

You can start hitting the French Broad in late April, and it often fishes well until early October. July and August can be awesome because a drought here means good water clarity. The best flows for this river run from about 700 to 1,100 CFS.

## Season & Limits

For the latest information contact the North Carolina Wildlife Resources Commission, via the Web at www.ncwildlife.org or call (919) 707-0010.

## Nearby Fly Fishing

Alternative fishing locales include the Davidson, and just over the state line in Tennessee, the South Holston.

## Accommodations & Family Activities

There are more places to stay and activities for families to do in Asheville than you can imagine. The Western North Carolina Fly Fishing Expo (www.wncflyfishingexpo.com) is also held here each November and is really worth a visit. Attending this show is a great way to stay up on all things related to western North Carolina fly fishing.

Make sure to take time to visit the Biltmore Estate. This iconic home was built for George Vanderbilt and at the time was the largest home in America. The place was so large it required its own brick factory and a special rail spur just to deliver materials. I'm still not sure how old George, his wife, and their only daughter managed with only 34 bedrooms. All total, the square footage of Biltmore equals 4 acres and sports 43 bathrooms! Guests can fly fish with a guide or even shoot sporting clays during their visit.

Biltmore
Asheville, North Carolina
www.biltmore.com
1-800-411-3812

## Fly Shops & Guides

Curtis Wright Outfitters
Asheville, North Carolina
www.curtiswrightoutfitters.com
(828) 274-3471

Davidson River Outfitters
Pisgah Forest, North Carolina
www.davidsonflyfishing.com
1-888-861-0111

Fishwater River Guides
Asheville, North Carolina
www.fishwaterguides.com
(828) 279-0959

Hunter Banks
Asheville, North Carolina
www.hunterbanks.com
1-800-227-6732

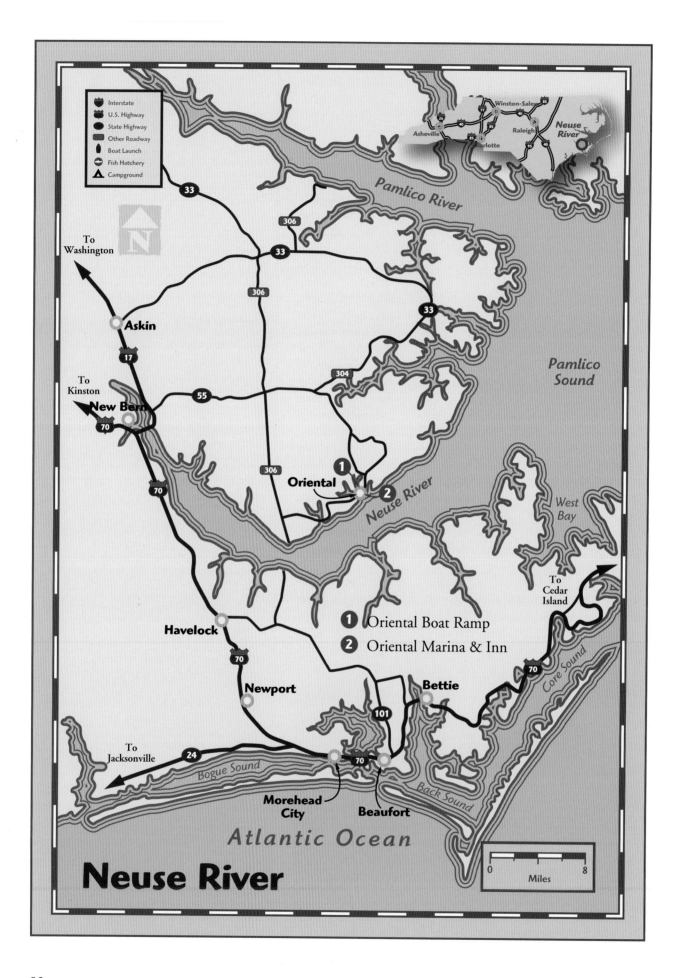

Interstate
U.S. Highway
State Highway
Other Roadway
Boat Launch
Fish Hatchery
Campground

To Washington

Askin

To Kinston

New Bern

Oriental

**①** Oriental Boat Ramp
**②** Oriental Marina & Inn

Havelock

Newport

Bettie

To Jacksonville

Morehead City

Beaufort

Pamlico River

Pamlico Sound

West Bay

To Cedar Island

Core Sound

Neuse River

Bogue Sound

Back Sound

Atlantic Ocean

Winston-Salem
Asheville
Raleigh
Charlotte
Neuse River

0          Miles          8

# Neuse River

# Neuse River

The Neuse River stretches more than 250 miles and flows completely within the Tar Heel State. It was home to Native Americans—the Neusiok tribe, from whom the river gets its name—for hundreds of years before it became an important commercial waterway and saw action during the Civil War. Among the two dozen or so ironclads built by the Confederate Navy, the *CSS Neuse* was designed to protect the rivers of eastern North Carolina in general and the Pamlico Sound in particular. The ship was instrumental at the Battle of Wyse Forks in March of 1865, when Gen. Jacob Cox led Union forces from New Bern in an effort to meet up with Gen. William T. Sherman on his famed march to the sea. The *CSS Neuse* fired on advancing Union forces in a rearguard action, allowing Confederate troops to safely evacuate the town of Kinston and fall back to Goldsboro. Unfortunately for the ship's crew, this action trapped them behind enemy lines. Because the *CSS Neuse* could not be moved swiftly to safety, the ship's crew scuttled her to keep her from falling into Union hands. The ship's powder magazine exploded soon after the ship was set

## Types of Fish
The primary fish sought here are red drum, specks, striped bass, and flounder with seasonal catches of black drum, weakfish, bluefish, and Spanish mackerel. Closer to New Bern, anglers can come into contact with many freshwater species including largemouth bass, pickerel, hickory shad, crappie, and jumbo white perch.

## Known Hatches & Baitfish
In the upper reaches of the Neuse you'll find all manner of minnows, frogs, damselflies, and terrestrials such as hoppers. Toward the mouth of the river you'll find menhaden, shrimp, crab, and glass minnows.

## Equipment to Use
*Rods:* 6- to 9-weight rods, 9 feet in length.
*Reels:* Mechanical and large-arbor reels.
*Lines:* Fast intermediate and floating lines matched to rod, as well as sinking-tip lines in the 200- to 300-grain range.
*Leaders:* 2- to 20-pound leaders from 7 to 10 feet should work just fine for floating lines, 4- to 6-foot leaders are sufficient for sinking lines.
*Wading:* Not applicable here.

*Continued*

*Capt. Gary Dubiel with a beefy redfish caught on the Neuse River just outside the historic seaside town of Oriental, North Carolina. Photo courtesy Capt. Gary Dubiel.*

*Protected shorelines and grass beds are great ambush points for predator fish. The Neuse River fishes well when high wind blows other areas. Photo by Beau Beasley.*

Dubiel's Red-Ducer

ablaze. It rested beneath the waters of the Neuse for nearly a century before it was raised in 1963.

Capt. Gary Dubiel, owner of Spec Fever Guide Service, has been guiding on the Neuse River for ten years. He's learned what works through a long process of trial and error: "I think the sheer vastness of this area can really complicate things for an angler. The Neuse is seven miles wide at its mouth where it empties into the Pamlico Sound, so it's easy to be overwhelmed if you don't have a game plan." If the name Gary Dubiel sounds familiar, it should: He's been a guest on *George Poveromo's World of Saltwater Fishing, Versus, The Sportsman's Channel,* and even *The Discovery Channel* in Europe. He's also a sought-after speaker. Despite his popularity, Captain Gary remains approachable even by the novice—most likely because he has earned his stripes the hard way, one guided trip at a time.

The Neuse is a river—but its water changes in salinity from fresh to brackish to nearly all salt as it wends its way to the Sound. Its habitat is diverse, and so should your methods and tactics be when fishing here. Those tactics will vary significantly depending upon when you're fishing and the species you're targeting. If you decide to focus on drum or speckled trout, you will likely be blind-casting to oyster bars or the seemingly never-ending grass-lined shores. Water clarity is also a tactical factor. Though at times you'll see nervous water or even breaking fish, the water is tea colored—and so the advantage goes to the fish. As a result, anglers are never sure when a violent strike might come, which leaves one a bit edgy. Anglers who put in their time, however, are likely to go home with a Neuse River Grand Slam of drum, flounder, and speckled trout all in the same day. If the wind is up, simply head upriver and you'll soon be casting poppers and large streamers to aggressive largemouth bass. Stripers often push up into this water, too, because apparently no one's told them that they are supposed to stay near the Sound. Best of all, the Neuse isn't located near major cities or interstates, which means that it sees little fishing pressure. You can fish here all day and not see another boat.

*Drum often fall for good streamer patterns such as Dubiel's Red-Ducer. Photo by Beau Beasley.*

### Flies to Use
Clouser Deep Minnow, sizes 2/0-4; Cowen's Baitfish, 1; Dubiel's Lil' Haden, 1/0-2; Dubiel's Red-Ducer, 1/0-2; Dubiel's Finesse Fly, 1/0; Lefty's Deceiver, 3/0-2; Lefty's Half and Half, 3/0-2; various Poppers, 3/0-4.

### When to Fish
Year-round although late January and February fishing can be influenced by hard cold fronts.

### Season & Limits
Limits and sizes will depend on species and the time of year when you're fishing. To get a full listing go to www. ncwildlife.org.

### Nearby Fly Fishing
One of the best alternatives to fishing the Neuse is the Pamlico Sound or the Crystal Coast.

### Accommodations & Family Activities
The 875 full-time residents of historic Oriental, the "Sailing Capital" tucked into North Carolina's southeastern corner, are easily outnumbered by the town's visitors and their many watercrafts moored in the town harbor. The town's peculiar name comes from the steamship *Oriental,* lost during the Civil War near Bodie Island Lighthouse about 30 miles above Cape Hatteras. In 1886 the postal service opened its first local office here, in what was then known as Smith's Creek. According to local lore, the wife of the first postmaster found the nameplate of the *Oriental* on the beach while visiting friends on the Outer Banks, and upon her return home began campaigning for the name change. Today, the town's museum displays an original bronze porthole from the sunken *Oriental.* This small town is not high on creature comforts but some true gems can be found if you look for them. Anglers taking on the Neuse River often stay at the Oriental Marina & Inn, which has a great restaurant that serves up wonderful local seafood. Anglers can even get picked up right at the dock by Captain Dubiel. For those wanting a great cup of coffee to start out the day stop by The Bean, a wonderful coffee shop within walking distance of the marina.

Oriental Marina & Inn
Oriental, North Carolina
www.orientalmarina.com
(252) 249-1818

The Bean
Oriental, North Carolina
www.thebeanorientalnc.com
(252) 249-4918

### Guides & Fly Shops
Great Outdoor Provision Company
www.greatoutdoorprovision.com
Raleigh, North Carolina
(919) 833-1741
Wilmington, North Carolina
(910) 343-1648

Orvis
Raleigh, North Carolina
www.orvis.com/raleigh
(919) 792-9200

Spec Fever Guide Service
Oriental, North Carolina
www.specfever.com
(252) 249-1520

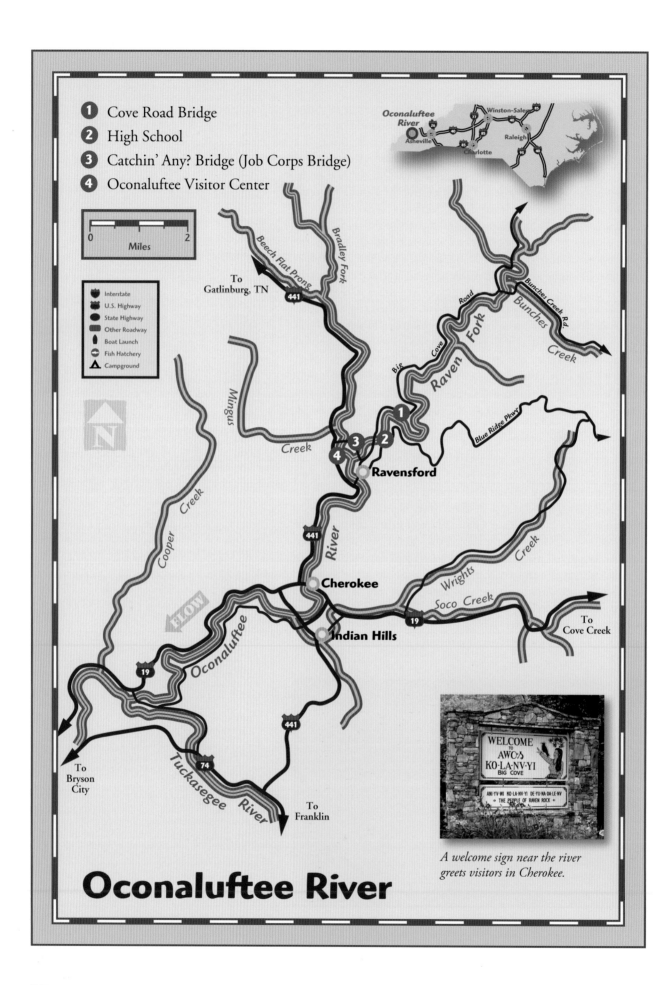

1 Cove Road Bridge
2 High School
3 Catchin' Any? Bridge (Job Corps Bridge)
4 Oconaluftee Visitor Center

Oconaluftee River

Asheville
Winston-Salem
Charlotte
Raleigh

0 Miles 2

Interstate
U.S. Highway
State Highway
Other Roadway
Boat Launch
Fish Hatchery
Campground

N

Beech Flat Prong
Bradley Fork
To Gatlinburg, TN
441
Cove Road
Big
Raven Fork
Bunches Creek Rd.
Bunches Creek
Mingus Creek
1
Blue Ridge Pkwy
3 2
4
Ravensford
Cooper Creek
441
River
Wrights Creek
FLOW
Cherokee
Soco Creek
19
To Cove Creek
Indian Hills
19
Oconaluftee
441
74
Tuckasegee River
To Bryson City
To Franklin

WELCOME TO AWC's KO·LA·NV·YI BIG COVE
ANI·YV·WI KO·LA·NV·YI DE·YU·NA·DA·LE·NV
THE PEOPLE OF RAVEN ROCK

*A welcome sign near the river greets visitors in Cherokee.*

# Oconaluftee River

# Oconaluftee River

## Types of Fish
Anglers typically find big rainbows and browns here.

## Known Hatches
Blue-winged olives, blue quill, stonefly, March brown, midge sulfur, light Cahill, quill Gordon, and assorted terrestrials.

## Equipment to Use
*Rods:* 4- to 6-weight, 8 to 9 feet in length.
*Reels:* Standard trout reel.
*Lines:* Weight-forward floating lines, matched to rod.
*Leaders:* 4X to 6X, 9 feet in length.
*Wading:* You can get by with hip boots in some places but chest waders are a better bet.

## Flies to Use
*Drys:* Adams, sizes 14-20; Blue-winged Olive, 14-20; Elk-Hair Caddis, 14-20; Flying Ant, 10-18; Gelso's Little Black Stonefly, 16-20; Light Cahill, 14-20; Little Yellow Sally, 14-20; March Brown, 10-14; Quill Gordon, 12-22; Stimulator, 12-20; Steeves's Attract Ant, 16-20; Sulfur, 16 to 18.

*Continued*

"Catching anything?" asked a voice from above, as Eugene Shuler and I stood fishing below the Job Corps Bridge on the Oconaluftee River. It's a commonly asked question of local anglers, as the bridge is restricted to foot traffic, and folks peer over and get curious. In fact, it's such a commonly asked question that the overpass is known to locals as the "Catchin' Any? Bridge"

Oconaluftee is Cherokee for "riverside"—but it ought to mean "stream full o' trout." The "Lufty" is stocked almost weekly throughout the year. As if on cue, Shuler set his hook into a nice fish and let his screaming reel and deeply bent rod do all the talking. Not long after he brought his fish to hand I also landed a nice rainbow, though I missed the chance at several others.

The Lufty actually begins in the Great Smoky Mountains National Park—America's most visited national park—and boasts a healthy population of native brookies. Although the cover can be tight in spots, very good access exists all along Route 441. The river eventually connects with the Raven Fork, and here the Lufty lies entirely in Cherokee Indian Reservation property. Excellent access for visiting anglers begins near Cove Landing Road and

*Anglers from Virginia, North Carolina, and Tennessee fish this river in a variety of ways, but nymphing is often the most effective. Photo by Beau Beasley.*

*Eugene Shuler, of Fly Fishing the Smokies Guide Service, fishes this river often. Fishing here can't help but bring a smile when hooking up with rainbows such as this one. Photo by Beau Beasley.*

Shuler's Carolina Midge

continues all the way to the Tuckasegee River. The place that draws the most attention from fly anglers is the 2.2-mile section of catch-and-release, fly-fishing-only water.

The Lufty is relatively small but provides plenty of water for the trout that call it home. Wading is quite easy, and the flow really isn't much of a problem even when the river is running a bit high. That said, anglers should use caution when wading here just as they would in any other river. Be sure to work the pools thoroughly. "These fish stack up in places at times," Shuler told me as we made our way downstream. "So once you find a good pool, you might be surprised at how many trout will respond to your pattern." That said, these fish, like any trout, can be unforgiving, so keep stealth and good casting in mind when fishing here.

Shuler and I had a pretty good day here, and his Carolina Midge really seemed to do the trick—though he was quick to point out standard patterns with a dropper can be just as effective if you fish them correctly. This river is open to fishing all year long, and the fish don't seem to mind the cold weather. If you brave the chilly winds of January and February, you might just have the river all to yourself.

A few words of caution are in order if you wish to try your luck on the Lufty. First, along with the fish, a small local herd of elk also call the river home. They are relatively accustomed to—though fairly unenthusiastic about—people, to the extent that the local high school near the river had to build a special fence to keep the elk from grazing there. Unexpectedly walking up on an elk can be frightening for both parties; keep your eyes open. Second, when on tribal land, consider yourself a guest and act accordingly. The Cherokee Nation is a sovereign authority and as such has its own tribal law enforcement officers and game wardens. Just a few weeks before I arrived, someone had been caught without a license and using bait in the fly-fishing-only section. The Cherokee authorities straightened out his little red wagon with a fine of more than $1,000.

*The Cherokee Nation has its own hatchery near the Oconaluftee River and protects its waterways with tribal police. Don't make the mistake of fishing here without a license. Photo by Beau Beasley.*

## Flies to Use *(continued)*

*Nymphs & Streamers:* BH Hare's Ear, sizes 14-20; BH Prince Nymph, 14-20; Coburn's Inchworm, 12-14; Finn's Golden Retriever, 6-10; Matuka, 4-10; Pheasant Tail, 14-20; Rainbow Warrior, 12-16; Shuler's Carolina Midge, 16-20; Woolly Bugger, 6-10.

## When to Fish
Open all year.

## Season & Limits
For the latest information on the Lufty, contact Cherokee Fish and Game (828-438-1601). You will need a catch-and-release special-use permit, which costs $20 annually, plus a fee of $7 a day. You don't need a North Carolina fishing license to fish tribal land.

## Nearby Fly Fishing
The Tuckasegee River is an easy drive from the Lufty. There's also great fishing all over the Great Smoky Mountains National Park.

## Accommodations & Family Activities
The town of Cherokee offers a host of lodging options. I had a great stay at the Microtel Inn & Suites, which is only a stone's throw from Rivers Edge Outfitters. There are plenty of activities for young and old alike in Cherokee. I highly recommend the outdoor drama *Unto These Hills*, a play the whole family will enjoy. For an entire listing of all the activities available to visitors while staying in Cherokee go to www.cherokee-nc.com.

Microtel Inn & Suites
Cherokee, North Carolina
www.microtelinn.com
(828) 497-7800

## Fly Shops & Guides
CCS Fly Fishing Outfitters
Cherokee, North Carolina
www.ccsflyfishing.com
1-888-243-5274

Fly Fishing the Smokies
Bryson City, North Carolina
www.flyfishgatlinburg.com
(828) 421-0172
(828) 488-7665

Highland Hiker
Highlands, North Carolina
www.highlandhiker.com
(828) 526-5298

Hookers Fly Shop
Sylva, North Carolina
www.hookersflyshop.com
1-877-518-7369

Nantahala Outdoor Center
Bryson City, North Carolina
www.noc.com
1-888-905-7238

Rivers Edge Outfitters
Cherokee, North Carolina
www.riversedgeoutfittersnc.com
(828) 497-9300

Waynesville Fly Shop
Waynesville, North Carolina
www.waynesvilleflyshop.com
(828) 246-0306

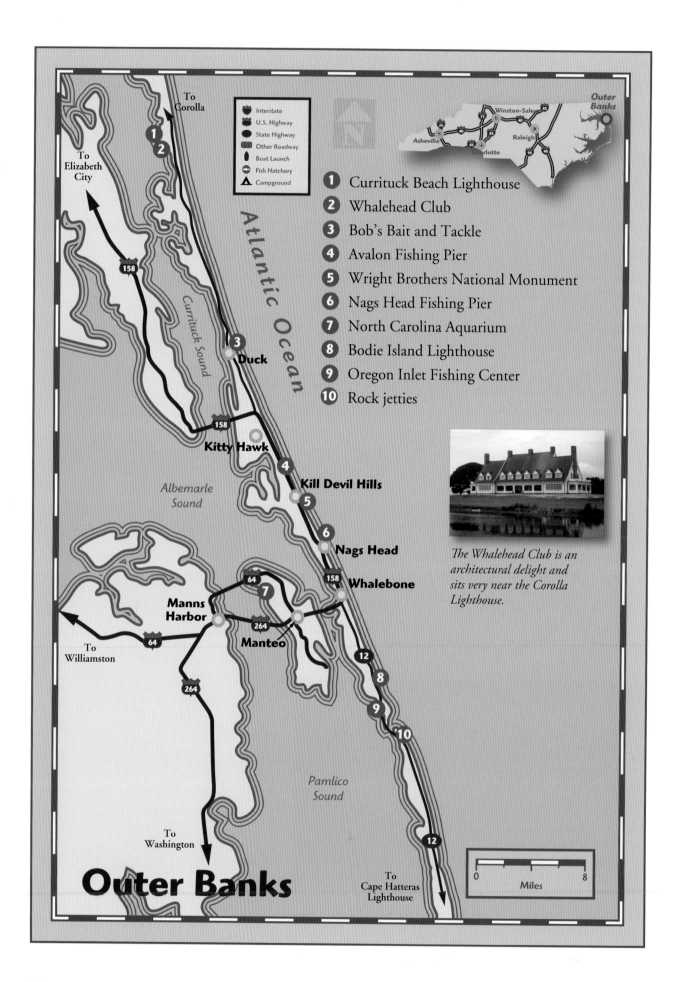

**Legend**
- Interstate
- U.S. Highway
- State Highway
- Other Roadway
- Boat Launch
- Fish Hatchery
- Campground

1 Currituck Beach Lighthouse
2 Whalehead Club
3 Bob's Bait and Tackle
4 Avalon Fishing Pier
5 Wright Brothers National Monument
6 Nags Head Fishing Pier
7 North Carolina Aquarium
8 Bodie Island Lighthouse
9 Oregon Inlet Fishing Center
10 Rock jetties

*The Whalehead Club is an architectural delight and sits very near the Corolla Lighthouse.*

To Corolla

To Elizabeth City

Atlantic Ocean

Currituck Sound

Duck

Kitty Hawk

Albemarle Sound

Kill Devil Hills

Nags Head

Whalebone

Manns Harbor

Manteo

To Williamston

To Washington

Pamlico Sound

To Cape Hatteras Lighthouse

**Outer Banks**

Miles
0          8

# Outer Banks

**R**ich in history, North Carolina's Outer Banks remain a favorite destination, year in and year out, for thousands of tourists from all over the country. Singles, families, and die-hard anglers all love the Outer Banks. It was on these windswept beaches—and at the Nags Head Pier in particular—that my own father introduced me to saltwater fishing when I was a boy. Each fall my family would come down from Virginia and while away the hours at the pier, on the beach, among the rocks, or on the sand dunes. My father worked construction for most of my life and never had much money, so our annual beach vacation was a big deal for us all. Those family vacations are some of my best childhood memories, so I definitely count myself among the longtime Outer Banks fans.

In the late 17th century, the Outer Banks played host to a much less pleasant group of tourists—pirates who lived and robbed with impunity in these barrier islands for many years. Generally, when we think of pirates we think of Jolly Roger–waving high-seas brigands—but not all pirates lived at sea. Some sent lighted signals to unsuspecting ships intentionally directing them into dangerous shoals. Thus duped, the wayward vessels would strike the rocks and take on water. Often the pirates tied a lantern

## Types of Fish
Bluefish, cobia, gray trout, speckled trout, flounder, croaker, drum, false albacore, Spanish mackerel, amberjack, sharks, the occasional dolphin, and other Gulf Stream species.

## Baitfish
Menhaden, eels, glass minnows, shrimp, squid, and crabs.

## Equipment to Use
*Rods:* 6- to 12-weight rods, 9 to10 feet in length.
*Reels:* Mechanical and disc-drag large-arbor reels.
*Lines:* Fast-intermediate lines, matched to rod, as well as 200- to 400-grain sinking lines.
*Leaders:* 10- to 30-pound-test leaders, 7- to 10-foot leaders for intermediate lines, 4- to 7-foot leaders for sinking-tip lines. Wire bite tippets for sharks and winter blues. 25-pound fluorocarbon bite tippet for small bluefish, Spanish mackerel, and cobia.
*Wading:* Anglers can wade here near Oregon Inlet Fishing Center.

## Flies to Use
Bruce's Crystal Shrimp, size 1/0; Clouser Minnow, 2/0-4; Dubiel's Red-Ducer 1/0-2; Dubiel's Lil' Haden, 1/0-2; Lefty's Deceiver, 3/0-2; Lefty's Half and Half, 3/0-2; Blados's Crease Fly, 1/0-2; Bunny flies for sharks and cobia, epoxy baitfish for Spanish mackerel and albies.

## When to Fish
The best fishing is from early April until mid- to late December.

*Continued*

*Fish such as this beautiful dorado will hit fly patterns presented correctly. Once they do hit, hold on and pray your knots hold. Photo by Brian Horsley.*

*Capt. Brian Horsley holds a fly-caught Spanish mackerel, just one of many species he catches while fishing the Outer Banks. He and his wife, Sarah Gardner, are the best-known guides in the Outer Banks. Photo courtesy Flat Out Charters.*

Bob's Banger

around the head of an old horse and led the animal up and down the beach. From their vantage point at sea, sailors believed that the light from shore was a lighthouse or small safety beacon. Only after they were shipwrecked and boarded by the cunning pirates did the hapless crews discover how they'd been duped. This nautical sleight of hand gave Nags Head its name.

Perhaps the best way to fish the Outer Banks is with a guide. Even avid fly-fishing guides carry light-tackle rods here because the wind is such an unpredictable variable. Some clients simply can't cast into the wind or adjust to the unsteady casting platform of a moving boat. The guides are the experts on this fishery, and many have lived here all their lives. You needn't call a guide and ask him what patterns are working and where. If you book a trip, you'll learn all that, and you can rest assured you'll have all the gear and flies that you need. Numerous guides service the Outer Banks, and two of the best fly guides I know are Captains Brian Horsley and Sarah Gardner. Both are experienced anglers who operate their boats with more skill than most folks can drive a car. They're also accomplished writers and photographers, and chances are that if you've read an article about the Outer Banks, they wrote it.

For those who prefer to wade, one of my favorite spots is near the Bodie Island Lighthouse. Park in the visitors' lot, and walk down the service road that faces the Sound. The lighthouse will be at your back. Wade out here, but be careful as the floor drops away without much notice. Two large propellers mounted into the ground at the Oregon Inlet Fishing Center parking lot also mark a good spot. Walk out toward the bridge or Sound from here, but again, wade carefully. The large jetty on the southern side of the bridge is also a good location from which to fish.

Beach access is also available, but check with local officials to avoid stumbling into federal bird sanctuaries.

*Bodie Island Lighthouse is well worth a visit, and the parking lot leads to some good wading access. Photo by Beau Beasley.*

*Dorado are just one of the many species pursued on the Outer Banks. Photo by Brian Horsley.*

### Season & Limits
Open all year. Limits and sizes will depend on species and the time of year that you're fishing.

### Nearby Fly Fishing
Croatan Sound, Roanoke Sound, Currituck Sound, and Pamlico Sound.

### Accommodations & Family Activities
There are so many things to see and do with your family in this area, it's hard to know where to begin. For a great look into the history of the Outer Banks be sure to visit the first grand house of the Outer Banks: the Whalehead Club (www.whaleheadclub.com). Built in the 1920s by industrialist Edward Collings Knight Jr., this 21,000-square-foot house is not to be missed. You can also visit the nearby Currituck Beach Lighthouse in Corolla. Other great sights include the outdoor drama, *The Lost Colony* (www.thelostcolony.org) and the very children-friendly North Carolina Aquarium on Roanoke Island (www.ncaquariums.com).

Surfside Motel
Nags Head, North Carolina
www.surfsideobx.com
1-800-552-7873

Sam and Omie's Restaurant
Nags Head, North Carolina
www.samandomies.net
(252) 441-7366

### Guides & Fly Shops
Bob's Bait and Tackle
Duck, North Carolina
(252) 261- 8589

Frisco Rod & Gun
Frisco, North Carolina
www.friscorodgun.com
(252) 995-5366

Orvis
Raleigh, North Carolina
www.orvis.com/raleigh
(919) 792-9200

Outer Banks Fly Fishing
    Flat Out Charters
    Fly Girl Charters
Nags Head, North Carolina
www.outerbanksflyfishing.com
(252) 449-0562

Rio Mar Fly Fishing
Kill Devil Hills, North Carolina
www.fish-riomar.com
(252) 202-7962

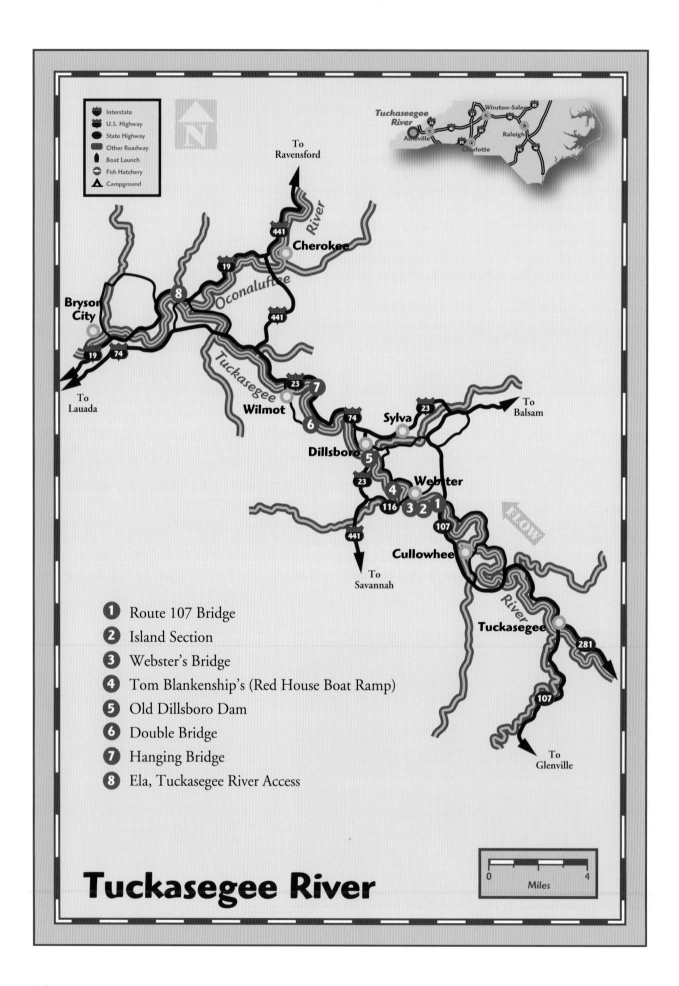

**Legend**
- Interstate
- U.S. Highway
- State Highway
- Other Roadway
- Boat Launch
- Fish Hatchery
- Campground

N

Tuckaseegee River

To Ravensford

441

Cherokee

19

Oconaluftee River

8

441

Bryson City

19  74

To Lauada

Tuckasegee River

23

7

Wilmot

6

74

Sylva

23

To Balsam

Dillsboro

5

23

Webster

4

116

3  2  1

441

107

FLOW

Cullowhee

To Savannah

River

Tuckasegee

281

107

To Glenville

① Route 107 Bridge
② Island Section
③ Webster's Bridge
④ Tom Blankenship's (Red House Boat Ramp)
⑤ Old Dillsboro Dam
⑥ Double Bridge
⑦ Hanging Bridge
⑧ Ela, Tuckasegee River Access

Tuckaseegee River
Asheville  77  Winston-Salem  85
40  85  Raleigh
Charlotte  95  40

0                4
Miles

# Tuckasegee River

# Tuckasegee River

The Tuckasegee River is one of the best-known trout rivers in the entire Southeast, and it comes by that reputation honestly. In the Cherokee language, the river's name means *place of turtles*—a fairly inauspicious moniker for a grand dame of a water big enough to fit right in the American West. The Tuck, which runs just outside the southern borders of the Great Smoky Mountains National Park in North Carolina, has a long and colorful history that still binds local residents to the water. The Cherokee, for example, believe that the ancient earthwork mound of Kituwah on the Tuckasegee near Bryson City is the original birthplace of the Cherokee Nation and served as its spiritual center and the source of a sacred fire many ages ago. The question before the Cherokee today is how to protect and preserve this ancient and sacred spot in the face of encroaching development.

The Tuck is a tailwater fishery that begins flowing out of Cedar Cliff Reservoir and eventually empties into Fontana Lake. Between the two you'll find many miles of unsurpassed water.

## Types of Fish
Anglers typically find rainbows, big browns, nice smallies, and carp here as well.

## Known Hatches
Blue-winged olives, blue quill, stonefly, March brown, midge, sulfur, Cahill, quill Gordon, and assorted terrestrials.

## Equipment to Use
*Rods:* 5- to 8-weight, 8 to 9½ feet in length.
*Reels:* Standard trout reel.
*Lines:* Weight-forward floating lines matched to rod.
*Leaders:* 3X to 5X, 9 to 12 feet in length.
*Wading:* You will surely need waders here and a wading staff wouldn't hurt.

## Flies to Use
*Drys:* Adams, sizes 14-20; Blue-winged Olive, 14-20; Elk-Hair Caddis, 14-20; Flying Ant, 10-18; Gelso's Little Black Stonefly, 16-20; Light Cahill, 14-20; March Brown, 10-14; Quill Gordon, 12-22; Stimulator, 12-20; Steeves's Attract Ant, 16-20; San Juan Worm, 12-14; Sulfur, 16-18.

*Continued*

*The Tuck has plenty of hungry trout hiding in and around the rock structures all along this river. Photo by Beau Beasley.*

*Though the Tuck is a large river, anglers have good wading opportunities along much of its length. Photo by Beau Beasley.*

Rainbow Warrior

Beginning about 300 yards downstream of the Route 107 Bridge, anglers can launch their boats directly off South River Road. This is very good water, and this stretch marks the beginning of the delayed-harvest section. Anglers will find plenty of rainbows and brookies—but the bulk of the fish will be browns. Brown trout positively *thrive* in this section of the river, and because the state puts more than 20,000 trout in the delayed-harvest section each year, it's not hard to see why it is so popular with anglers. As a matter of fact, in the early spring you may find dozens of cars parked along the road at this spot. By the first of June, the delayed-harvest section turns into an all-tackle section, and the pressure is tough again for a few weeks—and then it subsides, leaving fly anglers the chance to explore again. In many cases, these are not dumb stockers. Plenty of fish summer over and then become naturalized.

Just downstream of Route 107 a large island appears, and boating anglers often step out here to stretch their legs. One could easily spend a day here working the water on and around this island given its significant length. Your next good access point is Webster's Bridge. An alternative launching point is Tom Blankenship's place, known as the Red House Boat Ramp. Simply check in with Tom and pay your fare. Anglers floating downstream will be happy to hear that a major impediment to their travels has recently been removed: The old Dillsboro Dam has been taken down, and all that remains are excellent rock structures below the waterline and along the banks to reduce bank erosion. Another boat landing is available where Scotts Creek intersects the river just below the old dam site.

Anglers will find top-notch trout fishing in the Tuck. The river warms, however, as it closes in on Bryson City, at which point bass reign supreme. Smallies start showing up in pretty good numbers below Barker's Creek and continue all the way to Fontana Lake.

The Tuck is an excellent fishery and the many rock structures that are easily seen during low-water hold trout that use the rock structures to ambush smaller baitfish. If you haven't fished the Tuck yet, you don't know what you're missing.

*Browns and rainbows are both common on the Tuck, but brown trout are the main targets. Photo by Beau Beasley.*

## Flies to Use (continued)

*Nymphs & Streamers:* BH Hare's Ear, sizes 14-20; BH Prince Nymph, 14-20; Copper John, 14-18; Clouser Minnow; 2-6, Finn's Golden Retriever; 6-10, Howell's Big Nasty, 4-6; Matuka, 4-10; Midges, 18-22; Pheasant Tail Nymph, 14-20; Rainbow Warrior, 12-16; Shuler's Carolina Midge, 16-20; Woolhead Sculpin, 2-6; Woolly Bugger, 4-8; Zonkers, 4-8.

## When to Fish
Open all year.

## Season & Limits
For the latest information contact the North Carolina Wildlife Resources Commission (www.ncwildlife.org) or call (919) 707-0010.

## Nearby Fly Fishing
The Tuckasegee is within easy driving distance of the Oconaluftee River and many other fine streams in the Great Smoky Mountains National Park.

## Accommodations & Family Activities
Anglers wishing to stay near the river would be hard pressed to find a place closer or nicer than the Dillsboro Inn. The beautiful B&B is the perfect place to use as a base of operation to fish in a variety of locations, assuming that you can ever tear yourself away from the Tuck. Granny's Kitchen in Cherokee is also a great place to eat.

Dillsboro Inn
Dillsboro, North Carolina
www.dillsboroinn.com
1-866-586-3898

## Fly Shops & Guides
CCS Fly Fishing Outfitters
Cherokee, North Carolina
www.ccsflyfishing.com
1-888-243-5274

Curtis Wright Outfitters
Weaverville, North Carolina
www.curtiswrightoutfitters.com
(828) 645-8700

Fly Fishing the Smokies
Bryson City, North Carolina
www.flyfishgatlinburg.com
(828) 421-0172
(828) 488-7665

Highland Hiker
Highlands, North Carolina
www.highlandhiker.com
(828) 526-5298

Hookers Fly Shop
Sylva, North Carolina
www.hookersflyshop.com
1-877-518-7369

Nantahala Outdoor Center
Bryson City, North Carolina
www.noc.com
1-888-905-7238

Rivers Edge Outfitters
Cherokee, North Carolina
www.flyfishcherokee.com
(828) 497-9300

Waynesville Fly Shop
Waynesville, North Carolina
www.waynesvilleflyshop.com
(828) 246-0306

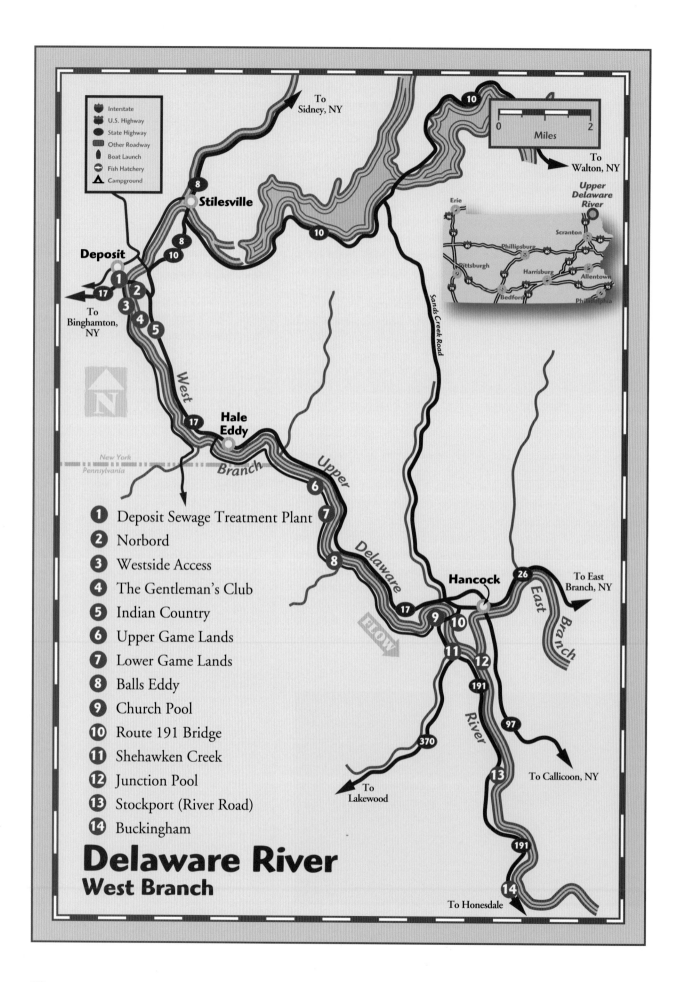

To
Sidney, NY

Interstate
U.S. Highway
State Highway
Other Roadway
Boat Launch
Fish Hatchery
Campground

10

0        Miles        2

To
Walton, NY

Upper
Delaware
River

Erie

Scranton

Phillipsburg

Pittsburgh          Harrisburg

Allentown

Bedford          Philadelphia

8
Stilesville

8
10

Deposit

1
17          2
3
4
5

To
Binghamton,
NY

West

N

17
Hale
Eddy

New York
Pennsylvania

Branch

Sands Creek Road

Upper

6
7

Delaware

8

17          9
Hancock          26          To East
Branch, NY

East

10

FLOW

11

Branch

**1** Deposit Sewage Treatment Plant
**2** Norbord
**3** Westside Access
**4** The Gentleman's Club
**5** Indian Country
**6** Upper Game Lands
**7** Lower Game Lands
**8** Balls Eddy
**9** Church Pool
**10** Route 191 Bridge
**11** Shehawken Creek
**12** Junction Pool
**13** Stockport (River Road)
**14** Buckingham

12

191

97

River

370

To
Lakewood

13          To Callicoon, NY

191

14

To Honesdale

# Delaware River
## West Branch

98

# Delaware River, West Branch

The Delaware River is named after Thomas West, 3rd Baron De La Warr. West arrived in Jamestown from England in 1610 just in time to convince the colonists not to throw in the towel on the whole New World project. He served as the first governor of the Virginia Colony and as a result a bay, the state of Delaware, and a tribe of Indians bear his name. Lord De La Warr was a tough administrator and though not overly popular, he is credited with providing much-needed structure and for helping to save the fledgling colony that would go on to become a nation.

The West Branch, East Branch, and the Main Stem of the Delaware are generally what is referred to as the Upper Delaware River System.

If there's a water in the Mid-Atlantic that epitomizes what a great trout water should be, it's the Delaware. In the excellent *Fly-Fishing Guide to Upper Delaware River,* author Paul Weamer exhorts his readers to think of this waterway as more than your typical trout stream. "The Upper Delaware stretches anglers. If the Upper Delaware doesn't humble you or teach you something new, then you're either not paying attention or not trying hard enough." I couldn't agree more. The Delaware can provide you with the best day of trout fishing you've ever had—or it can chew you up

## Types of Fish
Anglers come here for the wild browns and rainbows, and are rarely disappointed. You can, however, also catch stripers and shad in the spring.

## Known Hatches
Hatches on the Delaware River are nothing short of spectacular. Some of the better-known hatches here include blue-winged olive, Hendrickson, big and little sulfur, Grannom/apple caddis, March brown, green drake, brown drake, slate drake, quill Gordon, caddisflies, light Cahill, trico, and little black, brown, and golden stoneflies. Terrestrials are also here in good numbers, especially ants and beetles.

## Equipment to Use
*Rods:* 5- to 6-weight, 9 to 10 feet in length.
*Reels:* Solid disc-drag reel, and yes definitely bring that large arbor.
*Lines:* Weight-forward floating lines matched to rod, sinking-tip lines are also helpful.
*Leaders:* George Harvey–style slack leader 4X to 6X, 9 to 15 feet in length.
*Wading:* Chest waders will give you the most options here.

## Flies to Use
*Drys:* Blue-Winged Olive, sizes 16-18; Little Blue-Winged Olive, 22-26; Brown Drake, 10; CDC Caddis, 14-18; Green Drake, 10; Elk-Hair Caddis, 14-16; Cahill, 14-16; Slate Drake, 12-14; Rusty Spinner, 10-18; Sulfur Parachute, 14-20; Steeves's Japanese Beetle, 14-16; Steeves's Attract Ant, 18-20.

*Continued*

*Drift boats are a common sight on the Delaware and allow anglers to cover a great deal of water in a single day. Photo by Beau Beasley.*

*Guide Wayne Aldridge, owner of River of Life Outdoor Adventures, displays a healthy Delaware brown trout. Photo by Beau Beasley.*

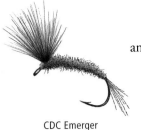

CDC Emerger

and spit you out. While it's true that conditions beyond your control, such as wind and low water flows, may take their toll, the angler's ability—and in some cases inability—to meet the Delaware River's exacting standards will eventually tell the tale.

I was introduced to the Delaware by Wayne Aldridge, owner of River of Life Outdoor Adventures of Deposit, New York. Wayne and I spent many hours fishing the river together, and I can say without a doubt that the Delaware has no equal anywhere on the East Coast. I can still remember the fight of the first trout I landed with Wayne: "Let him run, Beau," coached Wayne. "These are really strong fish, and if you put too much pressure on him too soon, he'll break you off. Most people don't know what fighting a wild fish is like, and they're pretty surprised when that first run comes along—and even more surprised at the second." Wayne was right. I've never landed a fish so small that fought so hard. It was only about 14 inches long, but I'd have sworn that I was trying to land a striper on a 5-weight.

Fishing with a guide like Aldridge who has a drift boat makes the Delaware a much more manageable fishery, most obviously because you can cover more water. When the river is a bit high, anglers can simply fish from the boat. A watercraft also allows anglers the option of fishing islands or sand bars not reachable from the shore. I enjoyed fishing around the large grass beds that sprout up along some of the small islands during the summer. Fishing from a drift boat is fun, but getting out and stretching your legs while hop-scotching from one good spot to another is also a great way to fish this river.

Fishing the Delaware can be tough because the hatches are so strong and so varied that anglers are often confused about what to use. CDC Emergers are a pretty good all-around choice. I also had good luck with white streamers, most likely because of the strong alewife population the trout feed on here.

Whether you choose to fish the mighty Delaware with a guide or by yourself, I urge you to experience this river firsthand. You might want to do a few calisthenics to warm up a bit before hitting the river, because this enormous water will definitely stretch you.

*Paul Weamer is a guide, author, and recognized expert on the Delaware River. Photo courtesy Paul Weamer.*

## Flies to Use (continued)
*Nymphs & Streamers:* BH Hare's Ear, sizes 12-20; CDC Emerger, 16-18; Copper John, 14-20; Flashback Hare's Ear, 16-20; Golden Stone, 18-20; Pheasant Tail Nymph, 12-20; Stroup's Sulphur Nymph, 14-18; Woolly Bugger, 6-10; Green Drake Nymph, 8-10; Zebra Midge, 18-20; Zonker, 2-6.

## When to Fish
The border water section of the West Branch and the main stem of the Delaware are open year-round. Contacting the local fly shops for the latest info is always a good move.

## Season & Limits
For the very latest information on fishing the Delaware, visit the Pennsylvania Fish and Boat Commission at www.fish.state.pa.us. You can also visit the New York State Department of Environmental Conservation on the web at www.dec.ny.gov/outdoor/fishing.html.

## Nearby Fly Fishing
Alternatives to fishing the Upper Delaware include the lower main stem of the Delaware. Also consider fishing the Beaverkill River and Willowemoc Creek in New York.

## Accommodations & Family Activities
The Upper Delaware offers a plethora of activities for anglers and non-anglers alike. I enjoyed not only fishing with Wayne Aldridge but also staying at his Lighthouse Lodge facility. Some anglers enjoy fishing here so much they purchase second homes so they can fish here more often. Below, I've listed just some of the shops and lodges where you are sure to get good information on the Upper Delaware.

Lighthouse Lodge
Deposit, New York
(607) 467-4215

## Fly Shops & Guides
Border Water Outfitters
Hancock, New York
www.borderwateroutfitters.com
(607) 637-4296

Al Caucci Fly Fishing
Starlight, Pennsylvania
www.mayfly.com
(570) 635-5897

Delaware River Club
Starlight, Pennsylvania
www.thedelawareriverclub.com
(570) 635-5880

River of Life Outdoor Adventures
Deposit, New York
www.river-of-life.com
(607) 743-5696

West Branch Angler and Sportsman's Resort
Hancock, New York
www.westbranchangler.com
(607) 467-5525

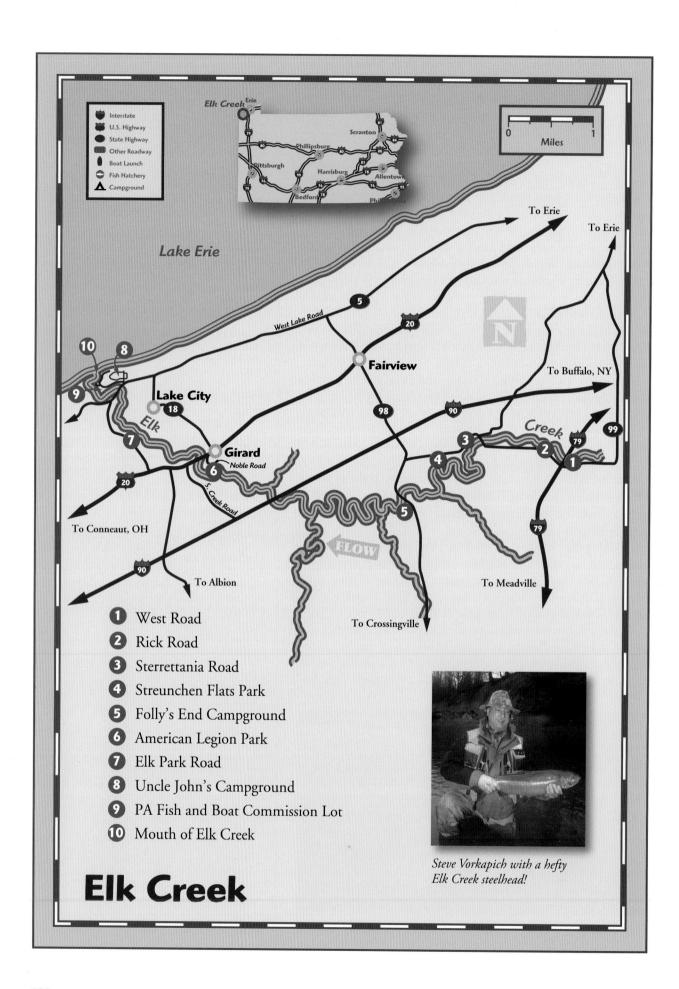

**Legend:**
- Interstate
- U.S. Highway
- State Highway
- Other Roadway
- Boat Launch
- Fish Hatchery
- Campground

Lake Erie

Elk Creek
Erie

Scranton

Phillipsburg

Pittsburgh

Harrisburg

Allentown

Bedford

Miles
0 — 1

To Erie

To Erie

West Lake Road

Fairview

To Buffalo, NY

N

Lake City

Elk

Creek

Girard
Noble Road

S. Creek Road

To Conneaut, OH

To Albion

FLOW

To Crossingville

To Meadville

1. West Road
2. Rick Road
3. Sterrettania Road
4. Streunchen Flats Park
5. Folly's End Campground
6. American Legion Park
7. Elk Park Road
8. Uncle John's Campground
9. PA Fish and Boat Commission Lot
10. Mouth of Elk Creek

*Steve Vorkapich with a hefty Elk Creek steelhead!*

# Elk Creek

# Elk Creek

The East boasts its fair share of fine steelhead streams, but few of those waters have the credibility—or the fish—of Elk Creek in northwestern Pennsylvania. As the largest tributary of Lake Erie, the Elk holds more water and more fish than many of the surrounding streams. The fish here are fresh from Lake Erie and once hooked, fight like there's no tomorrow. I well remember my surprise at nearly being at eyeball level with the first jumping steelhead I ever saw. I was glad I got a good look at it, because it was the last time I saw it—the steelie broke me off on his leap to freedom.

Steve Vorkapich, inventor of Float Master Indicators, introduced me to the Elk and spent nearly a day and a half showing me the ropes before I finally got the hang of it. It was on Elk Creek that Steve noticed many anglers spent more time rigging and re-rigging their rods than they did fishing. He also noticed too many of the indicators on the market moved up and down the leader when anglers didn't want them to—or worse, the leaders were cast off the line completely. This led him to develop his own line of indicators that are easy to move, never leave a kink in your leader, and won't move unless you move them. "Steelheaders are constantly making adjustments with their set-ups and the changing

## Types of Fish
Fly anglers typically fish here for hard-fighting steelhead. You can catch brown trout here and smallies close to the mouth of Lake Erie.

## Known Hatches
The hatches here are pretty much limited to stoneflies and the occasional caddis.

## Equipment to Use
*Rods:* Fast-action 6- to 7-weight, 9 to 10 feet in length.
*Spey Rods:* 6- to 7-weight 11 to 13½ feet in length.
*Reels:* Sturdy disc-drag-equipped reel with a large arbor.
*Lines:* Weight-forward floating lines matched to rod, sinking-tip lines can also be useful.
*Leaders:* Tapered leaders, 1X to 4X, 9 to 12 feet in length.
*Wading:* Chest waders will give you the most options here.

## Flies to Use
*Drys:* Yellow Stimulator, sizes 8-10, used in tandem with smaller nymphs as droppers.

*Nymphs & Streamers:* Black Pheasant Tail, sizes 12-16; Egg-Sucking Leech, 4-10; Eggs (various colors), 6-12; Karl's Moby Goby, 6-8; Pink Lady, 10-16; Soft Hackle, 14-18; Woolly Bugger, 6-10; Sucker Spawn 8-12.

*Continued*

*Local steelheader Mike Felege with a fresh Lake Erie steelhead. Photo by Beau Beasley.*

*Guide and author Karl Weixlmann has paid his dues in all types of weather to become proficient at finding and landing big steelhead. Photo by Jack Hanrahan.*

Pink Lady

river conditions. You might have to change your approach several times a day," says Steve. Karl Weixlmann, author and well-known local guide, agrees: "You need to change your approach with the prevailing conditions. To be successful here you need to have what I call carnal knowledge of the river, meaning that you need to spend time fishing this water and see what works and what doesn't. You just have to fish hard and pay your dues."

There are several places to pay those dues along Elk Creek, but finding a spot with any privacy won't be easy. The river draws thousands of conventional spin as well as fly anglers each year, so be ready to spend some time with guys who will sling just about any rig that will land steelhead, including bait. Two places that are quite popular with anglers are Folly's End Campground and Uncle John's Elk Creek Campground, which includes cabins. Folly's has a nice little fly shop and sells excellent Smith Brothers hot dogs to cold and hungry anglers. The shop is easily accessed off Route 98 and is inviting to everyone, but these guys have a wicked sense of humor. You're apt to get caught in the crossfire of friendly banter that occurs between owner Jim Phillips and his regular customers. Uncle John's campground also offers great access and even has webcams in the trees near the river so you can get a steelie fix before you head off to work.

Steve Brugger, owner of Lake Erie Ultimate Angler in Erie, believes the key to success is teaming up with someone who will show you the ropes, whether it be a guide or another seriously addicted steelheader. "Guys traveling here need to know these fish move a lot. They may be in one section of the river for a week, but after a good rain they may move much farther upriver," he says. "Local guides can save you a lot of time, and let's face it, we all want to be fishing where the fish *are,* not where they were."

There are no gimmicks in steelheading—you just have to go out to the river and learn the hard way. The good news is that once you get the hang of it, you can look the steelhead straight in the eye and let him know who's boss.

*Anglers fishing Elk Creek often need the help of another angler or guide, as landing these large fish often takes a toll on both anglers and fish. Photo courtesy Dan Pribanic, Chagrin River Outfitters.*

### When to Fish

Fall is the best time to fish here with November and December being prime time. It all comes down to how much cold you can stand. Fishing can last right through March. While some anglers return all they catch, many more don't.

### Season & Limits

Regulations vary widely depending on the time of the year and where you are on the creek. For the latest information on Elk Creek contact the Pennsylvania Fish and Boat Commission at www.fish.state.pa.us.

### Nearby Fly Fishing

Anglers fishing here can also hit Walnut Creek and Four Mile Creek. Fishing in Erie is also an option. For a more detailed map of the Lake Erie tributaries go to www.sgcmaps.com

### Accommodations & Family Activities

There are many activities for families to do in and around the Erie area. One of the best places to visit is Presque Isle State Park. Besides enjoying Lake Erie and the other wonderful scenery you can also fish in and around the banks of the Presque Isle.

While I was visiting Lake Erie I stayed at the El Patio Motel, a favorite hangout of anglers of every stripe. This motel is strategically located in Erie County and allows one to easily fish multiple locations. Plus, it is close to Joe Root's Grill.

Joe Root's serves all kinds of great food and local microbrewery beer which is quite good after a long day on the water. I highly recommend their local appetizer specialty, walleye nuggets.

El Patio Motel
Erie, Pennsylvania
(814) 838-9772

Joe Root's Grill
Erie, Pennsylvania
www.joerootsgrill.com
(814) 836-7668

Uncle John's Elk Creek Campground
Lake City, Pennsylvania
www.unclejohnselkcreekcamp.com
(814) 774-8672

### Fly Shops & Guides

Chagrin River Outfitters
Chagrin Falls, Ohio
www.chagrinriveroutfitters.com
(440) 247-7110

Folly's End Campground
Girard, Pennsylvania
www.follysend.com
(814) 474-5730

Gander Mountain
Erie, Pennsylvania
www.gandermountain.com
(814) 868-0880

Lake Erie Ultimate Angler
Erie, Pennsylvania
www.shopultimateangler.com
(814) 833-4040

Karl Weixlmann
Fly Fish Erie
Erie, Pennsylvania
(814) 836-8013

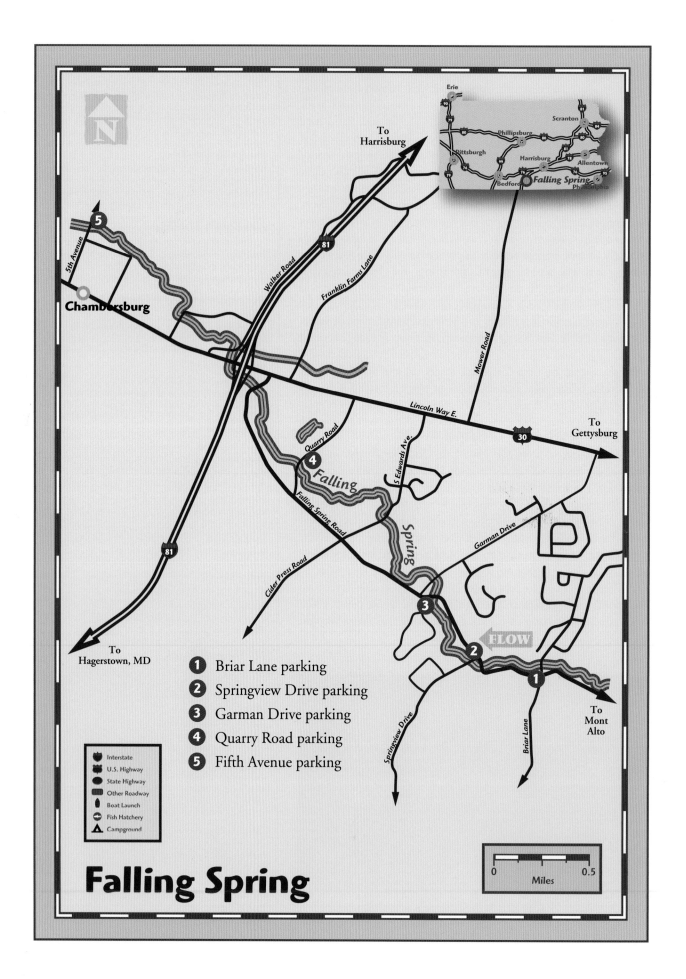

**N**

To
Harrisburg

Erie

90

79

Phillipsburg

Scranton

81

Pittsburgh

80

Harrisburg

Allentown

76

99

81

76

15

Bedford

**Falling Spring**

Philadelphia

81

5th Avenue

**5**

Walker Road

Franklin Farm Lane

Mower Road

**Chambersburg**

Lincoln Way E.

To
Gettysburg

30

Quarry Road

**4**

*Falling*

S. Edwards Ave.

Falling Spring Road

*Spring*

Garman Drive

81

Cider Press Road

**3**

**FLOW**

81

To
Hagerstown, MD

**1** Briar Lane parking

**2**

**2** Springview Drive parking

**1**

**3** Garman Drive parking

To
Mont
Alto

**4** Quarry Road parking

Springview Drive

Briar Lane

**5** Fifth Avenue parking

Interstate
U.S. Highway
State Highway
Other Roadway
Boat Launch
Fish Hatchery
Campground

0            0.5
Miles

# Falling Spring

# Falling Spring

### Types of Fish
Anglers will find wild rainbows here as well as good brown trout fishing.

### Known Hatches
Winter stonefly, Hendrickson, blue-winged olive, caddis, March brown, sulfur, light Cahill, white fly, terrestrials, and midges.

### Equipment to Use
*Rods:* Medium-action 4- to 5-weight, 9 feet in length.
*Reels:* Standard trout reel.
*Lines:* Weight-forward floating lines matched to rod.
*Leaders:* Leader should be 4X to 5X, 9 to 12 feet in length.
*Wading:* Chest waders will give you the most options here, but beware of the briars along the banks that can puncture your waders.

### Flies to Use
*Drys:* Ant, sizes 14-20; Blue-winged Olive, 18-22; Elk-Hair Caddis, 14-28; March Brown Parachute, 10-14; Letort Hopper, 14-16; Light Cahill, 22-26; Sulfur Parachute, 14-18; Sulfur Emerger, 14-18; Trico, 18-24.

*Continued*

Falling Spring, which runs through Chambersburg, Pennsylvania, may not be on the tip of every fly angler's tongue—but perhaps it should be. The drive north to Chambersburg from my home in Virginia took me through farmland and past Civil War battlefields in Virginia, West Virginia, and Maryland before crossing the Mason-Dixon line into Pennsylvania. It's an easy drive—and one fraught with history and marked by blood.

During the Civil War, Chambersburg was invaded no less than three times. In 1862, the town fell into the hands of Maj. Gen. J. E. B. Stuart, whose 1,800 cavalrymen burned various railroad buildings and captured 500 guns and some cannons as well. In 1863, a Virginia cavalry brigade entered the town and again set various railroad structures on fire as well as several local warehouses. Finally in July 1864, Gen. Jubal Early's cavalry of the Shenandoah Valley arrived. Brig. Gen. John McCausland ordered the city burned, and a great deal of Chambersburg was reduced to ashes. Chambersburg was the northernmost city razed by Confederate forces, and the slogan "Remember Chambersburg!" was a common Union battle cry.

*The township of Guilford has worked in conjunction with local conservation groups to preserve Falling Spring. Photo by Beau Beasley.*

*Beautiful willow trees and high grasses line the banks of Falling Spring. Photo by Beau Beasley.*

Mike's Simple Shrimp

Falling Spring has two distinct sections: The upper section is catch-and-release only beginning at the Geisel Funeral Home and ending 200 yards upstream of Briar Lane. Some of the popular access points may be found off of Briar Lane, Springview Road, Garman Drive, and Quarry Road. The delayed-harvest section is found downtown and can be accessed from Limekiln Drive, Coldbrook Avenue, and Fifth Avenue. While these areas might be less picturesque than the upstream section, you won't mind that quite so much when a healthy rainbow is running downriver. Falling Spring is one of the few Pennsylvania waters that holds a reproducing population of wild rainbows, so if that fish you lost seemed to fight much harder than the stockers you catch at home, that might be why.

The Falling Spring insect population is abundant and changes often. In the spring, think blue-winged olives and stoneflies. By late spring, the blue-winged olives are still around, but you'll also see sulfurs as well as black-and-tan caddis. Terrestrials are a significant source of food because of the high grass and vegetation. By the fall, Tricos start showing up while midges are a constant source of food all year. Anglers should keep a healthy supply of sow bugs or freshwater shrimp patterns on hand, like Mike Heck's Simple Shrimp.

Please think before you act when you fish Falling Spring: Don't leave even a hint of trash behind, and if you see litter that another unthinking angler left, please pick it up. I do this often and though it's not what I head to the river for in the first place, I have yet to meet a landowner who didn't appreciate my thoughtfulness. It's the least we can do for folks who donate their land to ensure public access. The Township of Guilford in particular has worked hard to gain easements for anglers and nature lovers alike, so keep this sacrifice and hard work in mind while you're streamside. Finally, don't break any tree branches to make it easier for you to cast in tight places. Not too long ago an angler on private property did just that. The owner had been willing to let him fish there unchallenged until the impromptu pruning took place. Needless to say the offending angler was promptly escorted from the property.

Battles still rage on Falling Spring today—but happily the only serious fighting is between anglers and the local trout.

*Fly anglers are welcome on Falling Spring, but be respectful of private property and remove trash. Photo by Beau Beasley.*

## Flies to Use (continued)

*Nymphs & Streamers:* BH Hare's Ear, sizes 14-20; BH Prince Nymph, 14-20; Brassie, 18-22; Coburn's Cress Bug, 16-20; Gray Scud, 14-18; Heck's Simple Shrimp, 12-18; Pheasant Tail Nymph, 12-20; JC's Electric Caddis Larva ,12-16; RS2, 18-26; San Juan Worm, 14; Sculpin, 6-10; Stroup's Sulphur Nymph, 14-18; Woolly Bugger, 6-10.

## When to Fish

Spring and fall are by far the best times to fish but summers can be good if there has been sufficient rain. Please respect the property owners who have graciously donated their land for public access, and leave nothing behind but great memories.

## Season & Limits

There is a private-water section that is posted from Edwards Avenue to Garman Drive, so keep your eyes open. For a complete list of all rules and regulations in Pennsylvania go to www.fishandboat.com, or call (717) 705-7930.

## Nearby Fly Fishing

Anglers fishing here can also hit Yellow Breeches and the Letort.

## Accommodations & Family Activities

Anglers can find places to stay and multiple restaurants in Chambersburg and Guilford Township. If you'd like to help support conservation efforts on Falling Spring please support Falling Spring Greenway, which is a 501(c)(3) organization and worthy of your contributions. Please contact Sam Small at (717) 709-7060 or Mike Heck at (717) 261-0070.

## Fly Shops & Guides

Tom Baltz Guide Service
Mount Holly Springs, Pennsylvania
baltzte@aol.com
(717) 486-7438

Beaver Creek Fly Shop
Hagerstown, Maryland
www.beavercreekflyshop.com
(301) 393-9090

Gander Mountain
Chambersburg, Pennsylvania
www.gandermountain.com
(717) 263-8433

Mike Heck's Trout Guides
Chambersburg, Pennsylvania
www.fallingsprings.com
(717) 816-7557

Keystone Country Store
Fort Loudon, Pennsylvania
www.keystonecountrystore.com
(717) 369-2970

Dusty Wissmath Guide Service
Mercersburg, Pennsylvania
www.dwflyfishingschool.com
(717) 328-9400 x3531

Yellow Breeches Outfitters
Boiling Springs, Pennsylvania
www.yellowbreeches.com
(717) 258-6752

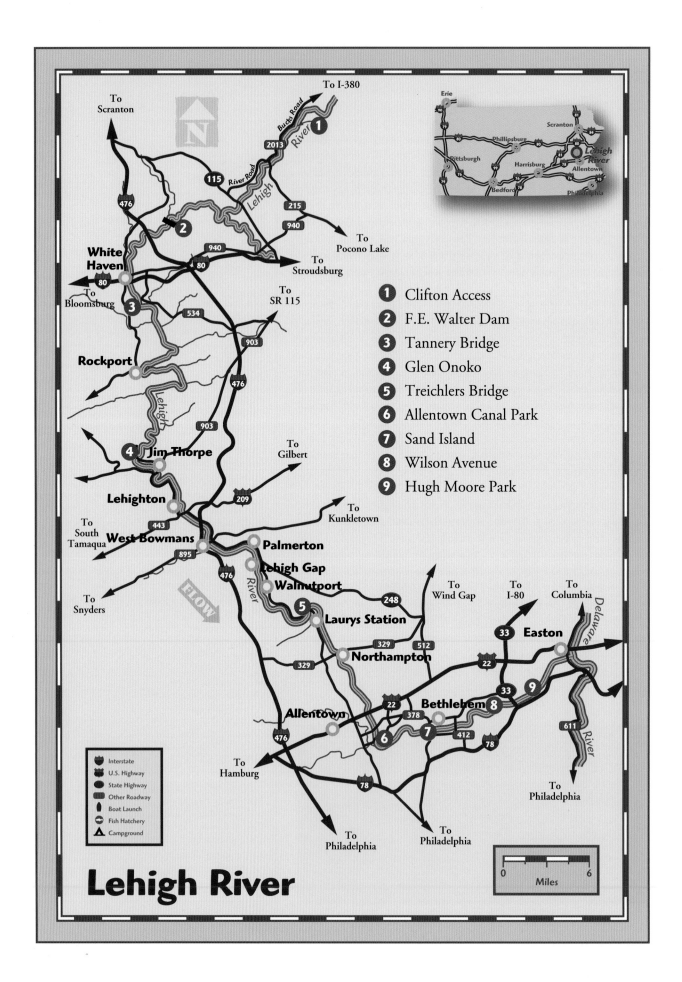

To I-380

To Scranton

Bucks Road

2013

Lehigh River

**1**

Erie

Scranton

Phillipsburg

Pittsburgh

Harrisburg

Lehigh River

Allentown

Bedford

Philadelphia

115

River Road

Lehigh

215

940

To Pocono Lake

476

**2**

940

80

To Stroudsburg

**White Haven**

80

To Bloomsburg

**3**

534

To SR 115

903

**Rockport**

476

Lehigh

903

To Gilbert

**4** **Jim Thorpe**

**Lehighton**

209

To Kunkletown

To South Tamaqua

443

**West Bowmans**

895

**Palmerton**

476

**Lehigh Gap**

River

**Walnutport**

248

To Wind Gap

To I-80

To Columbia

Delaware

To Snyders

FLOW

**5**

**Laurys Station**

329

512

33

**Easton**

329

**Northampton**

22

**Allentown**

22

378

33

**9**

**Bethlehem**

**8**

476

**7**

412

611

River

**6**

78

To Hamburg

78

To Philadelphia

To Philadelphia

To Philadelphia

**1** Clifton Access

**2** F.E. Walter Dam

**3** Tannery Bridge

**4** Glen Onoko

**5** Treichlers Bridge

**6** Allentown Canal Park

**7** Sand Island

**8** Wilson Avenue

**9** Hugh Moore Park

Interstate
U.S. Highway
State Highway
Other Roadway
Boat Launch
Fish Hatchery
Campground

0 Miles 6

# Lehigh River

# Lehigh River

A series of glacial bogs and marshes near Gouldsboro, Pennsylvania, forms the Lehigh River, which eventually flows into a reservoir created by Francis E. Walter Dam. The river then flows more than 100 miles across the state, eventually ending as a tributary of the Delaware River. Though quite small at its source, the Lehigh has become a hot spot for thousands of outdoor enthusiasts either plying her waters for trout or rafting her whitewater past some of the prettiest scenery in the Keystone State. In fact, some fly anglers claim that the Lehigh is the most underrated trout water in the East. My own experience leads me to believe that this may well be the case. One could fish the Lehigh for months and still have plenty to learn about it.

The smaller section of the river, which is easier to wade and fish than other sections, lies above the dam near White Haven. Anglers can access the river easily near Clifton by turning north off River Road (Bucks Road) to a gravel road leading to State Game Land 127. You will also find pullouts along River Road (Bucks Road), which runs adjacent to the river. Remember to get permission from local landowners before parking your car and heading to the river. At this writing, the Stanley Cooper Chapter of Trout

## Types of Fish
Anglers typically find rainbow trout and browns to tussle with and some brookies sprinkled in here and there. As the river heads southward, it warms considerably by the time it gets to Lehighton where smallies become the predominate fish.

## Known Hatches
Blue-winged olive, blue quill, golden stonefly, Grannom, Hendrickson, red quill, little brown stonefly, sulfur, slate drake, caddisfly, Cahill, gray fox, yellow sallies, brown drakes, inchworms, and terrestrials.

## Equipment to Use
*Rods:* 5- to 6-weight, 8½ to 9½ feet in length.
*Reels:* Disc-drag reel, some large-arbor applications.
*Lines:* Weight-forward floating lines matched to rod.
*Leaders:* 4X to 6X, 9 to 12 feet in length.
*Wading:* Chest waders are really needed here. Use extra caution when wading below the dam.

## Flies to Use
*Drys:* Blue-Winged Olive, sizes 14-20; Brown Stonefly, 14-16; Elk-Hair Caddis, 14-20; Flying Ant, 10-18; Hendrickson, 14-18; Light Cahill, 14-20; Red Quill, 14-16; Golden Stonefly, 8-12; March Brown, 10-14; Pale Evening Dun, 14-18; Quill Gordon, 14-20; Slate Drake, 10-14.

*Continued*

*The Lehigh River is easily accessible for wading anglers. Photo by Beau Beasley.*

*George Maciag fishes the Lehigh River as much as he can and often finds the trout in a ready mood. Photo by Beau Beasley.*

Letort Hopper

Unlimited is working with local landowners to gain permission for more public access. Below the F. E. Walter Dam the river changes dramatically and begins in earnest it's rush to meet the Delaware. From the very beginning, the river is large, and current is a real issue. Also it seems like someone has greased the rocks in this river, and walking across slippery bowling balls comes to mind. If you're fishing below the F. E. Walter Dam, be aware of the current. This is an ideal place to use your wading stick. If the dam is releasing water at 200 cubic feet per second, you're probably fine. If the release nears 350 cubic feet per second, you should head farther downstream.

This is all-tackle water, so don't be surprised by the spin anglers on this river. There are several boat launchings along the length of the Lehigh. I have not listed all of them on my map for this section because space does not permit it. One of the best areas includes Tannery Bridge, which has a 1 percent grade railroad bed that continues downstream for 29 miles all the way to the beautiful and historic town of Jim Thorpe. Some anglers walk or ride a bike on the railroad bed to gain better access to the river. If you do this, be sure to watch for trains. Other excellent spots include Glen Onoko and West Bowmans. By Lehighton the smallies take over, and they are found even farther upstream in hot, dry summers.

The Lehigh goes urban when it runs through Allentown and Bethlehem. You'll see a lot more people on the water as the river's wild surroundings give way to the hustle and bustle of city life. Many parks along the river provide access for anglers and paddlers taking on the Lehigh with canoes and other watercraft. The bottom end of the river also offers good bass fishing—and if your kids are with you, don't miss the Crayola Crayon factory near the landing at Easton, which sees nearly 300,000 visitors a year.

Looking for advice? Anglers upriver of the dam can get help from A.A. Outfitters and The Evening Hatch near Route 940. Downriver anglers can get help from L.L. Bean and A Sporting Lifestyle near Allentown.

*Both browns and healthy rainbows such as this one are abundant on the Lehigh River. Photo by Beau Beasley.*

### Flies to Use (continued)

*Nymphs & Streamers:* BH Goldilox, sizes 6-10; BH Hare's Ear, 14-20; BH Prince Nymph, 14-20; Flashback Hare's Ear, 14-18; George's Killer, 4-12; Green Weenie, 14-16; Matuka, 4-10; Muddler Minnow, 6-10; Pheasant Tail, 14-20; Sculpin, 4-8; Woolly Bugger, 6-10.

### When to Fish

Spring is prime time, but if cooler weather prevails the river will fish well nearly all year long. As the season warms you can pick up good smallies near Allentown.

### Season & Limits

For the very latest information on the Lehigh, contact the Pennsylvania Fish and Boat Commission at www.fish.state.pa.us.

### Nearby Fly Fishing

The Little Lehigh is certainly an option as is the Delaware and other Pocono waters.

### Accommodations & Family Activities

While fishing the Lehigh I had the pleasure of staying at The Village at Poconos in Long Pond. This excellent resort is directly across from the Pocono International Raceway.

The Village at Poconos
Long Pond, Pennsylvania
www.villageatpocono.com
1-800-276-2666

### Fly Shops & Guides

A.A. Outfitters
Blakeslee, Pennsylvania
www.aaoutfitters.com
1-800-443-8119

Cabela's
Hamburg, Pennsylvania
www.cabelas.com
(610) 929-7000

The Evening Hatch Fly Shop
Lake Harmony, Pennsylvania
www.eveninghatch.com
(570) 443-0772

Gander Mountain
Dickson City, Pennsylvania
www.gandermountain.com
(570) 347-9077

L.L. Bean
Center Valley, Pennsylvania
www.llbean.com/centervalley
(610) 798-4400

Orvis
Downingtown, Pennsylvania
www.orvis.com/downingtown
(610) 873-8400

Orvis
Plymouth Meeting, Pennsylvania
www.orvis.com/plymouthmeeting
(610) 825-1010

Rivers Outdoor Adventures
New Ringgold, Pennsylvania
www.riversflyfishing.com
(570) 943-3151

A Sporting Lifestyle
Allentown, Pennsylvania
www.asportinglifestyle.com
1-866-610-6611

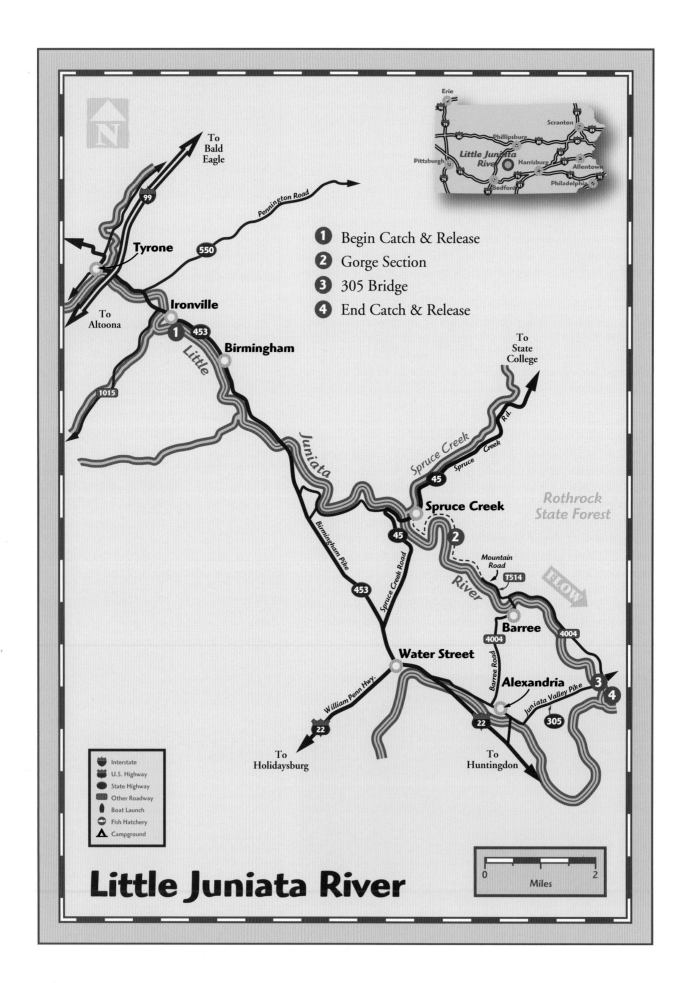

To Bald Eagle

99

Tyrone

To Altoona

550

Pennington Road

**1** Begin Catch & Release
**2** Gorge Section
**3** 305 Bridge
**4** End Catch & Release

Ironville

**1** 453

**Birmingham**

1015

Little

Juniata

To State College

Spruce Creek Rd.

Spruce Creek

45

**Spruce Creek**

**2**

Rothrock State Forest

Birmingham Pike

45

453

Spruce Creek Road

Mountain Road

T514

River

FLOW

Barree

4004

4004

Water Street

Alexandria

Barree Road

Juniata Valley Pike

**3**

**4**

305

William Penn Hwy.

22

22

To Holidaysburg

To Huntingdon

Interstate
U.S. Highway
State Highway
Other Roadway
Boat Launch
Fish Hatchery
Campground

0     1     2
Miles

# Little Juniata River

Erie
Scranton
Phillipsburg
Pittsburgh
*Little Juniata River*
Harrisburg
Allentown
Bedford
Philadelphia

# Little Juniata River

The Little Juniata River, or "Little J," is one of the most beloved trout streams of the entire Mid-Atlantic. Though this scenic stream certainly sees significant pressure, once one locates open water and lands a few fish, one comes to understand why the Little J has more than its fair share of addicts. Among those devotees is Eric Stroup, owner of Spruce Creek Fly Company and author of *Common-Sense Fly Fishing: 7 Simple Lessons to Catch More Trout.* Stroup's love for the Little Juniata is only eclipsed by his love for his young family. He is a superb fly tyer and fly caster whose passion for the Little J compels him to introduce as many folks to his river as he can. In addition to seemingly limitless patience, Stroup is also humble—in fact, rarely have I met a guide who has as much talent as he has but who so readily admits that he doesn't know it all. Instead Stroup routinely points to his mentor, the highly esteemed Charlie Meck, as the example of what a great fly angler should be.

The Little J, which starts out near Altoona and eventually empties into the Juniata River, has several attributes that boost

## Types of Fish
Anglers fishing here come for the wild browns and are rarely disappointed.

## Known Hatches
Blue-winged olive, sulfur, blue quill, caddis, Grannom, little black stonefly, light Cahill, midges, slate drake, yellow drake, and of course, terrestrials.

## Equipment to Use
*Rods:* Medium-action 4- to 5-weight, 9 feet in length.
*Reels:* Disc-drag reel, possible large-arbor applications.
*Lines:* Weight-forward floating lines matched to rod.
*Leaders:* George Harvey–style slack leader, 4X to 6X, 9 to 12 feet in length.
*Wading:* Chest waders will give you the most options here.

## Flies to Use
*Drys:* Blue-Winged Olive, sizes 16-24; Elk-Hair Caddis, 14-20; Grannom, 12-14; Cahill, 12-16; Slate Drake, 12-14; Sulfur Parachute, 14-18; Yellow Crane Fly, 18-20.

*Nymphs & Streamers:* BH Hare's Ear, sizes 12-20; BH Prince Nymph, 14-20; Flashback Hare's Ear, 16-20; Gray Scud, 14-18; Pheasant Tail Nymph, 12-20; Stroup's Sulphur Nymph, 14-18; Woolly Bugger, 6-10; RS2, 18-22; Walt's Worm, 12-16.

*Continued*

*The Little Juniata is chock full of wild brown trout that really know how to fight. Photo by Beau Beasley.*

*Guide and author Eric Stroup of Spruce Creek Fly Company fishes the Little Juniata hundreds of days a year. Photo by Beau Beasley.*

Stroup's Sulphur Nymph

its considerable appeal. First, most fly anglers ply the waters of a nice, 13½-mile-long all-tackle catch-and-release section that runs from Ironville to Petersburg. Second, the Little J is a fairly large river with significant flow and good holding structure. This allows the fish plenty of room to maneuver should they decide to run up or downstream, which I assure you they will if given the chance. Third, the river has plenty of good hatches, so these fish have lots to eat, which makes them both strong and selective.

What should you watch for while you're here? First, there are plenty of uneven rocks, originally used in the construction of the many train crossings that traverse this river. The rocks are often large and sit just above or below these crossings. While these provide excellent structure for the fish, they can be tough to negotiate around. Second, this is the place to break out your walking stick, and I'm not just talking to the "senior" anglers among us. You'll find a strong current on the Little J and inattentive anglers can easily be swept downstream.

Once these selective trout take your pattern, you're in for a real fight. These fish were either born here or were stocked as mere fingerlings. This means they are forced to adapt quickly to both the strong current and the much larger fish that view them as food. What this means for you is that the trout you have on the line is either wild or completely naturalized—and they don't fight like stockers that are put in when they have grown to be 9 to 12 inches long. These fish are hard to fool, and when they make a run for freedom they're all business—at which point that wading staff you decided not to bring starts to look pretty handy.

You'll find access points for the Little J at pullouts along Route 453. You can also fish the "Gorge" in Rothrock State Forest. To fish here, take State Road 4004 near Alexandria, and cross over the bridge at Barree. Turn left on to T-514 and drive to the end. To fish a different section below the forest, keep driving south on SR4004 until you reach the Route 305 Bridge near Petersburg. Park here and fish up or downstream.

Did I mention that you'll want a wading stick?

*Having your wading staff tethered to you allows you to keep both hands on the rod while fighting a fish. Photo by Beau Beasley.*

*Anglers fishing the Little Juniata are rarely disappointed with the wild brown-trout population.*

### When to Fish
Timing the Sulfur hatch in May can make for a killer trip. This stream never really closes because so much of this is catch-and-release only.

### Season & Limits
For the very latest information on the Little J, contact the Pennsylvania Fish and Boat Commission at www.fish.state.pa.us.

### Nearby Fly Fishing
In this part of Pennsylvania, good water abounds. Some great alternatives include Penns Creek and Spring Creek.

### Accommodations & Family Activities
Anglers fishing the Little J might consider attending one of Eric Stroup's Sulphur Schools held each spring. He and his wife, Tracey, also offer wellness weekends for couples, and these retreats offer remedies to common sports injuries. These classes combined with gourmet meals make for a great getaway weekend for anglers and non-anglers alike.

Spruce Creek Fly Company
Spruce Creek, Pennsylvania
www.ericstroupflyfishing.com
(814) 632-6129

### Fly Shops & Guides
Fly Fisher's Paradise
State College, Pennsylvania
www.flyfishersparadise.com
(814) 234-4189

Penns Creek Guides
Spring Mills Pennsylvania
www.pennscreekguides.com
(814) 364-9142

Spruce Creek Fly Company
Spruce Creek, Pennsylvania
www.ericstroupflyfishing.com
(814) 632-6129

Spruce Creek Outfitters
Spruce Creek, Pennsylvania
www.sprucecreekoutfitters.org
(814) 632-3071

TCO Fly Shop
State College, Pennsylvania
www.tcoflyfishing.com
(814) 689-3654

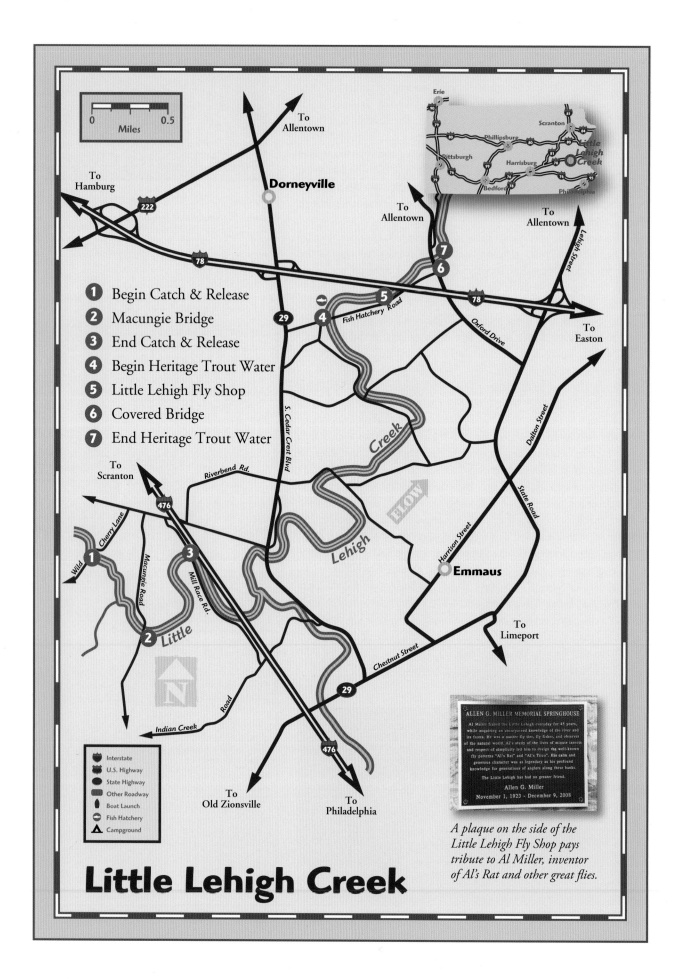

1 Begin Catch & Release
2 Macungie Bridge
3 End Catch & Release
4 Begin Heritage Trout Water
5 Little Lehigh Fly Shop
6 Covered Bridge
7 End Heritage Trout Water

To Allentown
To Hamburg
Dorneyville
To Allentown
To Allentown
222
78
29
Fish Hatchery Road
Oxford Drive
78
Lehigh Street
To Easton
S. Cedar Crest Blvd
Creek
Dalton Street
To Scranton
Riverbend Rd.
476
Cherry Lane
Macungie Road
Mill Race Rd.
Lehigh
State Road
Harrison Street
Emmaus
Wild
Little
FLOW
N
Indian Creek
Road
Chestnut Street
29
To Limeport
476
To Old Zionsville
To Philadelphia

Miles
0
0.5

Erie
90
79
80
Scranton
81
84
Phillipsburg
80
Little Lehigh Creek
Pittsburgh
Harrisburg
78
71
76
95
74
70
79
Bedford
78
Philadelphia

Interstate
U.S. Highway
State Highway
Other Roadway
Boat Launch
Fish Hatchery
Campground

ALLEN G. MILLER MEMORIAL SPRINGHOUSE

Al Miller fished the Little Lehigh everyday for 45 years, while acquiring an unsurpassed knowledge of the river and its fauna. He was a master fly tier, fly fisher, and observer of the natural world. Al's study of the lives of minute insects and respect of simplicity led him to design the well-known fly patterns "Al's Rat" and "Al's Trico". His calm and generous character was as legendary as his profound knowledge for generations of anglers along these banks.

The Little Lehigh has had no greater friend.

Allen G. Miller
November 1, 1923 - December 9, 2008

*A plaque on the side of the Little Lehigh Fly Shop pays tribute to Al Miller, inventor of Al's Rat and other great flies.*

# Little Lehigh Creek

# Little Lehigh Creek

It was on the famed Little Lehigh that I saw a brown trout worth $1,250. My friend George Maciag, an avid angler and retired school teacher, and I had decided to fish as much of the Little Lehigh as we could in a single day. We began at the top of the stream and eventually wound up near Mill Race Road. George had landed a small but colorful brown, and I'd decided to take a picture of him. George was having a hard time rearranging the fish in his net for the photo, so I leaned over to help. As I did, my precious Nikon camera leapt from its case and made a graceful and spirited dive into the river. George quickly released his fish, and we both made a mad scramble for my diva of a camera. It was too late: The camera was toast.

Perhaps it would be more accurate to say that it was on the Little Lehigh that I saw the brown trout that would *cost* me $1,250.

Little Lehigh Creek is probably one of the best-known trout streams on the East Coast and most certainly one of the best known in Pennsylvania. Though the stream has several sections, most anglers are familiar only with the famed trout water near the middle of the river. This area allows anglers to sight-fish for

## Types of Fish
Anglers typically find browns as well as rainbow trout in this river.

## Known Hatches
Little blue-winged olive, little blue quill, sulfurs, midges, tricos, and terrestrials.

## Equipment to Use
*Rods:* Medium action 3- to 5-weight, 7½ to 9 feet in length.
*Reels:* Standard trout reel.
*Lines:* Double taper in subtle colors—no oranges or bright greens.
*Leaders:* George Harvey–style slack leader, 6X to 8X, 10 to 15 feet in length.
*Wading:* In the Trout Heritage Water, no wading is allowed but chest waders can help you farther downstream.

## Flies to Use
*Drys:* Al's Trico, sizes 16-18; Ants, 14-16; Blue-winged Olive, 18-24; Crane Fly, 18-20; Pale Evening Dun, 14-18; Tan Caddis, 16-18; Trico, 18-22.

*Nymphs & Streamers:* Al's Rat, size 20; Copper John, 18-24; Honeybug Inchworm, 8-10; Pheasant Tail, 18-20; Stroup's Sulphur Nymph, 14-18. Zebra Midge, 20-24. In low-light or high-water conditions try Don's Sculpin, 8-10.

*Continued*

*Though the water near the park is tempting, wading in the river at Little Lehigh Parkway is prohibited. Photo by Beau Beasley.*

*The Little Lehigh Fly Shop is an institution in the Keystone State. Photo by Beau Beasley.*

*Rod Rohrbach knows the Little Lehigh like the back of his hand, and he can often be found in the shop tying various trout flies. Photo by Beau Beasley.*

Al's Rat

various trout, but you're not likely to catch one if you're not spot-on with the right fly and the right presentation.

If you do visit Little Lehigh Parkway, you'll no doubt see a small stone building sitting by the river. This building, an old spring house that's probably been there longer than you've been alive, is home to the Little Lehigh Fly Shop, which serves as fly-fishing central for all those who visit and pay homage to this stream. If you step inside the store you'll likely find shop owner Rod Rohrbach tying at his bench. Rod is an excellent tyer who knows the Little Lehigh very, very well. He is also a bit of a curmudgeon, so if you're expecting him to jump up from behind the bench to greet you with a bear hug, you've got a long wait ahead of you. Once you get to know him, however, you'll find that he grows on you. When I stopped in to say hi and mentioned that I was in the area doing research for my book, Rod replied, "Oh—you're from Virginia, right? No wonder you're up here fishing for trout. I would be too if I lived in Virginia."

This section of river—and more specifically the veteran anglers who *fish* this section of river—can teach you a lot about insects and their place in the ecosystem. If you're lucky, the old hands who regularly fish the Little Lehigh will be sitting out on an old picnic table in front of the shop tying flies and chatting about the recent fishing. Unfortunately you won't see Al Miller, who passed away in 2008. Al fished this river nearly every day for 45 years. To say that Al Miller knew something about flies and fly fishing the Little Lehigh is like saying that Frank Sinatra knew a little about singing. Fortunately Al's influence lives on in the patterns he created. His simple but effective Al's Rat and Al's Trico are still a mainstay on this stream. You'll find a brass plaque commemorating Al's contributions to the Little Lehigh fly-fishing community near the entrance to the Little Lehigh Fly Shop.

*An angler scopes out the best way to approach fishing by the footbridge just downstream from Little Lehigh Fly Shop. Photo by Beau Beasley.*

*The trout water here is inviting, but sloppy casters and anglers who allow their patterns to drag on the surface shouldn't bother coming.*

## When to Fish
Open all year.

## Season & Limits
A catch-and-release fly-fishing-only area exists from Wild Cherry Lane downstream to Mill Race Road. I remember this section in particular since this is where my camera went for a plunge. The next section that holds allure for fly anglers is near the Little Lehigh Fly Shop. This area allows no wading, is catch-and-release only, and allows no barbed hooks. The signs that are supposed to inform you of all these regulations are often covered by vegetation. This area lies near the heart of Allentown in a public park that serves as an oasis to anglers and non-anglers alike. This section stretches from the Fish Hatchery Road Bridge downstream to near the Oxford Dr. bridge.

## Nearby Fly Fishing
Anglers fishing here can also hit the Lehigh and the Monocacy.

## Accommodations & Family Activities
There is a host of activities a family can enjoy while visiting the city of Allentown. A nice park with a covered bridge lies just below the fly shop and is the perfect location for an evening stroll or a picnic. Also, the Museum of Indian Culture is within sight of the Little Lehigh Fly Shop and covers the history of the Lenape (Delaware) Indians.

Museum of Indian Culture
Allentown, Pennsylvania
www.museumofindianculture.org
(610) 797-2121

## Fly Shops & Guides
Little Lehigh Fly Shop
Allentown, Pennsylvania
www.littlelehighflyshop.com
(610) 797-5599

L.L. Bean
Center Valley, Pennsylvania
www.llbean.com/centervalley
(610) 798-4400

A Sporting Lifestyle
Allentown, Pennsylvania
www.asportinglifestyle.com
1-866-610-6611

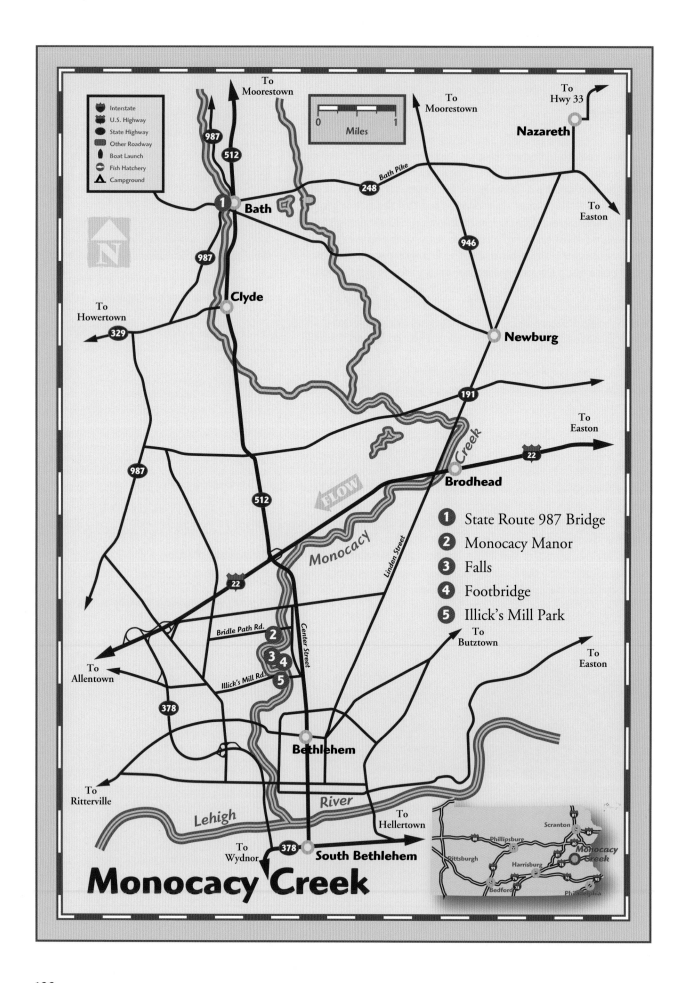

To Moorestown

To Moorestown

To Hwy 33

Interstate
U.S. Highway
State Highway
Other Roadway
Boat Launch
Fish Hatchery
Campground

Miles
0     1

Nazareth

Bath Pike

987

512

248

946

N

987

Clyde

To Howertown

329

Newburg

191

Creek

To Easton

22

987

512

Brodhead

FLOW

Monocacy

Linden Street

1. State Route 987 Bridge
2. Monocacy Manor
3. Falls
4. Footbridge
5. Illick's Mill Park

22

Bridle Path Rd.

2

Center Street

To Butztown

To Easton

To Allentown

3  4

Illick's Mill Rd.

5

378

Bethlehem

To Ritterville

River

To Hellertown

Lehigh

To Wydnor

378

South Bethlehem

# Monocacy Creek

Scranton
Phillipsburg
Monocacy Creek
Pittsburgh
Harrisburg
Bedford
Philadelphia

# Monocacy Creek

Illick's Mill is a beautiful stone structure built from rocks gathered from the creek. Many tourists visit the shops that now operate inside the mill. Photo by Beau Beasley.

It is not uncommon to see fly anglers spending their lunch hour fishing Monocacy Creek. Photo by Beau Beasley.

**M**onocacy Creek is a small but easily accessible water that has become quite popular with anglers and non-anglers alike. Many local fly fishermen still have not fished here, perhaps because they're put off by its partially urban setting. I'll grant you that plenty of great alternative waters exist, but turning one's nose up at readily accessible wild trout just because the scenery's not the most idyllic just doesn't make much sense. Yes, you read that right, modest Monocacy Creek boasts *wild* trout for those who will deign to fish for them.

I was introduced to this fishery by George Maciag, an avid fly angler and fly tyer who continually fiddles with his patterns to see what improvements he can make. George is a retired school teacher, but he finds that he's often busier now than he was when he worked full-time. "I try to fish as much as I can—and not just in Pennsylvania," he told me with a smile. "I'll admit that when I'm fishing in other places, folks look at me like I'm crazy when I tell them where I'm from. I guess Pennsylvania really is known for its good fishing." George teaches fly-fishing and fly-tying classes to dozens of eager young and not-so-young students at the L.L. Bean store in Center Valley. "I try to show people that fly fishing's

*Illick's Mill Park is popular with anglers and non-anglers alike. Families often picnic here and enjoy watching the fly anglers trying to tempt the local trout. Photo by Beau Beasley.*

George's Killer

not as hard as it seems. You just need to get some basics down, and then go out and enjoy yourself. It's really not that hard."

Barely 50 yards wide at its greatest breadth and lacking a dangerous current, the Monocacy is a small, pretty trout stream that makes the perfect water to hit on the way home from work for a few hours when you need a good trout fix. The creek begins above the town of Bath and plays host to a wild-trout population in a couple of locations before it turns into a put-and-take fishery from Illick's Mill on downstream. Near the head of the Monocacy, you'll find fewer people but a heavier canopy of trees. Watch for posted land. If you've got gumption, ask the homeowners in that area if they might allow you to park in front of their home or near their property to fish.

If you don't move too slowly, you can fish the entire length of Monocacy Creek in less than a day. Be forewarned: This isn't a stream that lends itself to long, graceful casts. Though long casts are possible on some sections of the river, here you'll do a fair amount of roll casting. George and I had a fine time fishing near Monocacy Manor, a Franciscan Retreat, located on Bridle Path Road. This area has great access to the river and affords plenty of room for backcasts. The bridge there also allows you to spot cruising trout. Near the end of our trip, George wanted to show me the nearby Illick's Mill Park. As it turned out, one of George's fly-fishing students was fishing the stream there but without success. "I like to sneak out during my lunch hour, but they don't seem to want to bite today," the rookie told me. As he and I chatted, George went to work casting—and within five minutes he'd landed a dandy rainbow. "That's why George has so many followers," the lunch-hour angler told me with a smile. George grinned sheepishly and said, "I told you. Once you get the basics down, it's not that hard. You just need to relax and have a good time."

*An angler fishing Monocacy Creek near Monocacy Manor. This area affords lots of room for backcasts. Photo by Beau Beasley.*

## Types of Fish
Anglers typically find wild browns and stocked rainbows here. Toward the mouth of the creek, a smallmouth bass might shoot up from the Lehigh River.

## Known Hatches
Hatches on the Monocacy are pretty much limited to blue-winged olives, sulfur, caddisfly, and tricos. Of course terrestrials can also be counted on as well.

## Equipment to Use
*Rods:* 3- to 4-weight, 7 to 8½ feet in length.
*Reels:* Standard trout reel.
*Lines:* Weight-forward floating lines matched to rod.
*Leaders:* 4X to 6X, 9 feet in length.
*Wading:* Hip boots unless you plan to wade in the river.

## Flies to Use
*Drys:* Blue-Winged Olive, sizes 16-20; Beetle, 16-20; Dusty's Deviant, 14-16; Elk-Hair Caddis, 14-20; Flying Ant, 10-18; Stimulator, 14-18; Trico, 18-22.

*Nymphs & Streamers:* BH Hare's Ear, sizes 14-20; BH Prince Nymph, 14-20; Copper John, 16-20; Flashback Hare's Ear, 16-18; George's Killer, 6-10; Green Weenie, 12-16; Woolly Bugger 6-12.

## When to Fish
July and August can be very difficult on Monocacy Creek. Most other times, the fishing can be quite good. As always, rain is a major factor.

## Season & Limits
A wild-trout population exists from State Route 987 Bridge to nearly two miles downstream. The next wild-trout section stretches from one-half mile above the Center Street Bridge (State Route 512) downstream nearly two miles to Illick's Mill. The rest of the river is a stocked trout fishery, ranging from Illick's Mill downstream to the Lehigh River. For the very latest information on Monocacy Creek, contact the Pennsylvania Fish and Boat Commission at www.fish.state.pa.us.

## Nearby Fly Fishing
If Monocacy Creek is crowded or fishing is slow, try the Little Lehigh or the Lehigh River, which are close by.

## Accommodations & Family Activities
Beginning anglers, in particular those who are trying to learn to roll cast, would enjoy spending time at Illick's Mill Park. This area is very popular with families.

## Fly Shops & Guides
Little Lehigh Fly Shop
Allentown, Pennsylvania
www.littlelehighflyshop.com
(610) 797-5599

L.L. Bean
Center Valley, Pennsylvania
www.llbean.com/centervalley
(610) 798-4400

Orvis
Downingtown, Pennsylvania
www.orvis.com/downingtown
(610) 873-8400

Orvis
Plymouth Meeting, Pennsylvania
www.orvis.com/plymouthmeeting
(610) 825-1010

A Sporting Lifestyle
Allentown, Pennsylvania
www.asportinglifestyle.com
1-866-610-6611

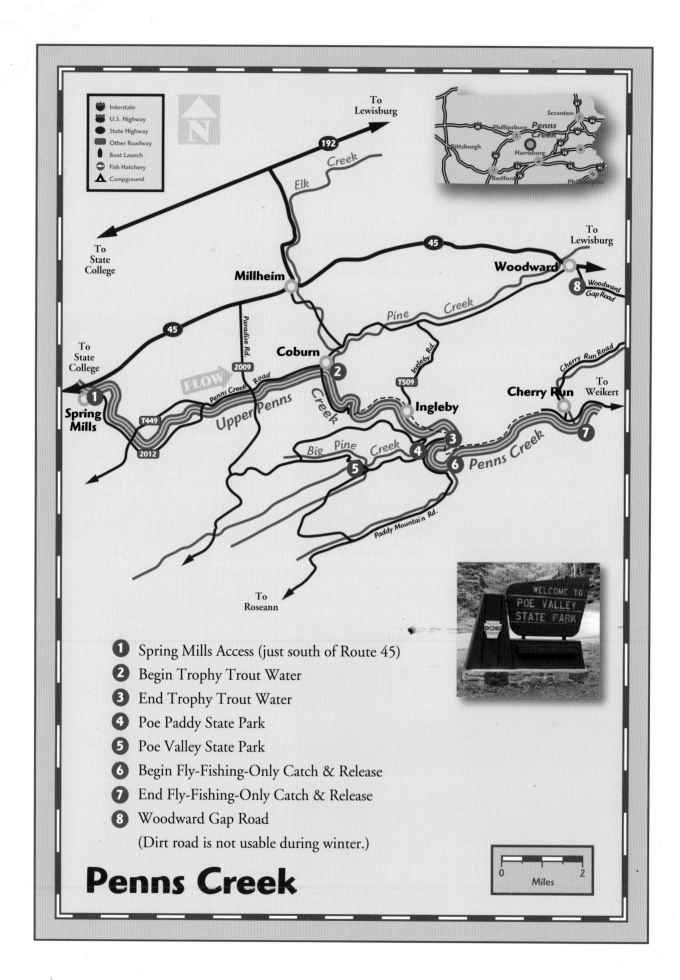

① Spring Mills Access (just south of Route 45)

② Begin Trophy Trout Water

③ End Trophy Trout Water

④ Poe Paddy State Park

⑤ Poe Valley State Park

⑥ Begin Fly-Fishing-Only Catch & Release

⑦ End Fly-Fishing-Only Catch & Release

⑧ Woodward Gap Road

(Dirt road is not usable during winter.)

# Penns Creek

# Penns Creek

Ah, the beloved and enigmatic Penns Creek. Many cherish it, but even those who do admit that Penns Creek anglers often struggle to find what works. Rookie anglers have been reduced to tears in their desperate search to determine exactly what finicky Penns Creek trout want to eat, and even seasoned veterans may be baffled. Oddly enough Penns Creek begins in Penns Cave in Centre County and, at its headwaters, is only a dozen or so yards wide. Though it starts out small and on privately owned property—which you have to pay to fish—it opens up to a much larger stream as it twists and turns on its way to the Susquehanna. Fortunately, the stream is accessible to the public and widens as it heads down through rolling farmland and wooded state-park land.

Penns Creek can be pretty easily broken into three sections—but this is where the ease ends. Near Spring Mills, Penns Creek widens and increases in flow near Route 45 as it makes its way downstream. This upper section is about seven miles long and is stocked trout water. The next section begins the all-tackle trophy trout water near Coburn and runs all the way to Poe Paddy State Park—again, about seven miles. This area is very popular and sees significant pressure, but the fishing remains good. From Poe Paddy at Swift Run to downstream for nearly four miles,

## Types of Fish
Anglers typically find browns here and the occasional rainbow. Smallies may be caught at the every end of the creek.

## Known Hatches
By far the best-known hatch here is the green drake that occurs in June. Other hatches include blue-winged olive, little black stonefly, quill Gordon, spring blue quill, Hendrickson, black quill, Grannom, caddis, March brown, giant stonefly, sulfur, slate drake, yellow drake, October caddis, terrestrials and tricos.

## Equipment to Use
*Rods:* 5- to 6-weight, 8½ to 9½ feet in length.
*Reels:* Disc-drag reel, possible large-arbor applications.
*Lines:* Weight-forward floating lines matched to rod.
*Leaders:* 5X to 8X, 9 to 14 feet in length.
*Wading:* Chest waders are a must here and a wading staff is also a good idea.

## Flies to Use
*Drys:* Big Slate Drake, sizes 6-8; Blue-winged Olive, 18-22; Elk-Hair Caddis, 14-20; Grannom, 10-14; Giant Stonefly, 8; Gray Fox, 12-14; Green Drake, 8-12; Hendrickson, 14-16; Light Cahill, 14-16; March Brown, 10-14; Quill Gordon, 12-18; Stroup's Sulphur Nymph, 12-20; Trico Spinner, 20-24; Yellow Drake, 10-12; and of course, terrestrials.

*Continued*

*Fishing can be quite good on Penns Creek, but keep in mind that the trout will use the river's current against you. Photo by Beau Beasley.*

Anglers should fish their way over to good water, rather than simply walking to the section of the stream they think holds fish. Many anglers miss good fishing opportunities by not following this approach. Photo by Beau Beasley.

Anderson's Bird of Prey

a catch-and-release-only area exists until it meets Cherry Run. Here is where most fly anglers duke it out with wild fish. This section of the river has high grass and is popular with snakes, so watch your step. You can most certainly fish well below Cherry Run all the way down to Weikert and beyond, but most fly anglers stay upstream of this section.

If all this great-sounding trout water seems too good to be true, there's a hitch. Penns Creek hatches are off the charts compared to other trout streams in Pennsylvania—or nearly anywhere else, for that matter. Penns is truly in a league of its own in this regard, which is why the fish are so darned hard to catch. With the sole exception of the Delaware River, no other trout water on the East Coast can rival Penns Creek's prolific hatches. Most anglers want to visit during the famed green-drake hatch in June, but in truth there are so many excellent hatches here that it would almost be easier to name the flies that don't hatch here than those that do. As if this isn't enough of a hatch-matching challenge, throw into the mix the fact that these trout have so many nymphs to eat that they don't readily rise to drys. And now you can see why fishing Penns Creek is such a challenge. The one plus is Penns has a great deal of open area for anglers to manage their backcasts. Of course, this can play against you as well if you don't approach the stream with stealth.

"Consistently rising trout are uncommon on Penns, but fish do occasionally rise to midges. Fishing with nymphs and streamers can also be excellent," says Paul Weamer, who manages TCO Fly Shop in nearby by State College. "Ants and beetles can also be helpful in the early spring, and Stimulators can help mimic golden stoneflies." He ought to know: Weamer and the venerable Charlie Meck co-authored *Pocketguide to Pennsylvania Hatches,* an excellent book that I highly recommend to any angler who hopes to get Penns Creek's tight-lipped trout to open up.

When fishing Penns Creek, keep an eye out for snakes in the tall grass along the shore. Photo by Beau Beasley.

*Penns Creek has an excellent population of brown trout.*

### Flies to Use (continued)

*Nymphs & Streamers:* Anderson's Bird of Prey, sizes 16-20; BH Hare's Ear, 16-22; BH Prince Nymph, 14-22; Copper John, 16-22; Muddler Minnow, 6-10; Pheasant Tail Nymph, 14-20; Slumpbuster, 6; Scud, 10-18; Sculpin, 4-8; Woolly Bugger, 6-10; Zonkers, 6-10; Zuddlers, 6-10.

### When to Fish

Any time you can go you should, but summer can be tough.

### Season & Limits

For the very latest information on Penns Creek contact the Pennsylvania Fish and Boat Commission at www.fish.state.pa.us.

### Nearby Fly Fishing

If Penns Creek is crowded, try fishing Spring Creek or perhaps the Little Juniata.

### Accommodations & Services

State College is a great jumping-off point for those anglers who want to fish Penns Creek. While in town you can also visit Penn State and some of the best fly shops in the Keystone State.

### Fly Shops & Guides

The Feathered Hook
Coburn, Pennsylvania
www.thefeatheredhook.com
(814) 349-8757

Fly Fisher's Paradise
State College, Pennsylvania
www.flyfishersparadise.com
(814) 234-4189

E. Hille
S. Williamsport, Pennsylvania
www.anglersupplyhouse.com
(570) 323-7564

Penns Creek Guides
Spring Mills Pennsylvania
www.pennscreekguides.com
(814) 364-9142

Spruce Creek Fly Company
Spruce Creek, Pennsylvania
www.ericstroupflyfishing.com
(814) 632-6129

TCO Fly Shop
State College, Pennsylvania
www.tcoflyfishing.com
(814) 689-3654

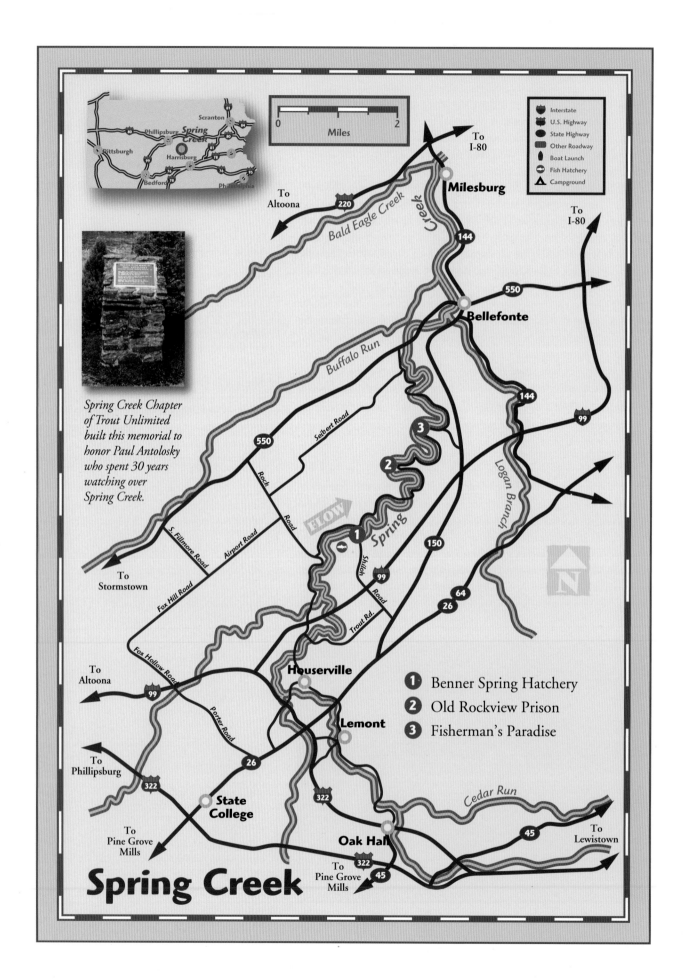

Spring Creek Chapter of Trout Unlimited built this memorial to honor Paul Antolosky who spent 30 years watching over Spring Creek.

Miles
0       2

Interstate
U.S. Highway
State Highway
Other Roadway
Boat Launch
Fish Hatchery
Campground

To I-80

Milesburg

To Altoona

Bald Eagle Creek

Creek

220

144

To I-80

550

Bellefonte

144

Buffalo Run

550

Seibert Road

99

3

2

Logan Branch

Rock

Road

1

Spring

FLOW

150

S. Fillmore Road

Airport Road

Shiloh Road

99

To Stormstown

Fox Hill Road

Trout Rd.

64

26

N

Fox Hollow Road

Houserville

To Altoona

99

Porter Road

Lemont

❶ Benner Spring Hatchery

❷ Old Rockview Prison

❸ Fisherman's Paradise

To Phillipsburg

26

322

Cedar Run

State College

322

45

To Lewistown

To Pine Grove Mills

Oak Hall

To Pine Grove Mills

322

45

# Spring Creek

# Spring Creek

spring Creek begins near Oak Hall, Pennsylvania, and runs in a northeasterly direction until it empties into Bald Eagle Creek. What lies between those two points are 22 miles of some of the best wild brown-trout fishing imaginable. This wonderful limestoner averages about two to three feet in depth, which makes it easy to wade. There are of course deeper pools with banks and deep undercut ledges because the river has normal shifts in its bed like other bodies of moving water. The catch-and-release-only Spring Creek is not a big intimidating river, but neither is it an English chalk stream that your average five-year-old could straddle with a foot on either bank. Perhaps one of the most delightful surprises awaiting the Spring Creek angler is that the water hasn't been stocked since the mid 1980s, and the trout are both wild and plentiful.

Though Spring Creek has suffered from industrial negligence, the most important occurred when the Nease Chemical Company near State College improperly stored kepone and mirex, two powerful insecticides used during the late 1960s and early 1970s in ant and roach baits. The toxins found their way into Spring Creek and, fearing a threat to public health, the Pennsylvania Department of Environmental Protection issued a warning to Spring Creek anglers: They could continue to fish the water but could not creel

## Types of Fish
Anglers typically find wild brown trout, and on a rare occasion, an escaped rainbow from one of the state's hatcheries is landed here.

## Known Hatches
Blue-winged olive, blue quill, trico, sulfur, caddisfly, Cahill, terrestrials. Midges are a very important hatch here.

## Equipment to Use
*Rods:* 4- to 6-weight, 8 to 9 feet in length.
*Reels:* Disc-drag reel.
*Lines:* Weight-forward floating lines matched to rod.
*Leaders:* 3X to 6X, 9 to 14 feet in length. George Harvey–style.
*Wading:* Chest waders are best used here.

## Flies to Use
*Drys:* Antolosky's Crane Fly, sizes 16-18; Black Beetle, 12-18; Blue-winged Olive, 18-22; Blue Quill, 16-20; Crane Fly, 16-18; Elk-Hair Caddis, 14-20; Flying Ant, 10-18; Light Cahill, 12-14; Trico, 24.

*Nymphs & Streamers:* Anderson's Bird of Prey, sizes 16-20; Copper John, 16-20; Green Weenie, 10-14; Hare's Ear Nymph, 14-22 Pheasant Tail Nymph, 14-20; Midge (cream; ginger dun/black), 24-28; Stroup's Sulphur Nymph, 12-20; Scud, 10-18; Sculpin, 4-8; Walt's Worm, 8-18; Wet Black Ant, 12-16; Woolly Bugger, 6-10 Zebra Midge, 18-22.

*Continued*

*Steve Probasco, editor in chief of* Eastern Fly Fishing, *tries his luck on Spring Creek. Photo by Beau Beasley.*

*Anglers fishing Spring Creek need to keep a tight line while nymphing in order to detect subtle hits. Photo by Beau Beasley.*

Walt's Worm

their catch and were advised not to eat the fish. Thus, catch-and-release-only fishing was introduced to Pennsylvania.

Spring Creek has significant hatches all year, so there are no silver-bullet patterns. The river is full of cress bugs, freshwater shrimp, and a host of insects that hatch throughout the year. The fish are well fed and fight like mad. One local pattern holds its own against the trout. Walt's Worm was created by Walt Young, a noted fly-tying expert from Altoona, Pennsylvania. This modest, straightforward pattern often gets results when other patterns don't. In general, keep your patterns small and your tippets smaller. These canny trout see more than their fair share of patterns—as a result, anglers might want to start out with a midge pattern since this hatch is so strong here.

One of the best features about fishing Spring Creek is its easy access. Multiple entry points exist, but two stand out. First, Fisherman's Paradise off Spring Creek Road offers excellent access and comes complete with a wheelchair-accessible pier. You'll find a no-wading section here, which starts near the hatchery outflow. A wire stretched across the river indicates the beginning of this section and it continues for just more than half a mile upstream. There is no wading allowed in this section of the creek. Another easy-access point is near Benner Spring, which anglers can find off of Shiloh Road, itself easily accessed off I-99. Plans are afoot to expand fishing access along an area now occupied by the Rockville Prison. If this occurs, anglers will be able to walk from Benner Spring up to Fisherman's Paradise.

The granddaddy of the dozen or so Pennsylvania fly shops whose customers regularly fish Spring Creek is Fly Fisher's Paradise in State College. Shop owner Steve Sywensky has fished Spring Creek for more than 40 years and says, "There are a lot of fish in that river. So it only stands to reason that you're going to come across a hungry one sooner or later. At the same time, the population is not so large that the fish are in poor health. Chances are every time you take a step, you just walked past a fish."

*Walt's Worm can be very effective when nymphing trout water. Photo by Beau Beasley.*

### When to Fish
Spring Creek can fish nearly every day of the year. Check with the local shops to get the latest information on what's going on where.

### Season & Limits
This is an all-tackle stream. No wading is allowed in the fly-fishing-only catch-and-release-only section near Fisherman's Paradise. For the very latest information on Spring Creek contact the Pennsylvania Fish and Boat Commission at www.fish.state.pa.us.

### Nearby Fly Fishing
If Spring Creek isn't fishing well you can always try Penns Creek or the Little Juniata.

### Accommodations & Family Activities
Anglers fishing Spring Creek have the option of booking a room with guide Eric Stroup, who makes things very easy as the deal is a total package. Visiting anglers could also stay with Mike Gruendler at Spring Creek House, which sits right on Spring Creek.

Spring Creek House
Bellefonte, Pennsylvania
www.springcreekhouse.com
(814) 353-1369

### Fly Shops & Guides
Mark Antolosky
Bellefonte, Pennsylvania
(814) 389-0051

Dennis Charney
Bellefonte, Pennsylvania
www.dennischarney.com
(814) 280-8171

Fly Fisher's Paradise
State College, Pennsylvania
www.flyfishersparadise.com
(814) 234-4189

E. Hille
S. Williamsport, Pennsylvania
www.anglersupplyhouse.com
(570) 323-7564

Penns Creek Guides
Spring Mills, Pennsylvania
www.pennscreekguides.com
(814) 364-9142

Spruce Creek Fly Company
Spruce Creek, Pennsylvania
www.ericstroupflyfishing.com
(814) 632-6129

Spruce Creek Outfitters
Spruce Creek, Pennsylvania
www.sprucecreekoutfitters.org
(814) 632-3071

TCO Fly Shop
State College, Pennsylvania
www.tcoflyfishing.com
(814) 689-3654

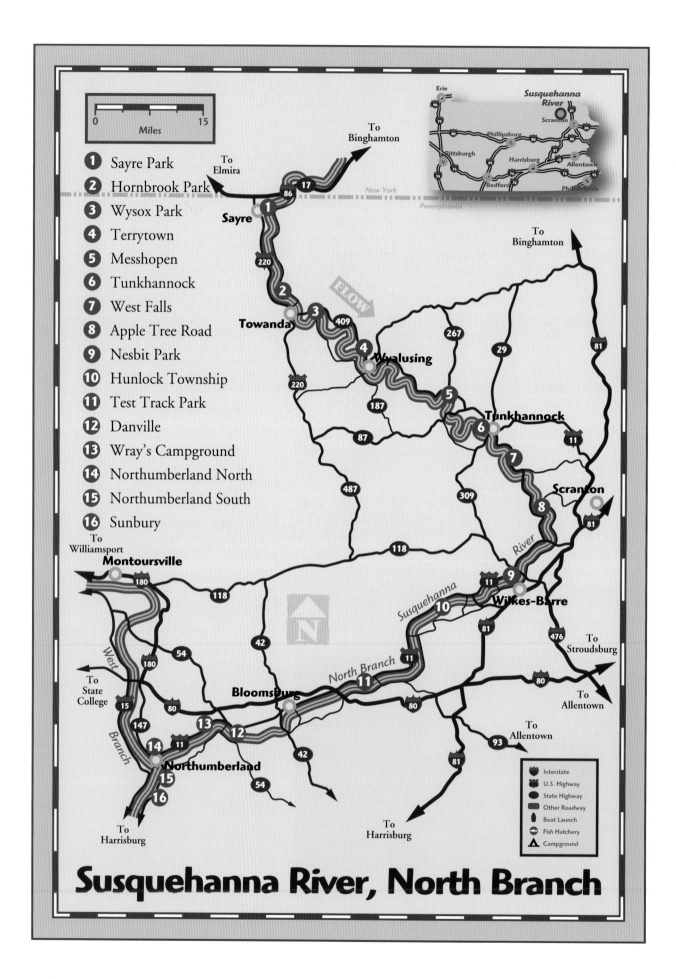

1 Sayre Park
2 Hornbrook Park
3 Wysox Park
4 Terrytown
5 Messhopen
6 Tunkhannock
7 West Falls
8 Apple Tree Road
9 Nesbit Park
10 Hunlock Township
11 Test Track Park
12 Danville
13 Wray's Campground
14 Northumberland North
15 Northumberland South
16 Sunbury

0 Miles 15

To Elmira
To Binghamton
To Binghamton
To Williamsport
To State College
To Harrisburg
To Harrisburg
To Stroudsburg
To Allentown
To Allentown

New York
Pennsylvania

Susquehanna River
Erie
Phillipsburg
Scranton
Pittsburgh
Harrisburg
Allentown
Bedford
Philadelphia

Sayre
Towanda
Wyalusing
Tunkhannock
Scranton
Montoursville
Wilkes-Barre
Bloomsburg
Northumberland

FLOW

West Branch
North Branch
Susquehanna
River

N

Interstate
U.S. Highway
State Highway
Other Roadway
Boat Launch
Fish Hatchery
Campground

# Susquehanna River, North Branch

# Susquehanna River, North Branch

can still remember the first time I drove across the Susquehanna River on my way to a fly-fishing show in New Jersey. It stretched out like a dark blue blanket winding its serpentine way seemingly forever into the distance. The local Algonquian Indians named the Susquehanna, though no one is certain what the name means. The grand old Susky—at 440 miles long, it's the longest river on the East Coast—is perhaps the most notable waterway in the Keystone State, which is really saying something considering that Pennsylvania is home to such fabled waters as Spring Creek, the Little Juniata, Elk Creek, Fishing Creek, and Penns Creek. Even still, Pennsylvanians, who are justifiably proud of their trout waters, love to brag about the mighty Susky. Having fished it, I can certainly see why.

A few years ago I floated the Susky with Brian Shumaker, owner of Susquehanna Guide Service in New Cumberland. He fishes a great deal on the main stem and the lower reaches of the Juniata River, a tributary of the Susky. Brian and I floated the river on his drift boat, and although the fishing was a tad on the slow side, the weather was great. We were having a good time fishing and talking about recent events when Brian felt a decidedly good thump on his line. He immediately set the hook, and a solid fight ensued. I was prepared to see a hefty smallmouth, but instead Brian brought a really nice walleye to hand—the first walleye I'd ever seen caught on a fly. "That's the thing about fishing

## Types of Fish
There are many types of fish to catch in the Susquehanna including shad, stripers, carp, walleye, and the occasional catfish. The main reason folks come here however is to take on the resident smallies.

## Known Hatches
Dragonflies, damselflies, and hellgrammites as well as crayfish and minnows are prevalent. Anglers may encounter numerous caddis and mayfly emergences throughout the season; the most notable is the white fly in mid-July to early August.

## Equipment to Use
*Rods:* 7- to 8-weight, 8 to 9 ½ feet in length.
*Reels:* Disc-drag reel, unless you are fishing for stripers. In this case you will need a large-arbor reel and plenty of 30-pound test backing. The same goes for carp.
*Lines:* Weight-forward floating, matched to rod. On sinking or sinking-tip lines a 4- to 5-foot piece of straight 2X tippet works well.
*Leaders:* 1X to 3X leaders, 9 feet in length.
*Wading:* Boating is the best way to fish the Susky, but kayaks and inflatable pontoon boats are also an option as there is plenty of shore access.

## Flies to Use
*Topwater:* Blockhead Poppers, sizes 4-6; BoogleBug, 2-10; Hickey's Condor, 6-10; Lefty's Bug, 1-4; Walt's Popper, 2-10; White Fly, 14.

*Nymphs & Streamers:* Bart-O-Minnow, size 2; Claw-Dad, 2-6; Clouser Crayfish, 4-8; Clouser Minnow, 1/0-6; Clouser Mad Tom, 4; Conrad's Bass Hair Nymph, 4;

## Flies to Use
Conrad's Hellgrammite, 4; Jail Bait, 2-6; Lefty's Deceiver, 2/0-6; Murdich Minnow, 2-6; Red and White Hackle Fly, 1/0-2; Skilton's Hellgrammite, 6.

*For Shad:* Tommy's Torpedo; sizes 4-6; Simmons's Shad Fly; 6; Scotts Golden Retriever, 6-10.

*Continued*

*Smallmouth bass are king on the Susquehanna.*
*Illustration by Alan Folger.*

*Though known for its smallmouth bass, carp in the Susquehanna are also a target for fly anglers. Lefty Kreh landed this one while fishing with guide Mike O'Brien. Photo by King Montgomery.*

Clouser Minnow

the Susquehanna," said Brian as he released the fish. "Folks come out here expecting to see big smallies, but the truth is that you never know for sure what you might catch out here because there are so many possibilities for quality fish."

The Susky has both North and West branches, with most of the anglers focusing on the North Branch as well as the main stem. Each has its own characteristics, and fish move in and around each of these branches. Their movements depend on weather conditions, times of year, and of course migrations of fish such as shad and stripers, not to mention the movement of the smallies. You don't need a watercraft, however, to have a great day on the Susky. I wet waded this river with my good friend, the late Steve Vlasak, and we enjoyed hop-scotching from one rock to the next. Casting crayfish patterns to every likely looking spot, we were able to catch and release several nice smallies. Wet wading can be fun, but it's not for everyone. Please don't venture out to the river if you're not in very good health. I hasten to add that wearing a life jacket is also a very good idea. You can increase your odds of success by focusing on drop-offs, seams in cross-currents, back eddies, and rock structures, all of which provide good ambush points for predator fish.

The Susky is a magnificent river, but like most big waterways, it's seen its share of hard times. Some believe that pollution has reduced the river's population of fish. One fish that seems particularly hard hit is the resident smallmouth bass population around Harrisburg. If you live in Pennsylvania or fish the Susquehanna, I urge you to make your voice heard so that this venerable water may be protected for future generations. Two organizations working to restore the Susky are PennFuture (www. pennfuture.org) and the Chesapeake Bay Foundation (www.cbf. org). Both groups can provide you with excellent advice on how to keep the mighty Susquehanna healthy for generations to come.

*Steve Vlasak, a friend of the author, with a smallie caught while wet wading the Susquehanna. Photo by Beau Beasley.*

## When to Fish
Other than the dead of winter nearly any day on the Susky can be good. Smallies respond best in water above 50 degrees.

## Season & Limits
Regulations on this river recently changed for the better. In October 2010, the Pennsylvania Fish and Boat Commission announced new catch-and-release-only regulations on the Susquehanna for all smallmouth bass. The new regulations affect the stretch of river from the inflatable dam near Sunbury in Northumberland County downstream to the Holtwood Dam in York County. This is a positive development that I am sure Bob Clouser and others who have fought for this river's health heartily embrace.

Contact the Pennsylvania Fish and Boat Commission at www.fish.state.pa.us. For the latest information and for a much more detailed map call (717) 705-7930.

## Nearby Fly Fishing
Alternative fishing locales exist in nearly all the tributaries of the Susky.

## Accommodations & Family Activities
Consider Harrisburg, Wilkes-Barre, Sunbury, Berwick, and perhaps a dozen or more other towns as a base of operations when fishing the Susky.

## Fly Shops & Guides
The list of guides and shops is only a partial listing of those that service this great river.

Bass Pro Shops
Harrisburg, Pennsylvania
www.basspro.com
(717) 565-5200

Clouser's Fly Shop
Middletown, Pennsylvania
www.clouserflyfishing.com
(717) 944-6541

French Creek Outfitters
Phoenixville, Pennsylvania
www.frenchcreekoutfitters.com
(610) 933-7200

Gander Mountain
Dickson City, Pennsylvania
www.gandermountain.com
(570) 347-9077

Gander Mountain
Harrisburg, Pennsylvania
(717) 671-9700

Gander Mountain
Pennsdale, Pennsylvania
(570) 546-1040

E. Hille
S. Williamsport, Pennsylvania
www.anglersupplyhouse.com
(570) 323-7564

An Irish Angler
Montoursville, Pennsylvania
www.flyfish-pa.com
(570) 220-0391

Susquehanna Guide Service
New Cumberland, Pennsylvania
www.susqriverguides.com
(717) 774-2307

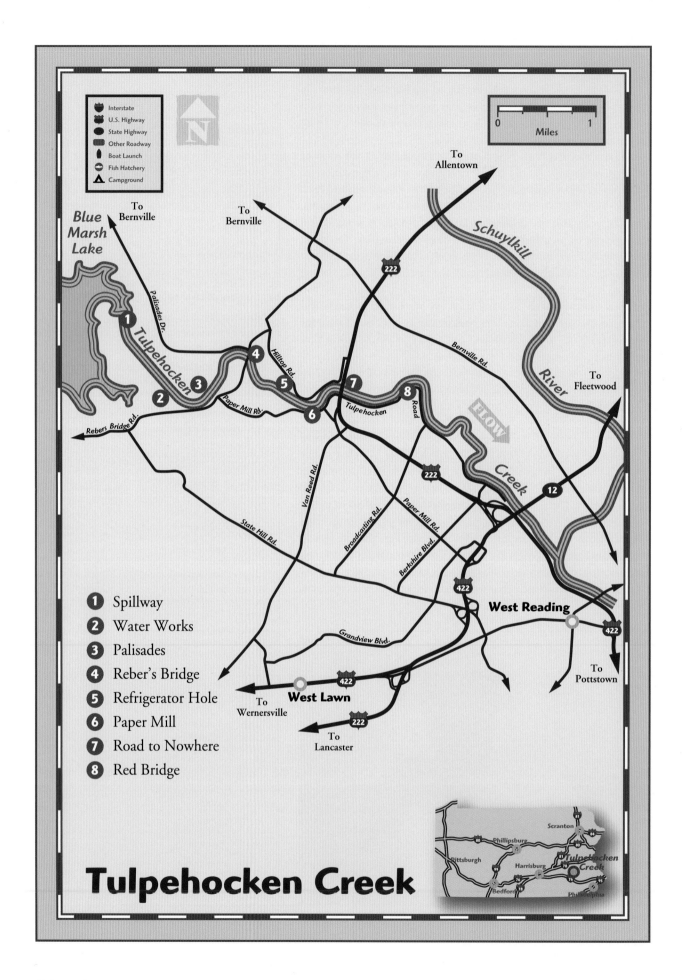

### Legend

- Interstate
- U.S. Highway
- State Highway
- Other Roadway
- Boat Launch
- Fish Hatchery
- Campground

N

0 Miles 1

To Allentown

To Bernville

To Bernville

To Bernville

Blue Marsh Lake

Schuylkill

River

To Fleetwood

Palisades Dr.

Tulpehocken

Hilltop Rd.

Paper Mill Rd.

Rebers Bridge Rd.

222

Bernville Rd.

Tulpehocken

Road

FLOW

Creek

12

Van Reed Rd.

State Hill Rd.

Broadcasting Rd.

Paper Mill Rd.

Berkshire Blvd.

222

422

West Reading

To Pottstown

422

Grandview Blvd.

422

West Lawn

222

To Wernersville

To Lancaster

1 Spillway
2 Water Works
3 Palisades
4 Reber's Bridge
5 Refrigerator Hole
6 Paper Mill
7 Road to Nowhere
8 Red Bridge

# Tulpehocken Creek

Tulpehocken Creek

Scranton

Phillipsburg

Pittsburgh

Harrisburg

Bedford

Philadelphia

# Tulpehocken Creek

ew fisheries in Pennsylvania are as well respected as Tulpehocken Creek. Located just outside Reading, its name means *place of turtles*—but it could just as easily mean "great stream with plenty of hungry trout." The Tully, as it is affectionately known in these parts, has quietly built a solid reputation as a strong trout fishery among a devoted following of anglers. Some of her suitors escape Philadelphia to get their required trout fix, while others aren't afraid to drive for hours if the right hatch is on. Browns and rainbows make up much of the targeted species in this stream, but other quarry call this tailwater fishery home as well. The trick is landing them, which is often harder than you think.

Tony Gehman, owner of Reading's TCO Fly Shop, knows this creek quite well, and he's nonplussed that so many anglers labor under the misapprehension that they should call it quits on the Tully during the dog days of summer: "Once late summer hits, lots of guys desert the river and put up their gear until the fall. This is a big mistake. While I don't encourage anglers to pursue trout during the extreme heat of the summer, stalking carp is something they could easily do." I agree with Tony completely, and if you think landing an angry brown is tough, try taking on a hefty carp

*Tony Gehman of TCO Fly Shop with a trout on the Tully. Photo by Chris Frangiosa.*

*Anglers who live in Philadelphia often fish Tulpehocken Creek because it's the closet trout water to the city. Photo by Beau Beasley.*

*Wading in the Tully is easy; it's tricking the trout that's tough. Photo by Beau Beasley.*

Zebra Midge

that has the current on his side. The first time I fished Tulpehocken Creek I was chasing carp with my good friend, the late Steve Vlasak. Steve was the consummate family-oriented fisherman. Though I considered him a trout fishing machine, Steve relished the challenge of going head-to-head with Tulpehocken carp. He was able to successfully drift small nymphs and egg patterns to lunker carp like no one else. It was a trip I'll never forget.

The access is excellent on Tulpehocken Creek, and because the stream lacks heavy current most of the time, wading is a breeze. Anglers need only park their car at one of several convenient locations and head to the river. Though most anglers come here for trout, some anglers do target stripers just below the spillway at Blue Marsh Lake. This area also affords lots of room for picnicking and other outdoor activities. All of this easy access and healthy trout water does lead to significant pressure, which readers should keep in mind when planning a trip here. Not to put too fine a point on it, Tulpehocken fish become highly selective. If you show up and throw a caddis or a Woolly Bugger at them with a clumsy cast, you might as well pack it in. When fishing does become tough, drop back to smaller patterns and even smaller tippets.

Nick Delle Donne, owner of The Evening Rise in Lancaster, enjoys fishing the Tully as much as the next guy but admits that it can be tough, especially for the beginner. "Standard as well as contemporary fly patterns and tactics will work here on occasion," he says, "but keen observation and presentation are keys to success." Tony Gehman and I fished the Tulpehocken in July 2010, and I'd describe the fishing as tough but pleasant. He and I both landed fish. His took drys, and I landed a nice brown on a nymph under the eerily named Road to Nowhere. Like most anglers who come here, I lost more trout than I landed—and who knows how many subtle takes I missed altogether?

*Steve Vlasak hooked up on the Tully with a carp. The fish was caught, photographed, and released. Photo by Beau Beasley.*

## Types of Fish

Brown trout, rainbows, muskies, carp, and even stripers call this creek home.

## Known Hatches

Blue-winged olives, sulfur, caddisfly, Cahill, green sedge, stoneflies, and terrestrials just to name a few. The trico hatch can look like a blizzard on a good day. Various baitfish and crayfish are found throughout the river.

## Equipment to Use

*Rods:* 4- to 6-weight, 7 to 9 feet in length.
*Reels:* Disc-drag reel, possible large-arbor applications.
*Lines:* Weight-forward floating lines matched to rod.
*Leaders:* 4X to 8X, 9 to 14 feet in length. George Harvey–style.
*Wading:* Chest waders are best used here.

## Flies to Use

*Drys:* Blue-winged Olive, sizes 14-22; Big Slate Drake, 8; Crane Fly, 18-20; Cased Caddis, 12-16; CDC Black Flying Ant, 12-14; Griffith's Gnat, 18-22; Letort Hopper, 10-16; Trico, 20-24; Yellow Drake, 12-14.

*Nymphs & Streamers:* Anderson's Bird of Prey, sizes 16-20; BH Hare's Ear, 14-22; BH Prince Nymph, 14-20; BH Olive Soft Hackle, 14-18; Clouser Deep Minnow, 6-10; Crane Larva, 12-18; Coburn's Inchworm, 12-14; Clouser Crayfish, 6-8; Muddler Minnow, 6-10; Pheasant Tail Nymph, 14-20; Pop Midge, 20-26; Scud, 12-18; Sculpin, 4-8; Stroup's Sulphur Nymph, 12-20; Woolly Bugger, 6-10; Zonker, 4-10; Zug Bug, 12-16; Zebra Midge, 16-20.

*Specialty Flies:* TCO Fly Shop in Reading has developed specialty patterns with an emphasis on CDC emergers just for this stream. Picking up a few before hitting the stream would be a very wise move.

## When to Fish

Tulpehocken Creek can be fished nearly every day of the year.

## Season & Limits

A delayed-harvest section exists from below the dam to the covered red bridge. For a complete list of all rules and regulations for this Pennsylvania stream go to www.fishandboat.com, or call (717) 705-7930.

## Nearby Fly Fishing

It's hard to find a time when fishing can't be done here, but if times are tough, you can try Blue Marsh Lake.

## Accommodations & Family Activities

Anglers fishing Tulpehocken Creek can find plenty of restaurants in nearby Reading. If you're in town for a few days you really should visit the Philadelphia Museum of Art in nearby Philly. If the steps at the museum look familiar, they should: They were featured in the movie *Rocky*.

## Fly Shops & Guides

The Evening Rise
Lancaster, Pennsylvania
www.theeveningrise.com
(717) 509-3636

Sporting Gentleman
Media, Pennsylvania
www.sportinggentleman.com
(610) 565-6140

TCO Fly Shop
Reading, Pennsylvania
www.tcoflyfishing.com
(610) 678-1899

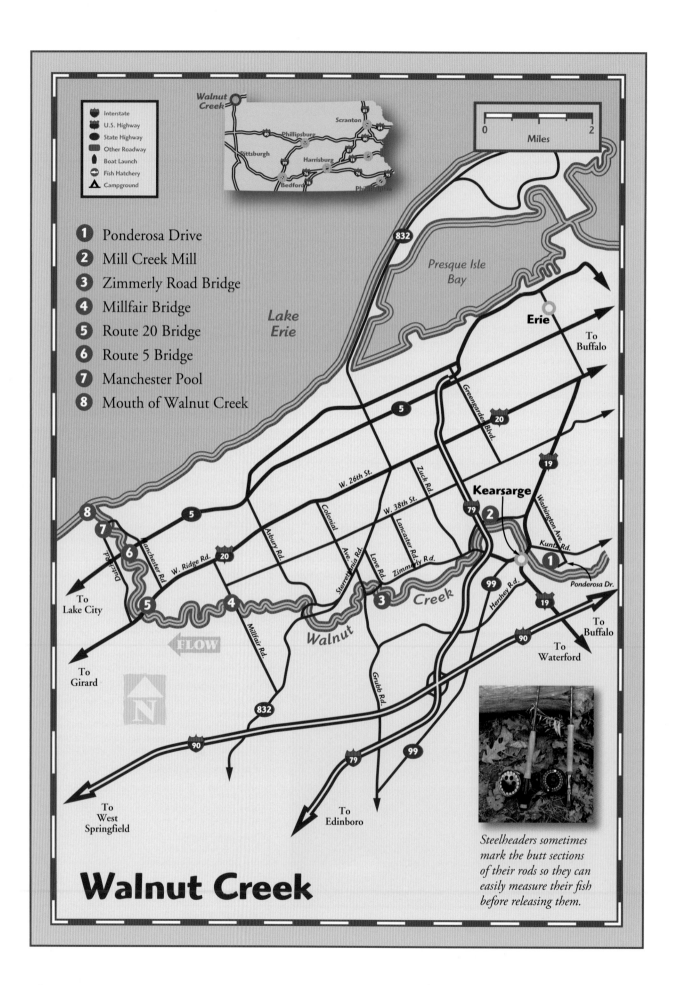

**Legend:**
- Interstate
- U.S. Highway
- State Highway
- Other Roadway
- Boat Launch
- Fish Hatchery
- Campground

1. Ponderosa Drive
2. Mill Creek Mill
3. Zimmerly Road Bridge
4. Millfair Bridge
5. Route 20 Bridge
6. Route 5 Bridge
7. Manchester Pool
8. Mouth of Walnut Creek

Walnut Creek

Scranton
Phillipsburg
Pittsburgh
Harrisburg
Bedford
Philadelphia

Miles
0    2

Presque Isle Bay

Lake Erie

Erie

To Buffalo

Greengarden Blvd

Kearsarge

Washington Ave.

Kuntz Rd.

Ponderosa Dr.

W. 26th St.
Zuck Rd.
Colonial
W. 38th St.
Asbury Rd.
Lancaster Rd.
Sterrettania Rd.
Love Rd.
Zimmerly Rd.
Hershey Rd.

Creek

To Buffalo

To Waterford

Dutch Rd.
Manchester Rd.
W. Ridge Rd.

To Lake City

Millfair Rd.

FLOW

Walnut

Grubb Rd.

N

To Girard

To West Springfield

To Edinboro

**Walnut Creek**

*Steelheaders sometimes mark the butt sections of their rods so they can easily measure their fish before releasing them.*

# Walnut Creek

Perhaps a bit overshadowed by her larger sister, Elk Creek, Walnut Creek is a water that steelheading anglers have enjoyed for generations. This tributary of Lake Erie has a strong run of steelies that begins as early as late September. Good numbers of fish generally start showing up by mid- to late October and continue strong through March. The run, however, can linger into April but the duration of the run is determined by water conditions. If the fall run begins early as a result of late-summer rains, steelheaders may find that their quarry is well upriver before the middle of March. This is precisely why anglers need to keep an eye on the weather and stay in touch with their local fly shops for the latest information.

Named for the stately trees that line its banks, Walnut Creek is a typical northwestern Pennsylvania steelhead stream with a slate rock bottom and the occasional jagged rock thrown in for good measure. Anglers may be lulled into a false sense of security, believing that they may wade with impunity (and greater speed) because the creek's shale bottom is flat. This is a mistake because even a relatively flat river bottom can become quite slick, and

## Types of Fish
Fly anglers typically fish here for hard-fighting steelhead and salmon. Smallies can't get beyond Manchester Pool, so this is a very small fishery for bronzebacks.

## Known Hatches
Hatches here are limited to stoneflies as well as a few caddis. Small baitfish are also present.

## Equipment to Use
*Rods:* Fast-action 6- to 7-weight, 9 to 10 feet in length.
*Spey rods:* 6- to 7-weight, 11 to 13½ feet in length
*Reels:* Large-arbor reel equipped with a sturdy disc drag.
*Lines:* Weight-forward floating lines matched to rod, sinking-tip lines can also be useful.
*Leaders:* Tapered leader 1X to 5X, 9 to 12 feet in length.
*Wading:* Chest waders will give you the most options.

## Flies to Use
*Nymphs & Streamers:* Egg-Sucking Leech, sizes 4-10; Eggs (various colors), 6-12; Gray Scud, 14-18; Karl's Moby Goby, 6-8; Pink Lady, 10-16; Woolhead Sculpin, 4-8; Woolly Bugger, 6-10; Sucker Spawn, 8-12.

## When to Fish
October to March is prime time. It all comes down to how much cold you can stand.

*Continued*

*The author is all smiles as he releases a hefty steelhead. Photo by Steve Vorkapich.*

*Steelhead fanatic and inventor of Float Master Indicators, Steve Vorkapich demonstrates how it's done on Walnut Creek. Photo by Beau Beasley.*

Egg-Sucking Leech

inattentive anglers may find themselves floating downstream if they aren't careful. Though few fly fishermen plan to go swimming when they're out steelheading, slips and falls are indeed common, which is why you should wear wading shoes with cleats or studs and have a change of clothes in your vehicle. This way the impromptu swim is an inconvenience rather than the end of your fishing trip.

Fishing Walnut Creek is not for the faint of heart. At the mouth of the creek is a huge parking lot along with a small boat ramp for anglers to gain access to Walnut Creek and Lake Erie. This is a very popular access point, and at the peak of the season, you may find anglers fishing nearly elbow to elbow. Most fishermen seem to take this in stride and will quickly give way to their fellow who shouts "fish on" and, with rod bent accordingly, races up or downstream trying to land his fish. If you don't want to see steelhead harvested, don't fish Walnut Creek. Some anglers return all that they catch, but many more do not.

Water conditions dictate the quality of the steelheading, according to Dan Pribanic, owner of Chagrin River Outfitters in Chagrin, Ohio. "The best conditions are when rivers are receding from recent rains, allowing fresh fish to enter the river," he says. "This also makes fish that are already in the river more active."

Pattern selections for anglers fishing the Walnut—or nearly any other Lake Erie tributary—are fairly obvious. If the river is up and dirty, use larger and brighter patterns so that steelhead can see your offering. If the water is low and clear, step your pattern down to a darker and much smaller size. Don't stay in one place too long; if you aren't getting any strikes, move on to better water. This means looking for seams or obvious depressions in the river. Broken water can also be a great staging area for fish.

Finally, be careful where you park and keep an eye open for posted land. It's tempting to park right on I-79 and I-90—it's also illegal. If the fishing is off on Walnut or if you have kids with you, take a moment out of your day to visit Trout Run. This area is closed to fishing, but you and your children will delight in the fish schooling by the hundreds and thousands to the local nursery water.

*Wading is an effective method for catching steelhead, but anglers need to dress warmly. Good woolen socks will help insulate feet from the frigid water. Photo by Beau Beasley.*

*Tributaries of Lake Erie, such as Walnut Creek, can produce healthy fish. Note the girth of this fish, beginning right behind its head.*

### Season & Limits

As with any waterway, access changes occur often, and I have not attempted to list every single access point. For a more detailed map of the Lake Erie tributaries go to www.sgcmaps.com. For the latest information on Walnut Creek, contact the Pennsylvania Fish and Boat Commission at www.fish.state.pa.us.

### Nearby Fly Fishing

Anglers fishing here can also hit Elk Creek, Four Mile Creek, fish around Presque Isle State Park, and of course Lake Erie.

### Accommodations & Family Activities

There are many activities for families in and around the Erie area. One of the best places to visit is Presque Isle State Park. Besides enjoying Lake Erie and the other wonderful scenery, you can also fish in and around the banks of the Presque Isle. While I was visiting Lake Erie I stayed at the El Patio Motel, a favorite hangout for anglers of every stripe.

El Patio Motel
Erie, Pennsylvania
(814) 838-9772

Joe Roots Grill
Erie, Pennsylvania
www.joerootsgrill.com
(814) 836-7668

### Fly Shops & Guides

Chagrin River Outfitters
Chagrin Falls, Ohio
www.chagrinriveroutfitters.com
(440) 247-7110

Folly's End Campground
Girard, Pennsylvania
www.follysend.com
(814) 474-5730

Gander Mountain
Erie, Pennsylvania
www.gandermountain.com
(814) 868-0880

Lake Erie Ultimate Angler
Erie, Pennsylvania
www.shopultimateangler.com
(814) 833-4040

Karl Weixlmann
Fly Fish Erie
Erie, Pennsylvania
(814) 836-8013

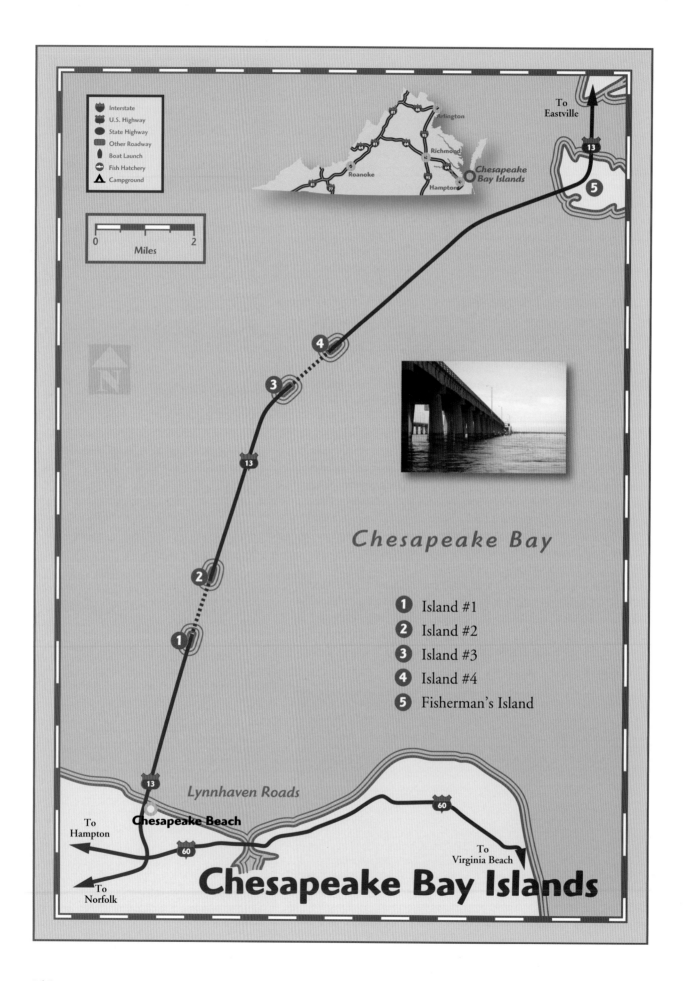

**Legend:**
- Interstate
- U.S. Highway
- State Highway
- Other Roadway
- Boat Launch
- Fish Hatchery
- Campground

0 — 2 Miles

To Eastville

13

5

Chesapeake Bay Islands

Arlington
Richmond
Roanoke
Hampton

4

3

13

Chesapeake Bay

2

1 Island #1
2 Island #2
3 Island #3
4 Island #4
5 Fisherman's Island

1

13

Lynnhaven Roads

60

Chesapeake Beach

To Hampton

To Virginia Beach

60

To Norfolk

# Chesapeake Bay Islands

# Chesapeake Bay Islands

### Types of Fish
Stripers, bluefish, cobia, gray trout, speckled trout, flounder, croaker, drum, spadefish, and false albacore can all be caught on the Bay.

### Baitfish
Menhaden, eels, spearing, glass minnows, shrimp, squid, and crabs.

### Equipment to Use
*Rods:* 8- to 10-weight rods, 9 to 10 feet in length.
*Reels:* Disc-drag reel, possible large-arbor applications.
*Lines:* Fast intermediate matched to rod, as well as 200- to 400-grain sinking lines.
*Leaders:* 10- to 30-pound-test leaders, 3 to 5 feet in length (wire leaders should be used if fishing for blues).
*Wading:* Not applicable. Use a seaworthy boat or kayak.

### Flies to Use
Bruce's Bay Anchovy, size 2; Bruce's Crystal Shrimp, 1/0; Clouser Minnow, 2/0-4; Dubiel's Lil' Haden, 1/0-2; Dubiel's Red-Ducer, 1/0-2; Lefty's Deceiver, 3/0-2; Lefty's Half and Half, 3/0-2; Russell's Mussel, 1/0 and 1; Tommy's Crease Fly, 2/0-2; Tommy's Eel Fly, 2/0 and 1/0.

### When to Fish
Fishing on the Chesapeake Bay offers so many opportunities that it's hard to know when to go. Ultimately it's a question of what you are fishing for. Many anglers pursue stripers here, which have good runs in the spring and fall. October through mid-December is prime time for big stripers. Keep in mind, that in the Bay, you can catch nearly everything.

*Continued*

Virginia's Chesapeake Bay has few equals. When Capt. John Smith arrived here in 1607, he found a maritime wonderland. Among other splendors, Smith noted oyster beds so large that they actually posed a threat to shipping. These massive structures were hidden below the waterline and could easily break through a ship's wooden hull if unwary mariners were to strike them. Smith also noted enormous schools of fish, so thick that he boasted to his friends back in England that his crew had caught all they could eat by merely lowering baskets into the water.

Today, anglers won't see the fish in the Bay in the numbers that Captain Smith experienced. Nevertheless, good fishing can still be had. Most popular of all among anglers are the Bay's renowned and resilient rockfish. Indeed, its hard-fighting striped bass are one of the Bay's few success stories: Their numbers plunged in the mid 1980s, but good conservation management has brought them back from the brink of destruction.

Stripers aren't the only fish in the Bay—not by a long shot. Many anglers also land bluefish, red and black drum, croakers, the occasional weakfish, and one of my personal favorites, the humble

*The author is captain of the Latitudes Charters Swim Team. Photo by Capt. Tommy Mattioli.*

Tommy's Eel

flounder. Essentially, something's always biting in the Bay. The trick is figuring out what it is, where it is, and what it wants to eat.

I have fished the Chesapeake Bay countless times with guides such as Capt. Tommy Mattioli, and its sheer size and fishing variety continue to amaze me. Rookie anglers may simply choose to look for the working birds—but remember that the Bay is massive. What do you do when you can't see any birds? My advice is to spare yourself the angst and hire a guide.

If ever the structure of a place played a role in finding fish, that place is the Chesapeake Bay, which has structure in spades: Start your search around the many bridges that cross the Bay. The four massive rock islands that support the 17-mile-long Chesapeake Bay Bridge-Tunnel are superb fish habitats. Here, anglers can improve their odds by casting close to the rocks with various streamers, capturing predator fish that patrol these waters nearly all year long.

The wind presents a challenge to novices and requires anglers to adjust their casting styles when using sinking lines. Years of casting a trout line into a mountain stream probably will not have prepared you for fishing the Chesapeake Bay. Anglers would do well to cast their sinking lines with about half the line's head still in the tip of the rod and by watching their backcasts. There's also no shame in making small rollcasts or in feeding line off the end of the boat into the current until you get the knack of casting heavy lines in adverse conditions.

Finally, a cautionary tale: The wind here can actually knock you right off your feet, which is exactly what happened to me one day when I was fishing with Capt. Tony Harding of Latitudes Charters. Yes, I landed right in the Chesapeake Bay. And yes, after he finished laughing at me, Tony pulled me into the boat. To this day, however, he teases me and jokes that I'm the captain of the Latitudes Charters Swim Team.

*Capt. Tommy Mattioli and photographer Robert Thomas with the big one that didn't get away. Black drum such as the one seen here like hanging out by the rock islands that support the Chesapeake Bay Bridge-Tunnel. Photo courtesy Robert Thomas.*

### Season & Limits
Open all year. Limits and sizes will depend on species and the time of year that you're fishing.

### Nearby Fly Fishing
If the weather is a little rough in the Bay, you can always opt for Rudee Inlet or the Lynnhaven River.

### Accommodations & Services
I like the city of Hampton, and when I'm there I make it a point to stay at Magnolia House, which is less than a mile from the Sunset Marina (www.sunsetboatingcenter.com) where anglers can meet their charters. Magnolia House was built in 1889 by a Virginia harbor pilot and sports many of its original fireplaces and wooden floors, as well as Grecian columns. Joyce and Lankford Blair are wonderful hosts who go out of their way to make you feel at home. Surfrider is a great seafood restaurant and is very close to Magnolia House.

Magnolia House
Hampton, Virginia
www.maghousehampton.com
(757) 722-2888

### Fly Shops & Guides
Bass Pro Shops
Ashland, Virginia
www.basspro.com
(804) 496-4700

Bass Pro Shops
Hampton, Virginia
(757) 262-5200

Capt. Chris Newsome
Bay Fly Fishing
www.bayflyfishing.com
(804) 815-4895

Green Top Sporting Goods
Glen Allen, Virginia
www.greentophuntfish.com
(804) 550-2188

Capt. Tony Harding
Latitudes Charters
www.flyfishtidalva.com
(540) 582-6396

Capt. Tommy Mattioli
Matty-J Charter Service
www.matty-j.com
(804) 314-2672

Orvis
Richmond, Virginia
www.orvis.com/richmond
(804) 253-9000

Cory Routh
Ruthless Fishing
www.ruthlessfishing.com
(757) 403-0734

Capt. Ed Lawrence
Speckulater Charters
www.speckulatercharters.com
(804) 693-5673

Wild River Outfitters
Virginia Beach, Virginia
www.wildriveroutfitters.com
1-877-431-8566

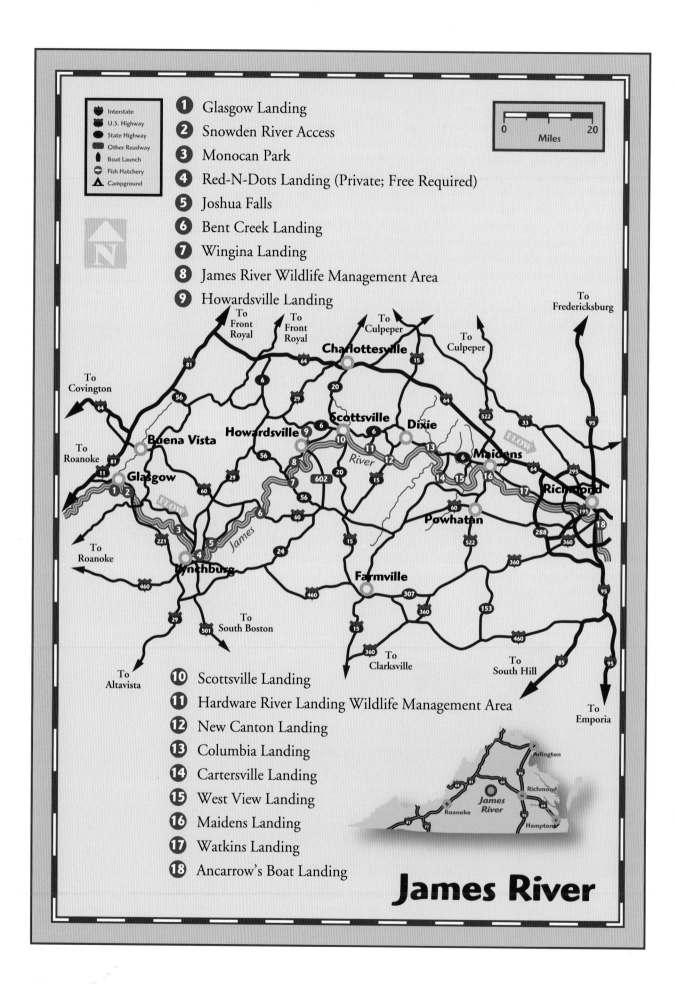

**Legend:**
- Interstate
- U.S. Highway
- State Highway
- Other Roadway
- Boat Launch
- Fish Hatchery
- Campground

1. Glasgow Landing
2. Snowden River Access
3. Monocan Park
4. Red-N-Dots Landing (Private; Free Required)
5. Joshua Falls
6. Bent Creek Landing
7. Wingina Landing
8. James River Wildlife Management Area
9. Howardsville Landing
10. Scottsville Landing
11. Hardware River Landing Wildlife Management Area
12. New Canton Landing
13. Columbia Landing
14. Cartersville Landing
15. West View Landing
16. Maidens Landing
17. Watkins Landing
18. Ancarrow's Boat Landing

**James River**

# James River

Before the Europeans arrived, Indians populated, traded on, and lived and died on the banks of the river they called Powhatan, named after their powerful chief. In 1607, Englishman John Smith and a group of fellow explorers sailed around what is now Cape Henry off the coast of Virginia. The explorers landed their small party not far up the Chesapeake Bay, astutely naming the village they established and the major river that led into the Chesapeake Bay after their sovereign, King James I of England and VI of Scotland—the same James who gave his name to the Authorized Version of the Bible. Jamestown would be the first permanent English colony in the New World, and the James River would prove to be the lifeblood of the colony.

Virginia's majestic James River, about 340 miles long, is one of the larger American rivers contained in a single state. The Upper James runs from the river's headwaters at the confluence of the Cowpasture and Jackson rivers in the foothills of the Allegheny Mountains over hills and rolling farmland and through the towns that have grown up through the centuries all along its banks, until it flows through Lynchburg. From Lynchburg, the Middle James meanders back and forth across the land until it arrives in Richmond, the capital of the Old Dominion. The Lower James comprises the

## Types of Fish
The river's namesake aside, smallies are king on the James. Anglers may also catch rock bass, carp, catfish, and the occasional muskellunge.

## Known Hatches
Dragonflies are a major hatch on this river; other important sources of food are crayfish and minnows, so consider throwing plenty of streamer patterns.

## Equipment to Use
*Rods:* 6- to 9-weight, 8 to 9½ feet in length.
*Reels:* Disc-drag reel, unless you are fishing for muskie. In this case you will need a disc-drag large-arbor reel and plenty of 30-pound-test backing.
*Lines:* Weight-forward floating, matched to rod. Sinking-tip lines work as well.
*Leaders:* 1X to 3X leaders, 9 feet in length, wire leaders will be needed for muskie fishing.
*Wading:* Boating is the best way to fish the James. Also consider kayaking or canoeing in conjunction with chest waders. Fish the banks and small islands as well.

## Flies to Use
*Topwater:* Chocklett's Disc Slider, size 1/0; Hickey's Condor, 6-12; Walt's Popper, 2-12;

*Nymphs & Streamers:* Claw-Dad, sizes 2-6; Chocklett's Gummy Minnow, 6; CK Baitfish, 1; Clouser Minnow, 1/0-6; Craft's Kreelex, 2-6; Finn's Golden Retriever, 6-10; Forage Fish, 6; Murray's Marauder, 6; Tommy's Torpedo, 6; Trow's Minnow, 1/0-6.

*Shad:* Clouser Minnow, size 6; BH Goldilox, 6; Tommy's Torpedo, 6.

*Tye Kreuger of the Orvis Company with a big catfish caught on the fly while wading the James River. Photo by Mark Sargent Photography.*

*Continued*

*The James River is the best-known small-mouth fishery in the Old Dominion. Here, spin and fly anglers often fish for shad just a few hundred feet from the city of Richmond. Photo by Mark Sargent Photography.*

Chocklett's Gummy Minnow

waters from the Fall Line in Richmond to the venerable Chesapeake Bay.

The James is flanked for miles at a time by large trees that cast tremendous shadows on the water. These silent sentinels are a haven for insects, which periodically fall into the water and provide the fish with a quick and easy meal. This is precisely why boating anglers cast to the shorelines and why surface flies such as poppers are so effective when cast under tree limbs. The trees also provide much-needed shade. Fish can't close their eyes, so they instinctively tend toward the river's shady spots. The water is often cooler here because of the trees, and anyone familiar with steamy Virginia summers knows that all right-thinking creatures make for shade during this time of year.

Some of the best structure on the James can't be seen from the shore. Great subsurface rock ledges run the breadth of the river in many places—the perfect hiding place for feeding fish. Some of the ledges are tiny, others are enormous, but all are prime spots for sinking-tip lines and baitfish or crayfish patterns worked slowly across the bottom. Timing your retrieve is crucial: Sometimes your prey wants an aggressive stripping action. On another occasion, only a slow, methodical retrieve will yield success.

What you catch largely depends on when you go. While smallies are caught throughout the river, shad and stripers are generally caught from about a mile above Richmond on down to the Bay. From about the end of March through the beginning of May, anglers are gunning primarily for shad. I still remember my first shad expedition on the James with Dale Huggins, who works at the Orvis store in Richmond. We had a grand old time catching and releasing scores of feisty shad. Anglers using large patterns are liable to land migrating stripers that follow the shad on their spring spawning run. Though shad are popular here, the smallies are what draws most anglers.

By the middle of May, smallies rule the river, so anglers change over to poppers. Occasionally catfish and carp will strike at insect and baitfish patterns.

It's true that, as a native son, I'm partial to this gem of the Old Dominion. But in my personal opinion, any day that you can spend on the James is a good day.

*L. E. Rhodes, a longtime guide on the upper James, wet wades near Scottsville. Photo by Beau Beasley.*

### When to Fish
Other than the dead of winter, nearly any day on the James could produce a good day of fishing.

### Season & Limits
The James is open all year.

### Nearby Fly Fishing
Alternative fishing locales include the Jackson River, the Shenandoah River, as well as the New River.

### Accommodations & Family Activities
Consider Richmond, Charlottesville, Roanoke, or Lynchburg as a base of operations when fishing the James. I recommend calling one of the shops listed below to get the latest on James River fishing before you hit the water. The activities available for families near this water are too numerous to list.

### Fly Shops & Guides
Albemarle Angler
Charlottesville, Virginia
www.albemarleangler.com
(434) 977-6882

Angler's Lane
Forest, Virginia
www.anglerslane.com
(434) 385-0200

Bass Pro Shops
Ashland, Virginia
www.basspro.com
(804) 496-4700

Dance's Sporting Goods
Colonial Heights, Virginia
www.dancessportinggoods.net
(804) 526-8399

Green Top Sporting Goods
Glen Allen, Virginia
www.greentophuntfish.com
(804) 550-2188

Chuck Kraft
Charlottesville, Virginia
(434) 293-9305

Mossy Creek Fly Fishing
Harrisonburg, Virginia
www.mossycreekflyfishing.com
(540) 434-2444

Blane Chocklett
New Angle Fishing Adventures
www.blanechocklett.com
(540) 354-1774

Orvis
Richmond, Virginia
www.orvis.com/richmond
(804) 253-9000

Orvis
Roanoke, Virginia
www.orvis.com/roanoke
(540) 345-3635

L. E. Rhodes
Scottsville, Virginia
www.hatchmatcherguideservice.com
(434) 286-3366

Glenn Sides
Richmond, Virginia
www.surfsides.com
(804) 358-8642

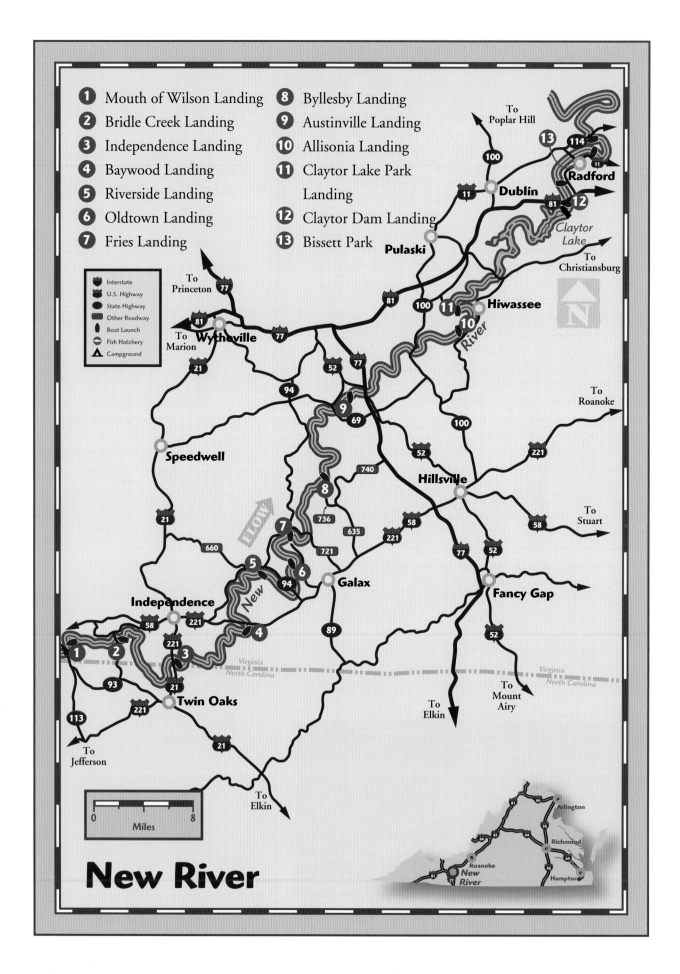

1 Mouth of Wilson Landing
2 Bridle Creek Landing
3 Independence Landing
4 Baywood Landing
5 Riverside Landing
6 Oldtown Landing
7 Fries Landing
8 Byllesby Landing
9 Austinville Landing
10 Allisonia Landing
11 Claytor Lake Park Landing
12 Claytor Dam Landing
13 Bissett Park

Interstate
U.S. Highway
State Highway
Other Roadway
Boat Launch
Fish Hatchery
Campground

Miles
0          8

# New River

154

# New River

The novel *Follow the River* by James Alexander Thom relates the incredible true story of 23-year-old Mary Draper Ingles who was kidnapped by Shawnee Indians in 1755 while her husband was out working in a remote part of their farm near what is now Virginia Tech. Ingles, her two young sons, and a few other captives were forcibly marched to a French and Indian village in present-day Ohio. Draper later fled from her captors after being taken into West Virginia on a salt-gathering expedition. Under cover of darkness, this incredible woman slipped into the night and began the long walk home. And a long walk it certainly was: She walked for about six weeks over more than 800 miles of mountainous terrain. No wonder then, that by the time she got home, she was mere skin and bones and her hair had turned completely white.

Mary Draper Ingles didn't know the way home. But she *did* know that if she followed the Ohio River to its confluence with the Kanawha, it would eventually lead her to her familiar New River—and to home.

The New River can be divided into an upper and lower section—and because the river flows north, the upper section is south of the lower section—with the midpoint being Claytor Lake. The upper New begins just four miles from the Virginia–North Carolina border and zigzags northward for more than 150 miles before it

## Types of Fish
Most anglers floating the New pursue smallies, but trophy walleye, white bass, and black crappie also call the New River home. Resident muskies and stripers can also be caught here.

## Known Hatches
Ants, beetles, crayfish, crickets, damselflies, dragonflies, frogs, hellgrammites, and hoppers. Don't miss the large spring migration of shad fry coming out of Claytor Lake, a major source of food for the larger fish in the New.

## Equipment to Use
*Rods:* 7- to 8-weight, 9 to 9½ feet in length.
*Reels:* Disc-drag reel, possible large-arbor applications.
*Lines:* Weight-forward floating, matched to rod. Sinking-tip lines can be useful.
*Leaders:* 1X to 2X leaders, 7½ to 9 feet in length.
*Wading:* The upper New River is best floated with a guide.

## Flies to Use
*Topwater:* Chocklett's Disc Slider, size 1/0; Walt's Popper, 2-6.

*Nymphs & Streamers:* Claw-Dad, sizes 2-6; Chocklett's Gummy Minnow, 6; CK Baitfish, 1; Clouser Minnow, 1/0-2; Forage Fly, 6; Smith's Creature, 2-6; Howell's Big Nasty, 6; Kreelex, 2; Trow's Minnow, 1/0-4.

*Continued*

*The New River is ironically thought to be one of the oldest rivers in the world, and anglers can easily lose themselves in its excellent scenery. Photo by Beau Beasley.*

*Mike Smith of Greasy Creek Outfitters floats the New River*
*hundreds of times a year. Photo by Beau Beasley.*

Smith's Creature

enters West Virginia. One unique characteristic of the upper New is that it lacks shore access, due primarily to the river's remoteness and the fact that much of it is surrounded by private land. As a result, fly anglers can expect to enjoy limited pressure on the New.

This river is still wild and untamed in many places, flanked with large rock gorges and heavily treed shoreline. New River anglers are unlikely to forget the scenery—and even less likely to forget those lunker walleyes and the aggressive smallies that routinely push 20 inches. I have also seen fly anglers take stripers here, and guides such as Blane Chocklett target the New's muskies when the weather and other conditions allow.

The lower section of the New River runs for 80 miles from the top of Claytor Lake all the way to the West Virginia state line. You can clearly see the dam at Claytor Lake from Interstate 81, and although dams are not generally thought of as friends to fishing, this dam has helped to prevent flooding and does generate electricity. Once the New River escapes from Claytor Lake, it begins its mad rush northward into West Virginia.

The New undergoes a dramatic personality change once it leaves the confines of Claytor Lake. The Lower New is much faster than the upper, with Class II and III rapids dotting the lower sections of the river. Anglers can look forward not only to great scenery but also to scores of hungry smallies eager to eat their flies. Anglers who do not quickly control their hooked fish may find said fish using the river's strong current against them—at which point, larger fish have the upper hand. The river boasts a great deal of structure, so investigate it well.

I've fished the New River with veteran guides Mike Smith and Shawn Hash, who each know the river well and regularly put their clients onto smallies larger than three pounds. A number of guides from Virginia, North Carolina, and West Virginia consider the New their home water, so if you're looking for angling assistance on this big river, strongly consider hiring an expert.

Smallmouth Bass by Alan Folger.

Smallies are the quarry of choice on the New River, but stripers and walleye can also be landed by fly anglers. Photo courtesy Mike Smith.

### When to Fish
Although you can fish the New River all year, the best times are April through October. Sometimes fly anglers may have to wait until May before action really heats up because the river is deep.

### Season & Limits
The New is open all year for fishing. Limits on sizes and amounts of fish will vary according to species.

### Nearby Fly Fishing
Anglers fishing the New can also try their hand at Claytor Lake, or drive a bit and fish White Top Laurel.

### Accommodations & Services
The Inn at Riverbend is a great B&B and their river view is unbeatable. Cascades Café opens at 6 a.m. for breakfast, has a fly shop next door, and can arrange for shuttle service as well.

Inn at Riverbend
Pearisburg, Virginia
www.innatriverbend.com
(540) 921-5211

Cascades Café
Pembroke, Virginia
(540) 626-4567

### Fly Shops & Guides
Greasy Creek Outfitters
Willis, Virginia
www.greasycreekoutfitters.com
(540) 789-7811

Blane Chocklett
New Angle Fishing Adventures
www.blanechocklett.com
(540) 354-1774

Mike Smith
New River Fly Fishing
www.newriverflyfish.com
(540) 789-7811

New River's Edge
Pembroke, Virginia
www.newriversedge.com
(540) 599-8382

Britt Stoudenmire
New River Outdoor Co.
www.newriveroutdoorco.com
(540) 921-7438

Shawn Hash
Tangent Outfitters
www.tangentoutfitters.com
(540) 626-4567

157

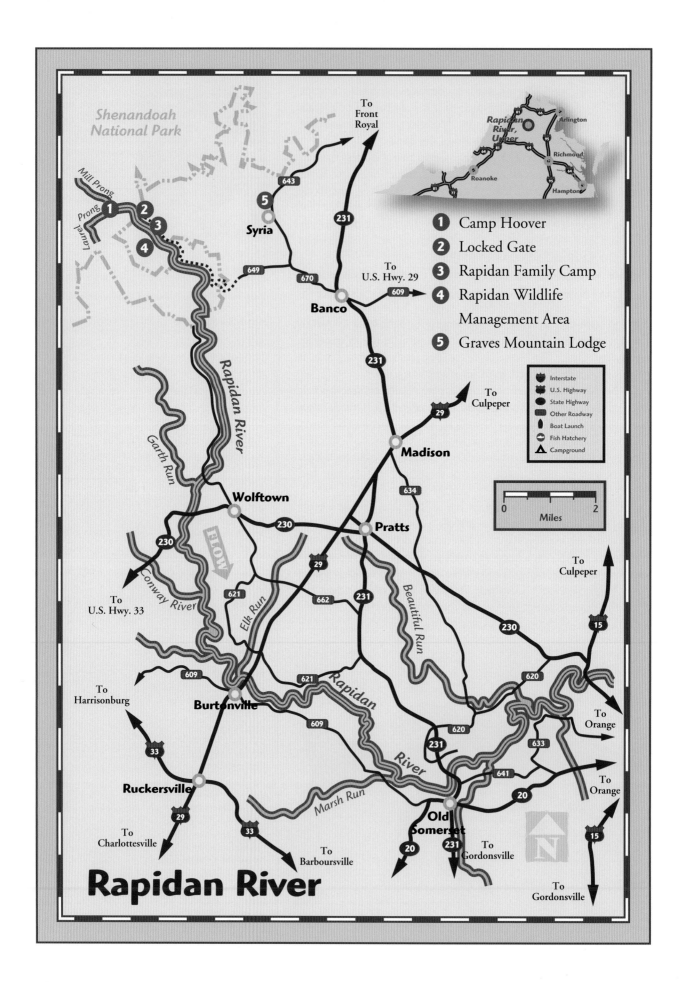

**Shenandoah National Park**

To Front Royal

643

5

231

Syria

To U.S. Hwy. 29

649        670

609

Banco

Mill Prong

Laurel Prong

1  Camp Hoover
2  Locked Gate
3  Rapidan Family Camp
4  Rapidan Wildlife Management Area
5  Graves Mountain Lodge

231

To Culpeper

29

Rapidan River

Garth Run

Madison

634

Wolftown

230        230

Pratts

FLOW

621        662        231        231

Beautiful Run

230

To Culpeper

15

Conway River

Elk Run

To U.S. Hwy. 33

609

621

Rapidan

620

To Orange

To Harrisonburg

609

Burtonville

620        633

To Orange

33

231        641

Ruckersville

River

20        To Orange

29

Marsh Run

Old Somerset

20        231        To Gordonsville        15

33

To Charlottesville        To Barboursville

To Gordonsville

**Rapidan River**

Interstate
U.S. Highway
State Highway
Other Roadway
Boat Launch
Fish Hatchery
Campground

0        Miles        2

Rapidan River, Upper

Arlington
Richmond
Roanoke        Hampton

N

# Rapidan River

**V**irginia's Rapidan River was named for England's Queen Anne, who reigned from 1702 to 1714. This river's original name was the Rapid Anne River but this was eventually shortened to Rapidan. Her Majesty was something of a friend to writers: In 1709, she issued the Statute of Anne, Great Britain's first copyright law, which gave authors rights to their work rather than publishers. Though Queen Anne never visited the river named for her, another head of state, Pres. Herbert Hoover, certainly did. Hoover, an avid fly angler, asked his aide, Lawrence Ritchey, to find him a trout stream within 100 miles of the White House that was above 2,500 feet (so that Hoover wouldn't have to fight mosquitoes). Ritchey eventually discovered the Rapidan River and recommended the place to his boss.

Rapidan Camp was the first complex set aside specifically as a presidential retreat. The main building, called the Brown House, presumably to set it apart from the White House, received such luminaries as Charles and Anne Morrow Lindbergh, Supreme Court Justice H. F. Stone, Mrs. Thomas Edison, Gov. Theodore Roosevelt Jr., British Prime Minister Ramsay MacDonald, and the great Winston Churchill, who was then Chancellor of the

## Types of Fish
This is wild brook-trout heaven.

## Known Hatches
Different fly hatches can occur throughout the year. These hatches include but are not limited to winter stoneflies, blue quills, blue-winged olives, Hendricksons, March browns, quill Gordons, caddisflies, Cahills, inchworms, and terrestrials.

## Equipment to Use
*Rods:* 3- to 4-weight, 6½ to 8 feet in length.
*Reels:* Standard trout reel.
*Lines:* Weight-forward floating, matched to rod.
*Leaders:* 4X to 7X leaders, 9 feet in length.
*Wading:* Hip waders are fine here.

## Flies to Use
*Drys:* Adams, sizes 14-20; Blue-Winged Olive, 14-20; Elk-Hair Caddis, 14-20; Flying Ant, 10-18; Gelso's Little Black Stonefly, 16-20; Light Cahill, 14-20; Little Yellow Sally, 14-20; March Brown, 10-14; Murray's Mr. Rapidan, 14-20; Pale Morning Dun, 14-20; Quill Gordon, 12-22; Stimulator, 12-20.

*Continued*

*The Rapidan has a strong population of brook trout, and all fish must be released immediately. Rich Hiegel casting drys to rising fish. Photo by Beau Beasley.*

*The Rapidan is the quintessential brook-trout stream and plays host to anglers as well as schoolchildren wishing to learn more about the environment. Photo by Beau Beasley.*

Murray's Mr. Rapidan

Exchequer across the pond. The camp even boasted a majestic stone fireplace built to be used in photo ops of visiting dignitaries. Hoover donated Rapidan Camp to the Commonwealth of Virginia when he left office in 1932. In 1935, it became a part of the Shenandoah National Park.

Anglers can access the Rapidan from Route 662 near Wolftown. Park at the end of the road, and then hike upstream. To fish higher in the park next to Camp Hoover, access the Rapidan from Route 649 (Quaker Run Road). This is a tough and winding road that doubles back on itself in places—and when the hard surface ends, you'll still have 7½ miles of rough road before reaching a locked gate. Take the time to walk upstream or downstream if you see a car parked on the side of the road. Distance makes good fishing pals. To view Camp Hoover (or take a Park Service tour of the place), park at the end of Route 649 by the locked gate, and then hike up the service road for about a mile. It can be a long walk to Camp Hoover, but it's worth it—and you can always fish on the way up.

The Rapidan is home to a healthy population of wild native brook trout that can entertain fly anglers all season long. The problem is landing them. These fish spook easily and won't tolerate poor presentations or sloppy footwork. Successful tactics run the gamut from casting drys along a foam line to plumbing the depths of small plunge pools. Be prepared to keep a low profile, and have plenty of extra patterns on hand—the surrounding tree branches are frequently hungry. On a side note, don't let a heavy rain put you off. The Rapidan often runs clear even soon after a downpour. The river bottom is mostly rock, so turbidity, while an issue, is not a big problem on this excellent water.

Though named for British royalty and made famous by an American president, the Rapidan River is a trout stream for the everyday angler. The river serves as a living classroom for Trout Unlimited's Tri-State Conservation Camp, held here each June. The camp, the sponsors of which include Dominion, L.L. Bean, and Orvis, has been so successful that it's now used as a model for similar programs. See page 202 for more details.

*The author has visited Camp Hoover on many occasions. For your first visit, you may enjoy a full tour offered free of charge by the National Park Service. Photo by Fire Capt. Tony Kostecka.*

## Flies to Use (continued)

*Nymphs & Streamers:* BH Goldilox, sizes 6-10; BH Hare's Ear, 14-20; BH Prince Nymph, 14-20; Coburn's Inchworm, 12-14; Green Weenie, 14-16; Mickey Finn, 6-10; Pheasant Tail, 14-20.

## When to Fish

Fishing is best on the upper Rapidan in the early spring and right through the fall.

## Season & Limits

You can fish the Rapidan year-round, but you can't harvest its trout.

## Nearby Fly Fishing

Numerous Shenandoah National Park streams are an easy drive from the Rapidan.

## Accommodations & Family Activities

Graves Mountain Lodge is a family-owned business, and their excellent meals served family style are not to be missed. Trout Unlimited's Tri-State Conservation & Fishing Camp held each June are open to boys and girls ages 13 through 17 from various backgrounds, and no experience is needed. Camp staff consists of retired and active doctors, nurses, environmental experts of every sort, fly-fishing guides, a professional biologist, and a former battalion chief from the fire department of Austin, Texas, who reminds me regularly that he still outranks me. The camp is successful primarily because of the selfless work of the staff members who often take vacation time to volunteer at the camp. Campers learn how to wade safely, tie their own flies, and of course, how to cast. A maximum of 24 campers attend each session and scholarships are available. The camp is nothing short of superb.

Graves Mountain Lodge
Syria, Virginia
www.gravesmountain.com
(540) 923-4231

Shenandoah National Park
Luray, Virginia
www.nps.gov
(540) 999-3500

Tri-State Conservation Camp
Camp Director Paul Kearney
www.tucamp.org
(540) 229-0563

## Guides & Fly Shops

Albemarle Angler
Charlottesville, Virginia
www.albemarleangler.com
(434) 977-6882

Angler's Lane
Forest, Virginia
www.anglerslane.com
(434) 385-0200

Mossy Creek Fly Fishing
Harrisonburg, Virginia
www.mossycreekflyfishing.com
(540) 434-2444

Murray's Fly Shop
Edinburg, Virginia
www.murraysflyshop.com
(540) 984-4212

Rhodes Fly Shop
Warrenton, Virginia
www.rhodesgiftandflyshop.com
(540) 347-4162

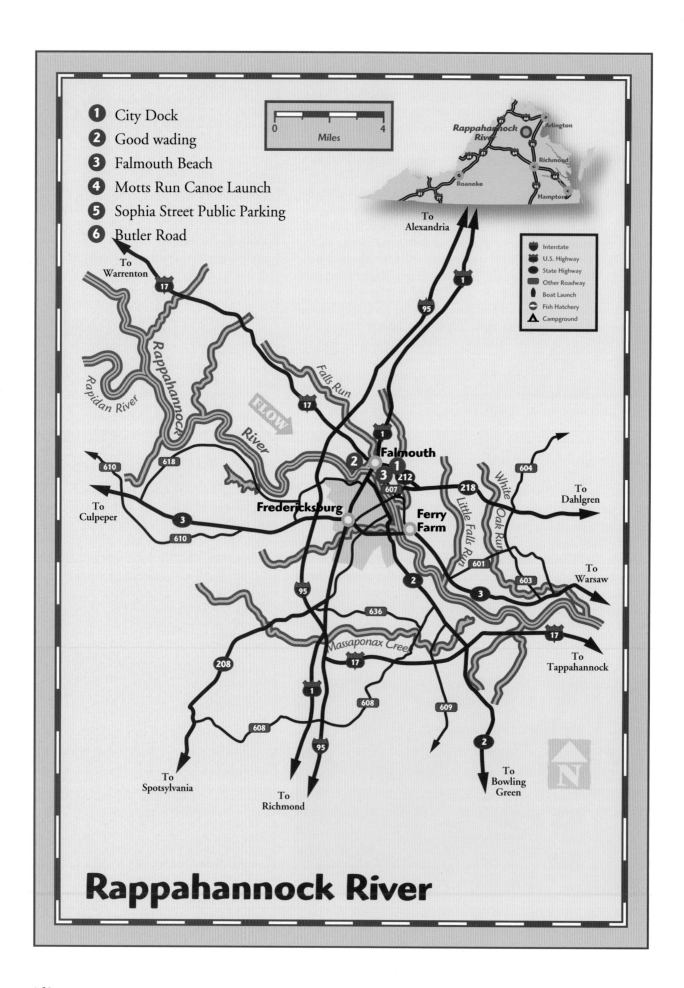

1 City Dock
2 Good wading
3 Falmouth Beach
4 Motts Run Canoe Launch
5 Sophia Street Public Parking
6 Butler Road

Miles
0                    4

Interstate
U.S. Highway
State Highway
Other Roadway
Boat Launch
Fish Hatchery
Campground

Rappahannock River

Arlington

Richmond

Roanoke

Hampton

To Alexandria

To Warrenton

17

95

1

Rapidan River

Rappahannock

River

FLOW

Falls Run

17

1

Falmouth

2

3 1

212

607

218

White Oak Run

604

To Dahlgren

610

618

610

To Culpeper

3

Fredericksburg

Ferry Farm

Little Falls Run

601

603

2

3

To Warsaw

95

636

2

Massaponax Creek

17

208

1

608

608

17

To Tappahannock

609

2

N

To Spotsylvania

To Richmond

To Bowling Green

# Rappahannock River

162

# Rappahannock River

## Types of Fish
Shad and stripers migrate annually, but anglers may prefer to go after the resident populations of smallmouth bass, bluegill, largemouth bass, perch, carp, or catfish.

## Known Hatches
Ants, beetles, crayfish, crickets, hellgrammites, and hoppers, as well as other baitfish and minnows call this river home. Many of the minnows that you see in the Rappahannock are actually shad fry prior to their migration to the Chesapeake Bay.

## Equipment to Use
*Rods:* 5- to 8-weight, 8 to 9 feet in length.
*Reels:* Standard reel for most species, large-arbor for stripers.
*Lines:* Primarily weight-forward floating, 200- to 300-grain sinking line for shad.
*Leaders:* 3X to 5X, 9 feet in length.
*Wading:* Chest waders are best. Float trips are also an option. Be forewarned: The Rappahannock is dangerous and anglers die here every year.

## Flies to Use
*For shad:* BH Goldilox, sizes 4-8; BH Woolly Bugger, 6-10; Crazy Charlie, 6-8; Simmons's Shad Fly, 4-6; Super Patuxent Special, 6-10; Tommy's Flash Torpedo, 4-6; Tommy's Torpedo, 4-6.

*Continued*

**V**irginia's Rappahannock, affectionately known as the Rapp, has a long and colorful history. The Algonquian Indians named the river *Rappahannock,* which, loosely translated, means rapidly rising and falling waters, no doubt referring to its daily tidal fluctuations as it empties into the Chesapeake Bay. Legend has it that George Washington was alongside the Rappahannock when he cut down that infamous cherry tree with his trusty ax and later came clean about the dirty deed. The first president grew up on Ferry Farm, his sister's nearby plantation, and no doubt fished the Rapp as a youth. Indeed, Virginia's spectacular cherry trees bloom at precisely the same time of year that the shad migrate up the Rappahannock. I like to think that George was merely fashioning his own fly rod.

From its humble beginnings in the Blue Ridge Mountains, past the famed Rapidan River and then to its final destination at the sea, the Rappahannock includes many miles of float- and wade-friendly fishable water. From the last week in March through the first week in May, fly anglers flock to the Rapp in search of hard-fighting shad. These scrappy fish, which migrate upriver by

*Shad are hard-fighting fish that migrate by the thousands from the Chesapeake Bay up the Rappahannock each spring. Photo by Jon Luke.*

*Fishing the Rappahannock can be wonderful, but please be careful: This is a dangerous river, and the current can be deadly. Photo by Mark Sargent Photography.*

Tommy's Torpedo

the tens of thousands from the Chesapeake Bay, may have lived as long as five years at sea before returning to the river to spawn. Urging the shad along en route to their own spawning grounds are striped bass, which feed heavily on the shad as they migrate upstream. And if anglers don't consider shad or stripers worthy opponents, the river boasts a healthy and active resident population of perch, bluegill, gar, and large and smallmouth bass.

Spin fishermen also favor the Rapp, particularly during shad season. Fly anglers should also expect to share water with all varieties of paddlers, from competition kayakers to day trippers killing an afternoon in their canoes. The city of Fredericksburg recently purchased a great deal of land adjacent to the riverbank, which picnicking families frequent throughout the summer—and anglers may meet a few of them capping their idyllic day with a river swim. Most of the time, though, there is plenty of water for everyone. Anglers should keep their eyes open for small watercraft and expect to be flexible in their positioning.

One of the prime locations for fishing the Rapp in Fredericksburg—and especially for fishing for shad—is just below and above the Route 3 bridge. I've occasionally parked my car at a local gas station on the southern side of the bridge, stepped in for a soft drink and perhaps a few crackers, and then, with snacks in hand, simply walked out to the bridge and scouted out the river. In the spring it's not uncommon to see schools of shad so thick that they black out the bottom of the river. Once you locate the fish, park your vehicle along River Road or in the public park downstream of the bridge. Old Mill Park and River Road afford excellent access, and anglers can simply walk up- or downstream.

A word of caution: Wade safely—the Rappahannock is dangerous, fast-moving water. Remember, too, that more than one angler has walked out onto rocks to reach a prime spot in the river only to find those same rocks submerged by tidal flows when he tried to exit the river. Yes, I've made this mistake myself and nearly had to swim back to shore. Anglers who are interested in the Rapp but who are bit intimidated by its size and power might prefer to take a beginner trip with a member of the Falmouth Flats Fly Fishers Club.

*Shad flies must be small, bright, and fished subsurface. Tommy's Torpedo is the author's favorite shad fly because it consistently produces good results. Photo by Jon Luke.*

## Flies to Use (continued)

*For smallies and stripers:* Claw-Dad, sizes 2-6; CK Baitfish, 1; Clouser Minnow, 1/0-6; Dover's Peach Fly, 6-10; Dubiel's Red-Ducer, 1/0-2; Hickey's Condor, 6-12; Lefty's Deceiver, 2/0-2; Lefty's Half and Half, 2/0-2; Murray's Lead Eye Hellgrammite, 6; Super Patuxent Special, 6-10; Walt's Popper, 2-12.

## When to Fish
Open all year.

## Season & Limits
For shad and stripers, prime time is the last week of March through the first week of May. From late May through the end of October is a good time to target smallies.

For a complete listing of laws check out the Virginia Department of Game and Inland Fisheries at www.dgif. virginia.gov.

## Nearby Fly Fishing
The Rapidan feeds into the Rappahannock and is a great fishery in its own right. You can also fish the James River, which is only an hour away. A good source of information is the Falmouth Flats Fly Fishers.

## Accommodations & Services
The bulk of the services for the Rappahannock will be found in the city of Fredericksburg. There is plenty to do here with all the Civil War history and with Old Town Fredericksburg to explore.

Fredericksburg-Stafford Park Authority
120 River Rd.
Fredericksburg, Virginia
(540) 373-7909

## Fly Shops & Guides
Bass Pro Shops
Ashland, Virginia
www.basspro.com
(804) 496-4700

Clore Brothers Outfitters
Fredericksburg, Virginia
www.clorebros.com
(540) 786-7749

Falmouth Flats Fly Fishers
Fredericksburg, Virginia
www.ffflyfishers.org
info@ffflyfishers.org

Friends of the Rappahannock
Fredericksburg, Virginia
www.riverfriends.org
(540) 373-3448

Gander Mountain
Fredericksburg, Virginia
www.gandermountain.com
(540) 548-1330

Green Top Sporting Goods
Glen Allen, Virginia
www.greentophuntfish.com
(804) 550-2188

Orvis
Richmond, Virginia
www.orvis.com/richmond
(804) 253-9000

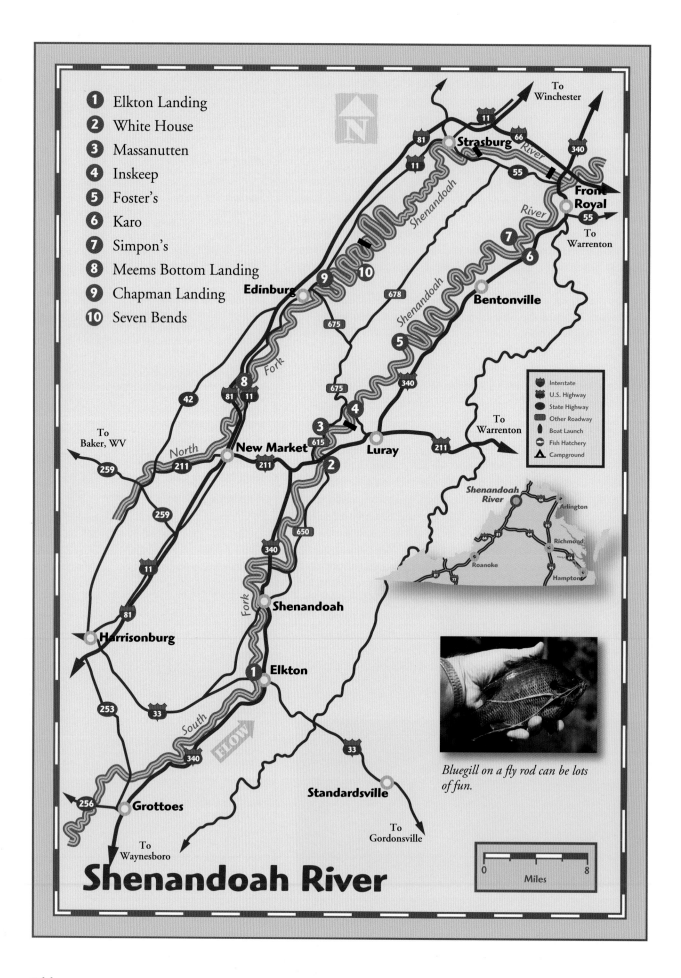

1 Elkton Landing
2 White House
3 Massanutten
4 Inskeep
5 Foster's
6 Karo
7 Simpon's
8 Meems Bottom Landing
9 Chapman Landing
10 Seven Bends

To Winchester

Strasburg

Front Royal

To Warrenton

Shenandoah

Edinburg

Bentonville

North

To Baker, WV

New Market

Luray

To Warrenton

Fork

Shenandoah

Harrisonburg

Elkton

South

FLOW

Grottoes

Standardsville

To Gordonsville

To Waynesboro

Interstate
U.S. Highway
State Highway
Other Roadway
Boat Launch
Fish Hatchery
Campground

Shenandoah River

Arlington
Richmond
Roanoke
Hampton

*Bluegill on a fly rod can be lots of fun.*

0       Miles       8

# Shenandoah River

## VIRGINIA

# Shenandoah River

S econd only to the mighty James, the Shenandoah is among the best known and most beloved warmwater fisheries in the state. Shenandoah Valley residents have long believed that the river's name means "daughter of the stars." Even if it's not true, her visitors have been almost as numerous as the stars—and as varied. From the Indians who lived here to the early pioneers who saw her as a vital trade route, the Shenandoah has been the lifeblood of tribes and settlements, and has played an integral part in the establishment and history of the Old Dominion. During the Civil War, both the Union and Confederate armies crossed her many times and, more than once, used the river's forks as a line of demarcation for advancements or retreats. Indeed, much of Virginia's history has been written on the banks of this beautiful river.

The North Fork of the Shenandoah rises in Rockingham County and snakes its way northward until it meets up with its sister, forming the main stem that then runs into West Virginia and eventually empties into the Potomac River near Harpers Ferry. The North Fork of the Shenandoah doesn't hold as much water as her counterpart—but plenty of good fishing is available on the North Fork for those who seek it. In the spring, the river can be pretty flush, but by late May the water begins to drop, and often by late June and into August, anglers can wet wade

### Types of Fish
By and large, anglers are chasing smallies when they fish the Shenandoah. Both forks of this river also offer healthy populations of sunfish, crappie, and largemouth. The carp fishing here can be awesome.

### Known Hatches
Ants, beetles, crayfish, crickets, damselflies, dragonflies, frogs, hellgrammites, and hoppers call this river home. You'll also find madtoms, sculpins, and various other baitfish and minnows.

### Equipment to Use
*Rods:* 3- to 8-weight, 8 to 9½ feet in length.
*Reels:* Disc-drag reel, possible large-arbor applications.
*Lines:* Weight-forward floating matched to rod, and occasional need for sinking-tip line.
*Leaders:* 3X to 5X, 9 feet in length.
*Wading:* Everything from hip waders to chest waders work here—and don't discount wet wading.

### Flies to Use
*Topwater:* Chocklett's Disc Slider, size 1/0; Hansen's Electric Frog, 6; Hickey's Condor, 6-12; Walt's Popper, 2-12.

*Nymphs & Streamers:* BH Goldilox, sizes 4-8; Chocklett's Gummy Minnow, 6; CK Baitfish, 1; Claw-Dad, 2-6; Clouser Minnow, 1/0-6; Finn's Golden Retriever, 6-10; Kreelex, 2-6; Murray's Lead-Eye Hellgrammite, 6; Murray's Marauder, 6; Super Patuxent Special, 6-10; Trow's Minnow, 1/0-6.

### When to Fish
Fishing takes places here between March and October. May through early July is prime time for this water, though low-water conditions can make fishing tough.

*Continued*

*King Montgomery is the warmwater columnist for* Fly Fish America, *and here, he shows off his expertise with a largemouth bass anyone would be happy to land. Photo courtesy King Montgomery.*

*Stargrass can become quite thick on the Shenandoah's low clear water during summer months. Fly patterns with weed guards are obviously helpful here. Photo by King Montgomery.*

Walt's Popper

without difficulty. In fact, during the dog days of summer, canoeing anglers might spend nearly as much time dragging their canoes around as they do floating in them.

The South Fork of the Shenandoah also begins in Rockingham County near Port Republic and is a much larger body of water than the North Fork. The South Fork sees more anglers and, of course, more rafts and canoes and kayaks because of its greater water volume. One of my favorite spots is Karo Landing, which affords good wading upstream and downstream. Multiple floats are available to Shenandoah anglers, and businesses such as the Front Royal Canoe Company will happily drop you off upstream and have you float back to their takeout. Some of my fondest memories are of fishing this way with the late Bob Guess, namesake of Mr. Bob's Lucky Day Lures, a well-known line of popping bugs. Bob is the man who taught me to fly fish. He and I had a fine time "testing" some of his excellent patterns on the Shenandoah.

Popping bugs are indeed great patterns to fish on the Shenandoah. Walt's Poppers are a fixture here and often produce excellent results. Master fly tyers Harry Murray and Blane Chocklett have also worked up creations that perform very well, especially around stargrass and the many islands throughout the river. I've also had much success with Jim Hickey's Condor, which mimics the strong blue damsel hatch that occurs here each summer.

In 2005, sections of the Shenandoah suffered a significant fish kill. Some experts estimated an 80 percent mortality rate for smallmouth bass and various sunfish. A task force involving several state and local agencies studied the issue diligently, but they were unable to pinpoint any single cause of the kill. Many suspect runoff from poultry operations near the river and other industrial pollution. I'm happy to say the venerable Shenandoah is making a strong comeback—but she still has a long way to go. For the latest developments on this, one of the Old Dominion's most sacred rivers, contact Jeff Kelble with Shenandoah Riverkeeper.

*Walt Cary has tied Virginia's best-known poppers for nearly 50 years. Walt's Poppers are a must on the Shenandoah. Photo by Beau Beasley.*

### Seasons & Limits

Check with local game laws for creel limits.

### Nearby Fly Fishing

Other options include fishing in and around the Shenandoah National Park.

### Accommodations & Services

By the Side of the Road B & B in Harrisonburg is a great place to stay if you're fishing the North Fork. Janice Fitzgerald is a delightful host, and her family will know how to make you feel like you're living in the lap of luxury. I stay there every time I can. The small town of Luray is nearly dead center of the South Fork and offers a good launching point for a boat. A great family outing can be had there visiting their underground caverns.

By the Side of the Road B & B
Harrisonburg, Virginia
www.bythesideoftheroad.com
1-866-274-4887

Luray Caverns
Luray, Virginia
www.luraycaverns.com
(540) 743-6551

Shenandoah Riverkeeper
Boyce, Virginia
www.potomacriverkeeper.org
(540) 837-1479

Front Royal Canoe Co.
Bentonville, Virginia
www.frontroyalcanoe.com
1-800-270-8808

### Fly Shops & Guides

Albemarle Angler
Charlottesville, Virginia
www.albemarleangler.com
(434) 977-6882

Angler's Lane
Forest, Virginia
www.anglerslane.com
(434) 385-0200

Gander Mountain
Winchester, Virginia
www.gandermountain.com
(540) 868-9312

Chuck Kraft
Charlottesville, Virginia
(434) 293-9305

Mossy Creek Fly Fishing
Harrisonburg, Virginia
www.mossycreekflyfishing.com
(540) 434-2444

Murray's Fly Shop
Edinburg, Virginia
www.murraysflyshop.com
(540) 984-4212

L. E. Rhodes
Scottsville, Virginia
www.hatchmatcherguideservice.com
(434) 286-3366

Rhodes Fly Shop
Warrenton, Virginia
www.rhodesgiftandflyshop.com
(540) 347-4162

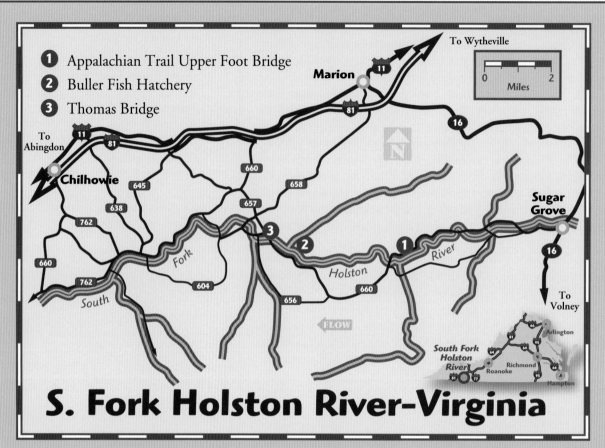

1 Appalachian Trail Upper Foot Bridge
2 Buller Fish Hatchery
3 Thomas Bridge

# S. Fork Holston River-Virginia

1 Osceola Island
2 TVA Road South
3 River Bend Road
4 Jack Prater's Livery Service

5 Big Springs Road
6 Weaver Pike Road
7 Rock Hold Road
8 Bluff City Boat Ramp

# South Holston River-Tennessee

# South Holston River

The South Holston River in Tennessee—the SoHo, to locals—is one of the best fisheries on the entire East Coast. Bold words, you say. Yes, they are—and they're words I'll stand by. The SoHo is a tailwater fishery that is regulated by the Tennessee Valley Authority (TVA) because of the power generated at the Holston Dam. Holston Lake, shared by Virginia and Tennessee, is fed from Virginia by the South Fork of the Holston. The diminutive South Fork emanates from southwestern Virginia and is popular with fly anglers because of its easy access and the occasional trophy trout that are landed here and then quickly released. Because many area anglers choose to fish both the South Fork of the Holston and the SoHo, anglers and guides often crisscross state lines. You may decide to begin your day near the Buller Fish Cultural Station in Virginia, where roll casts and tight cover are the norm, and then move downstream.

Fishing the SoHo begins just below the Holston Dam, which helps regulate the water flow. Much of the generation for the dam is done at night so as not to inhibit the public's access to the river or interfere with fishing and floating the river. That said, the TVA reserves the right to generate power whenever it feels the need, so be sure to call their number and coordinate your fishing trips accordingly. If you see the river rising unexpectedly while you're wading, make your way to the closest bank immediately. Knox

### Types of Fish
You'll find brookies in the South Fork of the Holston but mostly browns with some rainbows in the South Holston proper. Stripers run out of Boone Lake and enter the South Holston when it heats up.

### Known Hatches
The sulfur hatch runs from late May through the end of August. Other hatches include black flies, midges, blue-winged olive, ants, Japanese beetles, and crane flies.

### Equipment to Use
*Rods:* 5- to 9-weight, 9 to 9½ feet in length.
*Reels:* Disc-drag reel, possible large-arbor applications.
*Lines:* Weight-forward floating lines are the norm here.
*Leaders:* 4X to 7X leaders, 9 to 14 feet in length.
*Wading:* Chest waders are needed here. The SoHo is best floated but wading anglers can get good access off Big Springs Road and various locations below the weirs.

### When to Fish
Fishing on the South Holston is pretty good all year long, and veteran guides such as Patrick Fulkrod, Mike Adams, Bruce Wankel, and Blane Chocklett are often booked well in advance. Jimmy Dobes guides anglers also and specializes in fishing at night.

### Flies to Use
*Drys:* Blue-winged Olive, sizes 14-20; Elk-Hair Caddis, 14-20; Flying Ant, 10-18; Light Cahill, 14-20; Little Yellow Sally, 14-20; March Brown, 10-14; Mike's Magic Beetle, 10-12; PMD, 18-20; Sulfur Comparadun, 14-18.

***Continued***

*Bruce Wankel, owner of Virginia Creeper Fly Shop in Abingdon, Virginia, shows a young angler the ropes on the South Holston. Wankel is not only a good guide but a superb caster. Photo by Beau Beasley.*

*Knox Campbell displays a nice trout while fishing the sulfur hatch with the author. Photo by Beau Beasley.*

Mike's Magic Beetle

Campbell, who coordinates the South Holston River Fly Fishing Festival, was once stranded on an island for several hours because the river rose unexpectedly due to power generation. He was fishing in the early fall without waders and had to climb a tree on a small island. He remained in the tree for hours, waiting for the river to recede and avoiding the water to keep from becoming hypothermic. He looks back on the experience now and laughs but admits that, had it not been for that tree, the experience might not have been quite so funny. Calling ahead to the dam for the latest release information is always a good idea.

Patrick Fulkrod, a young and enthusiastic Orvis-endorsed guide who works at Mountain Sports Limited in Bristol, Virginia, introduced me to the South Holston via his comfortable raft. Patrick is a joy to fish with, and as we floated the SoHo one afternoon in June and tussled with the resident browns that thrive here, I was enthralled by the fog coming off the cold river—a fog that made the river appear to be smoking and that really didn't dissipate until almost lunchtime.

The South Holston is home to as many as 4,000 trout per river mile, and many of those fish are not your typical 12- to 14-inch river dwellers: "I once saw a huge brown eat a rainbow that was at least 13 inches long," says Patrick. "I know folks will think I'm exaggerating, but I know what I saw."

SoHo anglers have landed several fish longer than 16 inches in a single day, though that certainly won't be everyone's experience. But one thing is certain: The SoHo's wild browns fight like crazy. Anglers looking for adventure might consider night-fishing for big browns or stripers when power is being generated. Virginia, Tennessee, and North Carolina all have fly shops and excellent guides that support the SoHo. Consider booking a trip with one and save the tree climbing for your own backyard.

*Guide and author Cory Routh fishes the South Holston from a kayak. Thick fog is quite common here in the warmer months. Photo by Beau Beasley.*

## Flies to Use (continued)
*Nymphs & Streamers:* Articulated Minnows, sizes 2/0-4; BH Hare's Ear, 14-20; Bunny Leech, 1/0-6; Forage Fly, 6; Howell's Big Nasty, 6-10; Split Case Caddis, 16-20; Woolly Bugger, 2-6; Zebra Midge, 16-22.

## Season & Limits
For Virginia regulations, go to www.dgif.virginia.gov. For the Tennessee Wildlife Resource Agency, go to www.state.tn.us/twra.

## Nearby Fly Fishing
Anglers here can also fish the Watauga River.

## Accommodations & Family Activities
Consider attending the South Holston River Fly Fishing Festival held each year at River's Way in Bristol, Tennessee. If you go make sure you make it to Dip Dog Stand in Marion, Virginia, for a slice of Americana. Don't miss their milkshakes. The best boat launch on this river is located at Jack Prater's home. He can be reached at (423) 878-5345.

South Holston River Fly Fishing Festival
Bristol, Tennessee
www.southholstonflyfishingfest.com
(423) 538-0405

## Fly Shops & Guides
Mike Adams
Johnson City, Tennessee
www.adamsflyfishing.com
(423) 741-4789

Curtis Wright Outfitters
Weaverville, North Carolina
www.curtiswrightoutfitters.com
(828) 645-8700

Jimmy Dobes
Johnson City, Tennessee
(423) 773-8619

Fly Shop of Tennessee
Johnson City, Tennessee
www.flyshopoftn.com
(423) 928-2007

Patrick Fulkrod
Bristol, Virginia
(276) 492-9614

Holston Dam
www.tva.gov/sites/sholston.htm
1-800-238-2264 x4 then code 01

Hunter Banks Company
Asheville, North Carolina
www.hunterbanks.com
1-800-227-6732

Mahoney's
Johnson City, Tennessee
www.mahoneysports.com
1-800-835-5152

Mountain Sports Ltd.
Bristol, Virginia
www.mountainsportsltd.com
(276) 466-8988

South Holston River Fly Shop
Bristol, Tennessee
www.southholstonriverflyshop.com
(423) 878-2822

Virginia Creeper Fly Shop
Abingdon, Virginia
www.vcflyshop.com
(276) 628-3826

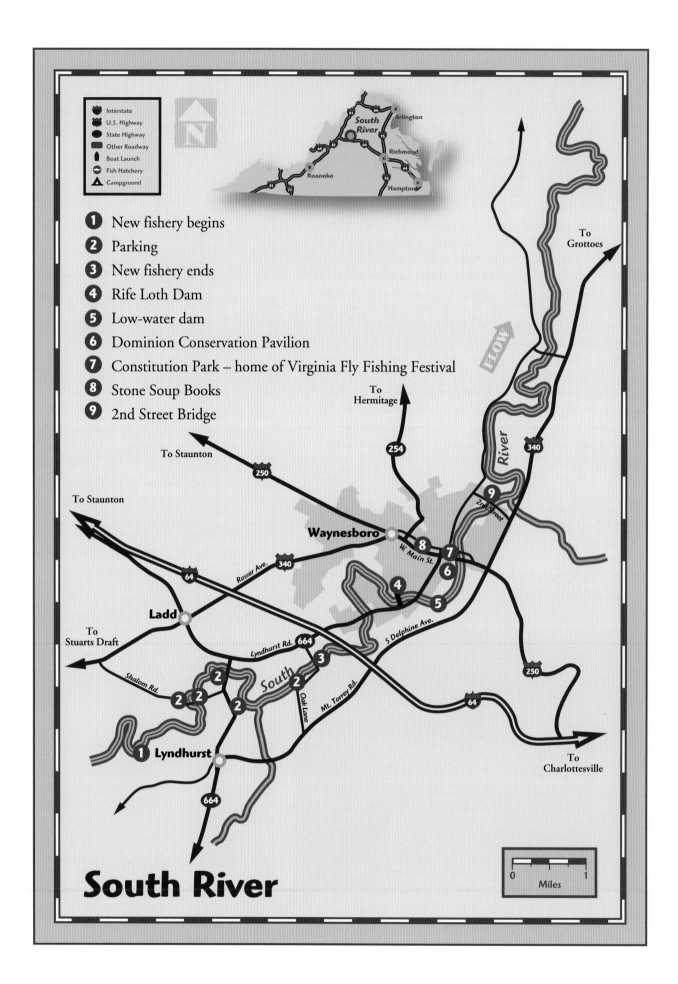

**Legend:**
- Interstate
- U.S. Highway
- State Highway
- Other Roadway
- Boat Launch
- Fish Hatchery
- Campground

1. New fishery begins
2. Parking
3. New fishery ends
4. Rife Loth Dam
5. Low-water dam
6. Dominion Conservation Pavilion
7. Constitution Park – home of Virginia Fly Fishing Festival
8. Stone Soup Books
9. 2nd Street Bridge

To Grottoes

FLOW

To Hermitage

To Staunton

To Staunton

Waynesboro

River

340

254

9

2nd Street

8
7
6
4
5

W. Main St.

Rosser Ave.
340
64

Ladd

To Stuarts Draft

Lyndhurst Rd.
664

South

S Delphine Ave.

3

2
2
2
2
2

Shalom Rd.

Oak Lane
Mt. Torrey Rd.

250

64

250

1  Lyndhurst

664

To Charlottesville

# South River

Miles
0                    1

# South River

Though a relatively small waterway, the South River has proven to be one of the most important fisheries in the state. It was the first urban trout fishery in Virginia and is home to the state's first Trout Unlimited chapter, which is still active. Nestled in Augusta County between the picturesque Blue Ridge Mountains, the South River has a long and colorful history that is still unfolding today. Winding first through farmland, the South River gathers steam from feeder creeks and eventually combines with the North River to form the South Fork of the Shenandoah.

It will come as no surprise that as an urban trout fishery (it runs right through the middle of downtown Waynesboro), the South River has seen its share of abuses in years past. Waynesboro old-timers recall that one day the river actually *caught fire!* Indeed, the South River was once little more than an industrial sewer: An old corduroy factory was located quite close by, and Waynesboro residents could track what color the plant was using that day by looking at the tint of the river. Happily, environmental laws have changed, and those days are long gone.

## Types of Fish
Rainbows and browns make up most of the coldwater fish here. The South River is also home to smallmouth bass, largemouth bass, bluegill, and the occasional carp.

## Known Hatches
Winter stonefly, blue quill, Hendrickson, March brown, little yellow stonefly, sulfur, quill Gordon, caddisfly, Cahill, inchworm, and terrestrials.

## Equipment to Use
*Rods:* 4- to 7-weight, 7 to 9 feet in length.
*Reels:* Standard trout reel.
*Lines:* Weight-forward floating lines matched to rod; sinking-tip lines will help in some places.
*Leaders:* 3X to 6X, 9 feet in length.
*Wading:* You can get by with hip boots, but you'll find chest waders useful in a number of places.

## Flies to Use
*Drys:* Adams, sizes 14-20; Blue-winged Olive, 14-20; Braided Butt Damsel, 10-12; Dusty's Deviant, 12-16; Elk-Hair Caddis, 14-20; Flying Ant, 10-18; Gelso's Little Black Stonefly, 16-20; Light Cahill, 14-20; Murray's Mr. Rapidan, 14-20; Stimulator, 12-20; Steeves's Attract Ant, 16-20; Steeves's Bark Beetle, 16-20; Steeves's Crystal Butt Hopper, 8-10.

*Continued*

*An angler prepares to take on the trout of the South River in downtown Waynesboro. The rock structures creating the riffles were purchased in part from funds generated by the Virginia Fly Fishing Festival. Photo by King Montgomery.*

*The South River, which runs through downtown Waynesboro, is one of Virginia's best-known urban trout streams. Photo by Beau Beasley.*

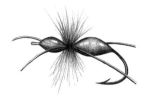

Steeves's Attract Ant

In the summer of 1999, a new hand was dealt to the South River from the business community, but this one was quite different from times past. A little-known non-profit group called Waynesboro Downtown Development Incorporated, tasked with promoting businesses near the city's center, decided to support a fly fishing festival as a means of drawing eco-tourists to the area. This was the genesis of the Virginia Fly Fishing Festival (VFFF), and the South River has now become the focal point for new anglers as well as old hands. The festival is now the largest outdoor fly-fishing event in the state and draws thousands of individual anglers from as far away as Georgia.

In 2007 some large rocks—actually considered construction trash—were installed with heavy equipment to provide the ideal habitat for local trout. Organizers used funds generated by the VFFF to help pay for the installation of the structure, and now anglers of all ages and abilities can benefit from these improvements. The structures are easily seen from the Main Street Bridge and are frequented by anglers.

The Virginia Department of Game and Inland Fisheries stocks the South River with rainbows and browns a few times each year, and a healthy population of bass, bluegill, and even carp call the water home as well. A delayed-harvest trout section exists in the river between the Second Street Bridge upstream to the base of the Rife Loth Dam, though anglers may have to bushwhack their way through some heavy growth along the banks. The river is easy to wade here, and locals are known to sneak out on their lunch hour for a quick trout fix.

In October of 2010 an exciting new development took place in the life of this river. The Virginia Department of Game and Inland Fisheries announced it had reached an agreement with 40 private land owners to open a new section for public fishing. This section, which is all on private property, spans nearly four miles and is set to open January 1, 2011. This area is located near the Waynesboro Nursery, is upstream from the fishery in town, and requires anglers to obtain a free permit before fishing. This historic arrangement could not have occurred without the leadership of the Shenandoah Valley Chapter of Trout Unlimited and local conservationist Urbie Nash. He along with these very generous landowners have opened a whole new chapter in the life of the South River. If you fish this new section of the river, be scrupulous in leaving no debris behind and thank any generous landowner you may encounter. While this portion of the river will hold mostly brown trout, the hope is to reintroduce a wild population of brookies eventually. Some anglers believe this river might produce brookies over a foot long if all goes well. Who knows, but it sure sounds good to me!

More than a decade ago Waynesboro Downtown Development had the vision and foresight to see what this river could mean to the community. What was once little more than an industrial eyesore is now the proving ground for thousands of would-be fly anglers, and the tiny town of Waynesboro is now trout central in the Old Dominion.

## Flies to Use (continued)

*Nymphs & Streamers:* BH Goldilox, sizes 6-10; BH Hare's Ear, 14-20; BH Prince Nymph, 14-20; Coburn's Inchworm, 12-14; Dover's Peach Fly, 6-10; Finn's Golden Retriever, 6-10; Forage Fly, 6; Green Weenie, 14-16; Matuka, 4-10; Mickey Finn, 6-10; Muddler Minnow, 6-10; Woolly Bugger, 6-10.

## When to Fish

The South River fishes best from April to mid-June, and then again from late September to mid-November.

## Season & Limits

To obtain permission to fish in the newly opened section of the South River above town, you'll need to pick up a free permit at Stone Soup Books in Waynesboro or Dominion Outdoors in Fishersville. This stream is open all year. Check with local game laws for specifics.

## Nearby Fly Fishing

The St. Mary's River and Mossy Creek are nearby alternatives, as well as several other streams in the Shenandoah National Park.

## Accommodations & Services

Waynesboro is home to the Virginia Fly Fishing Festival, which is held on the banks of the South River each April. The city can provide all the dining, lodging, and services you need. I've enjoyed staying at the Iris Inn and the Belle Hearth, two excellent B&Bs with very pleasant owners. For a great meal while you're in town or to pick up a good book, be sure to visit Stone Soup Books on Main Street.

Belle Hearth
Waynesboro, Virginia
www.bellehearth.com
(866) 710-2256

Iris Inn
Waynesboro, Virginia
www.irisinn.com
1-888-585-9018

Stone Soup Books
Waynesboro, Virginia
www.stonesoupbooks.com
(540) 943-0084

Virginia Fly Fishing Festival
Waynesboro, Virginia
www.vaflyfishingfestival.org
(703) 402-8338

## Fly Shops & Guides

Albemarle Angler
Charlottesville, Virginia
www.albemarleangler.com
(434) 977-6882

Angler's Lane
Forest, Virginia
www.anglerslane.com
(434) 385-0200

Dominion Outdoors
Fishersville, Virginia
www.dominionoutdoors.com
(540) 337- 9218

Mossy Creek Fly Fishing
Harrisonburg, Virginia
www.mossycreekflyfishing.com
(540) 434-2444

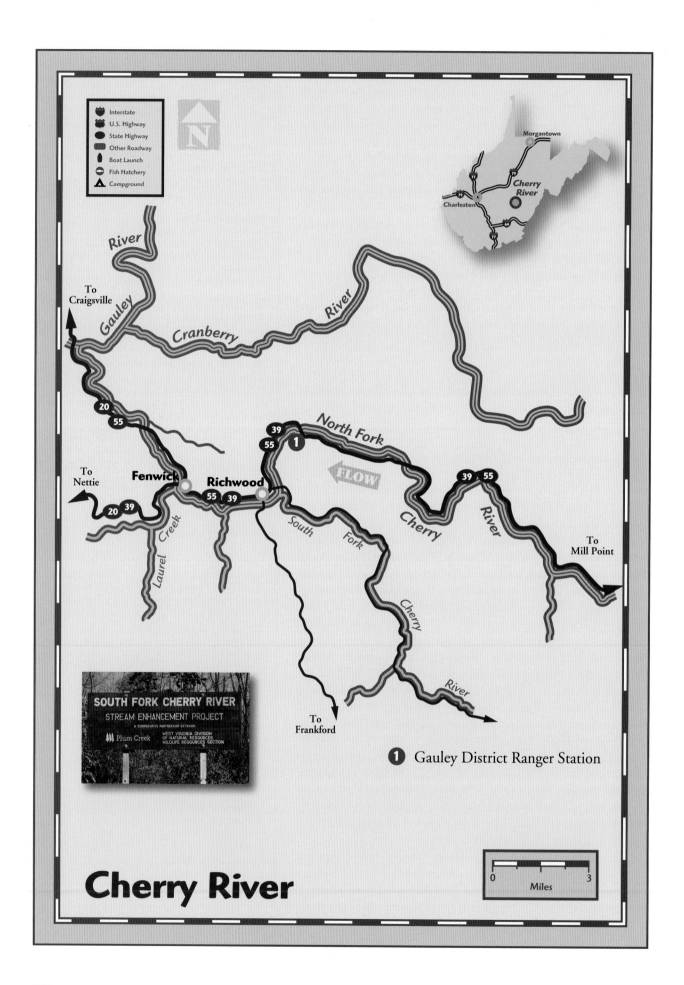

# Cherry River

Morgantown

Cherry River

Charleston

Legend:
- Interstate
- U.S. Highway
- State Highway
- Other Roadway
- Boat Launch
- Fish Hatchery
- Campground

N

River

Gauley

To Craigsville

Cranberry River

20
55

North Fork

39
55

1

FLOW

39 55

Cherry River

To Nettie

Fenwick

Richwood

55 39

20 39

Laurel Creek

South Fork

Cherry

River

To Mill Point

SOUTH FORK CHERRY RIVER
STREAM ENHANCEMENT PROJECT
A COOPERATIVE PARTNERSHIP BETWEEN
Plum Creek    WEST VIRGINIA DIVISION
OF NATURAL RESOURCES
WILDLIFE RESOURCES SECTION

To Frankford

**1** Gauley District Ranger Station

0    Miles    3

# Cherry River

Easily reached from Route 39, the North Fork of the Cherry River certainly isn't famous trout water. And it's true that this river contains primarily stocked fish. But what the Cherry lacks in wild fish it more than makes up for in beauty and accessibility.

Route 39 is a busy piece of road shuttling travelers to and from Richwood. This area was once a logging mecca, and Richwood still supports an active mill today, along with a sign that announces the town's 100-year history with the logging industry. On my last trip to the Cherry, I was shocked to see a Chinook helicopter parked just outside of town in a makeshift landing zone near the river. Someone from the local ranger station informed me that logging companies bid for the right to harvest certain sections of the surrounding Monongahela National Forest. Because no roads can be built into this remote area, today's lumberjacks hike in, cut down the trees, secure them with steel cables, and fly them out via helicopter.

Take note of the unusual rock formations along the banks of the Cherry. They're not there by accident: Locals built the miniature obelisks from river rock. A good point of reference for anglers is the Gauley District Ranger Station, which has a helpful staff, good bathrooms, and a small logging-history museum just off the

## Types of Fish
Both forks of the Cherry River contain stocked rainbows and browns. You'll also land a few brookies here as well.

## Known Hatches
Different fly hatches can occur throughout the day on the Cherry. These hatches include but are not limited to winter stoneflies, blue-winged olives, terrestrials, and other insects typical of a West Virginia mountain trout stream.

## Equipment to Use
*Rods:* 3- to 5-weight, 6½ to 9 feet in length.
*Reels:* Standard trout reel.
*Lines:* Weight-forward floating, matched to rod.
*Leaders:* 4X to 7X leaders, 9 feet in length.
*Wading:* Hip waders are fine here most of the time, but there are some sections where chest waders would be helpful. After mid-May, wet wading is very comfortable.

## Flies to Use
*Drys:* Adams, sizes 14-20; Blue-winged Olive, 14-20; Black Ant, 16-20; Elk-Hair Caddis, 14-20; Eastern Green Drake, 8 to 10; Gelso's Little Black Stonefly, 16-20; Flying Ant, 16-20; Light Cahill, 14-20; March Brown, 10-14; Pale Morning Dun, 14-20; Quill Gordon, 12-22; Rusty Spinner, 16-20; Stimulator, 12-20.

*Continued*

*An angler hooked up on the Cherry River. Photo by Beau Beasley.*

*Guide Gary Lang likes fishing the Cherry River as often as he can. Stimulators work well on the native trout. Photo by Beau Beasley.*

Stimulator

main information desk. The North Fork of the Cherry runs directly behind the ranger station and through the Monongahela National Forest. Local guides Gary Lang and Gil Willis introduced me to the Cherry, and there is no doubt that here, as on so many other waters, an angler really can't beat local knowledge. Indeed, local knowledge told me that the North Fork is more accessible than its southern sister. To some, however, lack of access is a good thing. Upon entering Richwood from the east, look for the commemorative logging sign. Turn left here on Main Street, left again on Water Street, and then right on Johnstown Road. Cross a small bridge, and go about a mile on Johnstown Road before it turns to gravel. This gravel road runs adjacent to most of the river. The rumble of the occasional logging truck is the only reminder of civilization. As you make your way to the water, you'll be driving through residential areas—so watch your speed.

This portion of the Cherry River, sometimes called the Plum Creek section, is a logging route. I found it a bit more productive than the North Fork, most likely because it's a little more off the beaten path. There are long pools here as well as good runs and riffles that allow you to make short casts with drys to the brookies that often strike with reckless abandon. You might notice many blown-down trees here—that is, medium-sized trees that have fallen into the river from erosion and wind. Where you see blown-down trees, you will likely find nice fat browns that have taken up residence under this wooden structure. Be armed and ready beginning with your first cast because these brown trout are not a forgiving lot and do not suffer fools with fly rods.

The Cherry is one of the few West Virginia rivers that most novice anglers can wade and fish themselves. If you take your time, you can easily spend the better part of a day fishing either fork of this river—and do so easily. While the Cherry isn't wild-trout water, and the fishing pressure can be more than one might desire, it is certainly worth a visit. And if you fish the Cherry on a weekday, you might well be fishing all alone.

*Visitors seem to enjoy erecting these rock obelisks in several locations along the North Fork of the Cherry River. Photo by Beau Beasley.*

## Flies to Use (continued)

*Nymphs & Streamers:* BH Goldilox, 6-10; BH Hare's Ear, 14-20; BH Prince Nymph, 14-20; Green Weenie, 14-16; Matuka, 4-10; Mickey Finn, 6-10; Muddler Minnow, 6-10; Pheasant Tail Nymph, 14-20; Sculpin, 8 and 10; Woolly Bugger, 6-10.

## When to Fish

Fishing is best on the Cherry in the early spring and in the late fall. The water level on the Cherry can get very low, so keep a low profile here. I've found it helpful to occasionally look down on the river from the higher banks on the South Fork of the Cherry to try to locate fish.

## Seasons & Limits

You can fish the Cherry River year-round. Be aware there are times when the South Fork is closed to the public. For a complete listing of regulations go to www.wvdnr.gov.

## Accommodations & Services

Richwood is the closest town to the Cherry River and seems to be struggling to find its place now that the heydays of logging have waned. The town, however, is rebuilding itself as a tourist destination and small restaurants can be found if you look hard enough.

## Family Activities

The area of Richwood is surrounded by the Monongahela National Forest and the famed Cranberry Wilderness Area. The town boasts the first and longest-running triathlon and also celebrates the Cherry River with a festival in August. Last, but certainly not least, the town has a Ramp Festival each year. Ramps are best described as wild onions and are certainly an acquired taste.

## Fly Shops & Guides

Cabela's
Triadelphia, West Virginia
www.cabelas.com
(304) 238-0120

Elk River Inn and Fly Shop
Slatyfork, West Virginia
www.ertc.com
1-866-572-3771

Elk Springs Resort
Monterville, West Virginia
www.elkspringsflyshop.com
1-877-355-7774

Evergreen Fly Fishing Company
Clarksburg, West Virginia
www.evergreenflyshop.com
(304) 556-7361

Gander Mountain
Charleston, West Virginia
www.gandermountain.com
(304) 746-6130

Gary Lang
Elkins, West Virginia
www.ertc.com/guidedflyfishing.htm
(304) 572-3771

Serenity Now Outfitters
Lewisburg, West Virginia
www.serenitynowoutfitters.com
1-877-983-4746

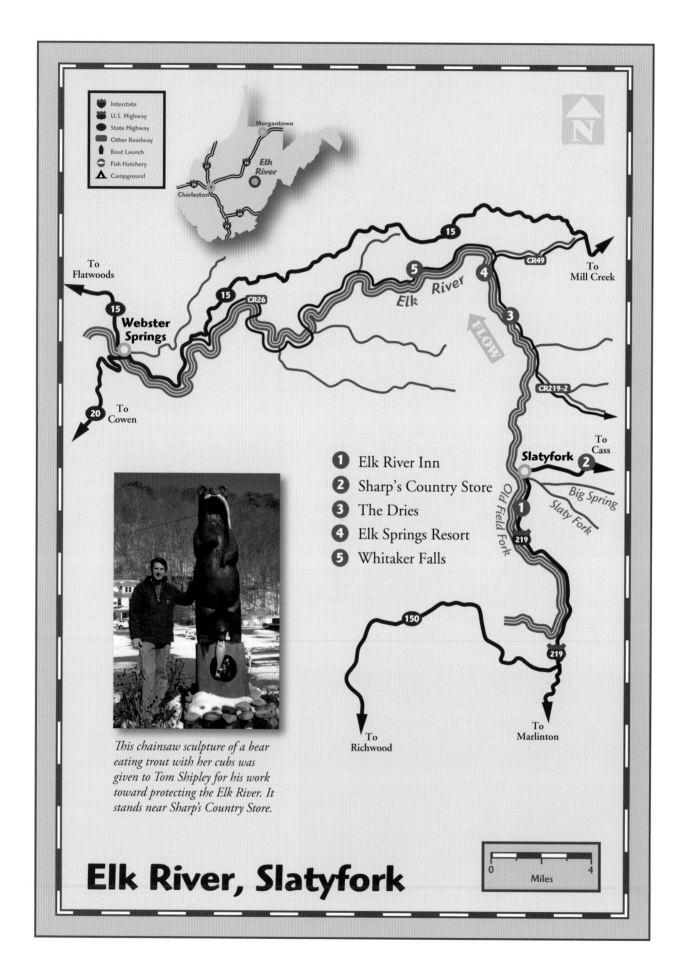

### Map Legend

- Interstate
- U.S. Highway
- State Highway
- Other Roadway
- Boat Launch
- Fish Hatchery
- Campground

Morgantown

Elk River

Charleston

**N**

To Flatwoods

To Mill Creek

15

CR49

15

CR26

5

Elk River

4

3

FLOW

Webster Springs

15

CR219-2

20

To Cowen

To Cass

**Slatyfork**

2

Big Spring

1. Elk River Inn
2. Sharp's Country Store
3. The Dries
4. Elk Springs Resort
5. Whitaker Falls

Old Field Fork

Slaty Fork

1

219

150

219

To Richwood

To Marlinton

*This chainsaw sculpture of a bear eating trout with her cubs was given to Tom Shipley for his work toward protecting the Elk River. It stands near Sharp's Country Store.*

# Elk River, Slatyfork

0     Miles     4

# Elk River, Slatyfork

### Types of Fish
Anglers typically find browns, a few rainbows, and wild brookies.

### Known Hatches
Blue quills, cream variant, gray fox, great autumn sedge, green drake, Hendrickson, March brown, light Cahills, little yellow stoneflies, sulfurs, and many more!

### Equipment to Use
*Rods:* 2- to 5-weight, 7 to 9 feet in length.
*Reels:* Standard trout reel.
*Lines:* Weight-forward floating lines matched to rod.
*Leaders:* 5X to 7X, 9 to 12 feet in length.
*Wading:* Chest waders are a must.

### Flies to Use
*Drys:* Blue-winged Olive, sizes 24-28; Blue-winged Olive Comparadun, 18-28; Black CDC V-wing Midge, 28-32; Black Flying Ant, 10-18; Gray Fox, 14; Gelso's Little Black Stonefly, 16-20; Light Cahill, 14-20; Mahogany CDC Comparadun, 16- 8; March Brown, 10-12; Quill Gordon, 12-22; Rusty Spinner, 12-28; Sulfur Spinner, 14-18; Usual, 14-18.

*Continued*

**K**nown as "The Lady" by those who know her best, the Elk River does indeed have her fair share of suitors, some of whom drive hundreds of miles for the chance to win her favor. The Elk boasts the largest area of native brook trout in West Virginia, and many consider her one of the best trout streams east of the Mississippi. If the native brookies don't grab you then the naturalized brown trout, some of which easily surpass 22 inches in length, certainly will. But brookies and browns are not the only game in town. Rainbows put in an occasional appearance and can be just as hard to bring to hand as the browns and natives.

The Elk begins where Old Field Creek and Big Spring merge just a few hundred yards downstream from the Elk River Inn off of Route 219 in the hamlet of Slatyfork. Gil Willis, an Orvis-endorsed guide and owner of the Elk River Inn, introduced me to this wonderful river several years ago, and I can honestly report

*Gil Willis, owner of Elk River Inn and Fly Shop, often fishes the upper catch-and-release section of the Elk. Photo by Beau Beasley.*

*The Elk River is by far the best wild-trout stream in West Virginia and goes by the moniker "The Lady." Unfortunately its future is far from certain unless West Virginians decide it's important enough to protect The Lady from poorly planned developments. Photo by Beau Beasley.*

Woolly Bugger

that I've never seen its equal. The river has a special-regulation catch-and-release-only section that begins at the headwaters and runs about 4½ miles downstream before the river literally disappears. In fact, the Elk flows through underground caves for several miles, leaving the river bed apparently empty at times as though it has dried up. This section, appropriately named "the Dries," runs with good flow when the water level is up in the spring.

Below the Dries is the second catch-and-release section of the Elk, where the water flows from three huge underground springs back to the surface. Elk Springs Resort and Fly Shop provides anglers good access to waters here. It's an easy walk from Dry Branch Road, which runs off of Route 219. This portion of the Elk continues as a catch-and-release section for two miles before it hits Rose Run Bridge. Access to the lower catch-and-release section on the Elk is easy from County Route 49, which is directly past Elk Springs Resort. Dave Breitmeier at Elk Springs will be glad to give you pointers if you stop in and ask.

The Slatyfork section of the Elk River faced a looming threat in 2005 when Pocahontas County commissioners planned to exercise what they believed to be their right of eminent domain to condemn the land around Sharp's Country Store and erect a huge sewage treatment plant primarily for the purpose of supporting the nearby Snowshoe ski resort. The resort's own plant had suffered myriad well-documented environmental violations ranging from unreported spills to high ammonia levels that are deadly to trout. The plant would have solved many wastewater issues for the rural area—but one bad break and raw sewage could have fouled the prestigious Elk River for years.

Tom Shipley, a member of the Sharp family who operates Sharp's Country Store and whose family has owned the land for nine generations, fought back. Shipley roused locals to his family's plight and to the environmental concerns of the plant. Shipley found support from 8 Rivers Safe Development, a cavers' organization, and TU Chapters across West Virginia that thought building a plant on karst posed a significant threat to the river. Shipley confronted members of the Pocahontas County Commission at public meetings and openly challenged the wisdom of such a plant. Eventually the county commissioners who had championed the eminent domain farm-seizure scheme were run out of office on a rail, and many local citizens and other stakeholders have now come forward to help craft a better plan.

In August 2010 a new legal action was brought by Ralph Beckwith, Russell Holt, and other local business interests along with Snowshoe Mountain Inc. This action might lead to the new plant being built at the headwaters of this river despite strong local opposition.

The Lady remains one of the premier, unmarred wild trout streams in the Eastern U.S. Let us hope that the good citizens of West Virginia continue to stay engaged and protect her, for she certainly deserves their attention.

*A sulfur struggles to break free of its shuck. Photo by King Montgomery.*

### Flies to Use (continued)

*Nymphs & Streamers:* Baetis Nymph, sizes 18-28; BH Soft Hackle Hare's Ear, 14-20; BH Soft Hackle Pheasant Tail Nymph, 14-18; BH Prince Nymph, 14-20; Copper John, 14-22; Copper Sulphate Nymph, 14-24; Cream Caddis Larva, 12-20; Gray Scud, 18-28; Midge Larvae Dun, 28-32; Woolly Bugger, 6-10; Zonker, 4.

### When to Fish

Any time you can get away to fish the Elk is a good time but early spring through June is very good. The fall is also an excellent time but be sure to check water conditions first.

### Season & Limits

The Lady is best approached like a classic Eastern freestone stream where stealth and matching the hatch counts. Below the area known as the Dries, the river is best approached as a spring creek that fishes well nearly all year long.

### Nearby Fly Fishing

Greenbrier River, Cherry River, and Williams River are nearby.

### Accommodations, Services, and Family Activities

I've stayed at the Elk River Inn many times and plan to go back. The only thing that rivals the fishing is Mary Willis's homemade muffins. Families staying here can also mountain bike and hike. Skiing is big here in the winter. Accommodations also can be found at Elk Springs Report. Sharp's Country Store is an institution and should not be missed. This place is as much a local museum as an old-time country store. If you're in luck, Tom Shipley will be on hand with some of his local maple syrup and country jams.

Sharp's Country Store
Slatyfork, West Virginia
www.sharpscountrystore.com
(304) 572-3547

8 Rivers Safe Development
Scott Depot, West Virginia
www.8riverssafedevelopment.com

### Guides & Fly Shops

Elk River Inn and Fly Shop
Slatyfork, West Virginia
www.ertc.com
1-866-572-3771

Elk Springs Resort
Monterville, West Virginia
www.elkspringsflyshop.com
1-877-355-7774

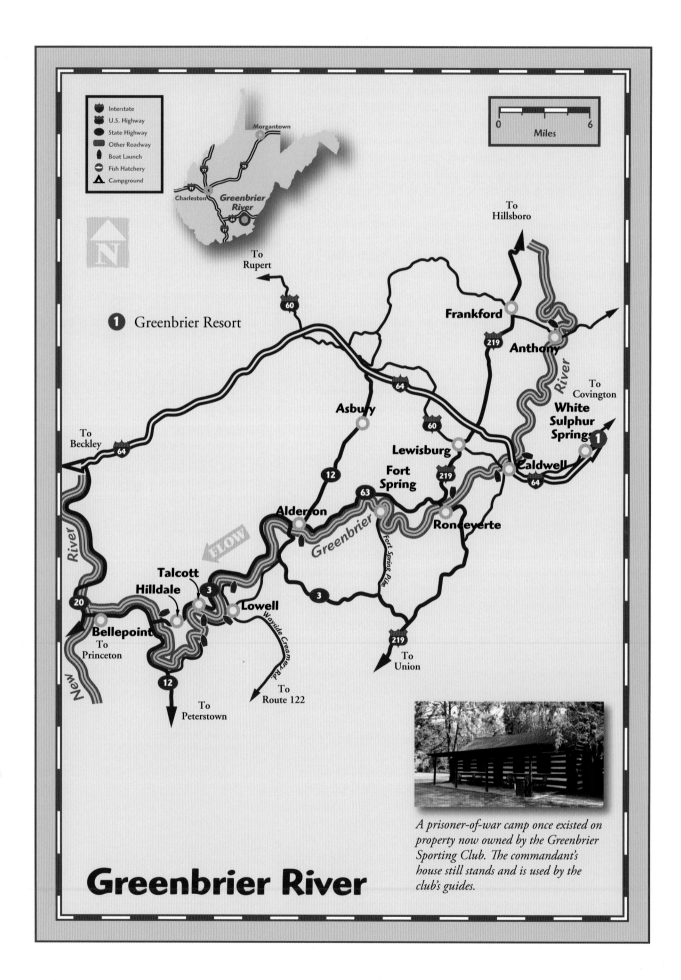

### Legend

- 🛡️ Interstate
- 🛡️ U.S. Highway
- ⬤ State Highway
- ▭ Other Roadway
- ⬥ Boat Launch
- ⬤ Fish Hatchery
- ▲ Campground

N

Morgantown

Charleston

Greenbrier River

To Rupert

60

To Hillsboro

**1** Greenbrier Resort

Frankford

219

Anthony

River

To Covington

64

**White Sulphur Springs**

60

**Asbury**

**Lewisburg**

**Fort Spring**

219

**Caldwell**

64

To Beckley

64

12

63

**Alderson**

*FLOW*

*Greenbrier*

**Ronceverte**

Fort Spring Pike

**Talcott**
**Hilldale**

3

3

**Lowell**

*Wayside Creamery Rd.*

219

To Union

20

**Bellepoint**
To Princeton

New

River

12

To Peterstown

To Route 122

# Greenbrier River

*A prisoner-of-war camp once existed on property now owned by the Greenbrier Sporting Club. The commandant's house still stands and is used by the club's guides.*

# Greenbrier River

The Greenbrier River originates in the mountains of Pocahontas County and meanders its way through high green mountain passes and tiny towns, inviting anglers and other outdoor enthusiasts to its banks. The name "Greenbrier" will forever be associated with the iconic, luxurious Greenbrier Resort, which has welcomed the rich, famous, and powerful (as well as the rest of us) to White Sulfur Springs since 1778. Owned by CSX, the grand hotel has a fascinating history, as does the verdant, wooded area surrounding the resort complex. During World War II, for example, the government used the remote, secluded area to intern prisoners of war from Rommel's Africa corps. The Greenbrier Sporting Club now sits on the land that was once home to these prisoners. Jacob Ott, an Orvis-endorsed guide who works in tandem with Kate's Mountain Outfitters, does business out of a cabin on resort property that was once the home of the POW camp's commandant. A pond adjacent to the cabin is often used as a classroom for beginner fly anglers visiting the resort.

For 30 years, the Greenbrier Resort operated as a top-secret location for an alternative seat of government should war or some other cataclysmic event threaten the government in Washington. The entire Congress could have been housed here underground

## Types of Fish
Smallmouth bass are more sought after than any other species on the Greenbrier, but you can also catch largemouth bass, carp, muskie, and the occasional trout.

## Known Hatches
Crayfish are seen pretty consistently throughout the river system, and it's a safe bet that patterns that mimic this profile will work most of the year. Frogs, as well as various baitfishes such as creek chubs and shiners, are spread throughout the river.

## Equipment to Use
*Rods:* 5- to 9-weight, 8 to 9½ feet in length.
*Reels:* Standard trout reel.
*Lines:* Weight-forward floating, matched to rod. Sinking-tip lines will work in some places.
*Leaders:* 2X to 5X leaders, 9 feet in length.
*Wading:* Anglers have the option of floating in several locations. Chest waders are another option, as is wet wading.

## Flies to Use
*Topwater:* Hickey's Condor, sizes 6-12; Walt's Popper, 2-12.

*Continued*

*Guide Gil Willis floats the Greenbrier River often and occasionally lands rainbows like the one pictured here. Trout sometimes head out of their mountain streams to the larger waters of the Greenbrier. Photo by Beau Beasley.*

*The Greenbrier River is quite large and easily handles drift boats. Photo by Beau Beasley.*

Forage Fly

in what was referred to as "the Bunker." One might be tempted to imagine that Congressmen had outfitted themselves with a posh hideaway, but that is not the case. One can tour the Bunker, and the area where our representatives would have lived for up to three months resembles nothing so much as a bunch of college dorm rooms. Members of Congress would have been permitted to bring one support staff member along with them to the Bunker; no plans were made to accommodate their families. Obviously the place was never used, and no doubt some other secure location now exists.

The Greenbrier River is nearly 200 miles long and presents serious opportunities for anglers of every stripe. A beautiful warmwater river with plenty of wide pools, runs, and riffles, the Greenbrier is calm water by West Virginia standards—the perfect water, in fact, for novice anglers or anyone who prefers fishing to white-knuckle rapids running. Though shallow in many places, the river's breadth allows for anxiety-free casts. Anglers wishing to wade the Greenbrier have lots of options as well because all public boat launches allow wading. Some of the better locations include where the river and the I-64 bridge intersect as well as the Caldwell boat ramp. Ronceverte is also a good location from which to wade or launch a boat, and it's about as close to serious civilization as you'll find on this river.

Greenbrier River float trips are very popular, and indeed this was how Gil Willis, owner of Elk River Inn, introduced me to the water. I was impressed with some of the torpedo-like smallies we saw, even if they did reject my patterns with a dismissive wave of the fin. About a year later, those smallies and I had a rematch, and the Big One really did get away. (No, *really!*) The truth is that you're never sure what you're going to bring to hand on the Greenbrier, as muskies will periodically enter the river from the New River, and trout will often venture out of mountain streams when they have a mind to do so. In fact, during my most recent fishing trip with Gil, I was certain that I had a nice smallie on the line. Imagine my surprise when I landed a very nice rainbow instead.

*Jacob Ott holds a nice muskie he caught on the Greenbrier River. Photo courtesy Jacob Ott.*

*In warmer months anglers frequently wet wade the Greenbrier. Photo by Beau Beasley.*

### Flies to Use (continued)
*Nymphs & Streamers:* BH Goldilox, sizes 4-8; CK Baitfish, 1; Claw-Dad, 2-6; Clouser Minnow, 1/0-6; Dover's Peach Fly, 6-10; Forage Fly, 6; Finn's Golden Retriever, 6-10; Howell's Big Nasty, 6; Kreelex, 2-6; Lefty's Deceiver, 2; Popovics's Surf Candy, 1.

### When to Fish
The Greenbrier River fishes well nearly all year but really heats up in late April and fishes well to the fall.

### Season & Limits
For a complete listing of regulations go to www.wvdnr. gov.

### Accommodations & Services
The General Lewis Inn and the Greenbrier Resort are conveniently located and offer excellent food and accommodations. The biggest nearby town, Ronceverte, practically sits on the river where Route 219 and Route 63 intersect.

General Lewis Inn
Lewisburg, West Virginia
www.generallewisinn.com
1-800-628-4454

Greenbrier Resort
White Sulphur Springs, West Virginia
www.greenbrier.com
1-800-453-4858

### Family Activities
There are plenty of touristy things to do, especially in White Sulphur Springs and in Lewisburg, which has a long history including significant ties to the Civil War. The Greenbrier Resort, while not the most affordable place for a family to stay, nonetheless has great tours. I highly recommend the Bunker Tour (www.greenbrier. com/bunker), which lasts 90 minutes and costs $30 for adults and $15 for children 10 and over. It is worth every penny; you'll hardly believe your eyes.

### Fly Shops & Guides
Elk River Inn and Fly Shop
Slatyfork, West Virginia
www.ertc.com
1-866-572-3771

Kate's Mountain Outfitters
White Sulphur Springs, West Virginia
1-800-624-6070

Serenity Now Outfitters
Lewisburg, West Virginia
www.serenitynowoutfitters.com
1-877-983-4746

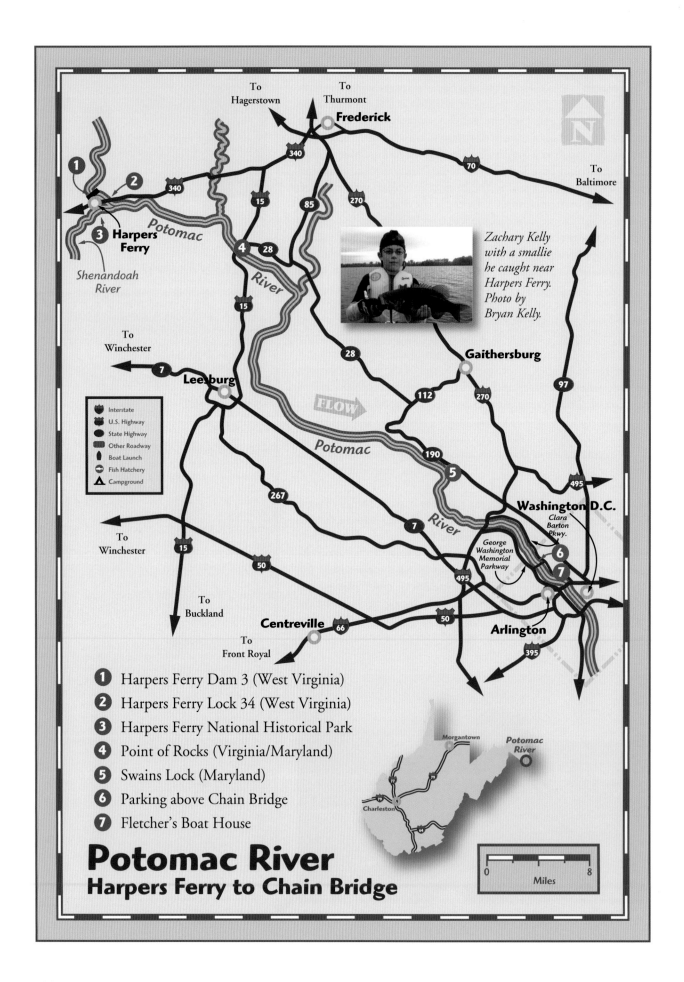

*Zachary Kelly with a smallie he caught near Harpers Ferry. Photo by Bryan Kelly.*

**Legend:**
- Interstate
- U.S. Highway
- State Highway
- Other Roadway
- Boat Launch
- Fish Hatchery
- Campground

1. Harpers Ferry Dam 3 (West Virginia)
2. Harpers Ferry Lock 34 (West Virginia)
3. Harpers Ferry National Historical Park
4. Point of Rocks (Virginia/Maryland)
5. Swains Lock (Maryland)
6. Parking above Chain Bridge
7. Fletcher's Boat House

# Potomac River
## Harpers Ferry to Chain Bridge

## WEST VIRGINIA

# Potomac River, Main Stem

## Harpers Ferry to Chain Bridge

In 1859, radical abolitionist John Brown threw gasoline on the political fire when he led 21 men, including some of Brown's own sons as well as free blacks—on a pre-dawn raid of the federal armory in Harpers Ferry. The band intended to overtake the armory, redistribute its weapons among the local slave population, and then lead a slave rebellion. After cutting the telegraph lines and seizing a train they were confronted by Hayward Shepherd, a freed slave who worked on the train as a baggage handler. Ironically, he was the first person killed in the raid. Brown's men captured some townspeople and made it to the armory, but by the following day the local militia had cut off their means of escape. Two days after the raid, militiamen had isolated the group and their few hostages to the armory's small fire station, which future annals would dub John Brown's Fort. A group of Marines stormed the fire station the next day and put down the rebellion. In fact, the makeshift commanding officer of the intrepid Marines—who had to scramble to the action and found themselves temporarily leaderless—was a well-respected Army colonel named Robert E. Lee, who happened to be on leave nearby.

Situated as it is at the confluence of the Potomac and Shenandoah Rivers, Harpers Ferry is a great jumping-off point for fly anglers. Most anglers come here to do battle with smallmouth bass, but you'll also find carp, various sunfish, and shad. With its variety of species and its spectacular scenery, the Potomac River makes a worthwhile trip—but where to begin? Anglers could spend

### Types of Fish
Smallmouth bass are king in this section of the Potomac, but you can also catch the occasional largemouth bass, carp, shad, striped bass, and unfortunately snakeheads towards the mouth of the river.

### Known Hatches
Hatches on the Potomac vary greatly depending on the size of the river. One hatch that doesn't vary is the white fly hatch that occurs in July.

### Equipment to Use
*Rods:* 6- to 9-weight, 8 to 9½ feet in length (Spey rods, 11½ to 13 feet).
*Reels:* Disc-drag, some opportunities for large arbor.
*Lines:* Weight-forward floating line matched to rod. Sinking-tip lines will work in some places.
*Leaders:* 2X to 4X leaders, 9 feet in length.
*Wading:* Chest waders are needed here; there are also multiple floats. Be sure to wear a personal flotation device when wading.

### Flies to Use
*Topwater:* Chocklett's Disc Slider, size 1/0; Hickey's Condor, 6-12; White Fly, 6-10; Walt's Popper, 2-12.

*Nymphs & Streamers:* CK Baitfish, 1; Claw-Dad, 2-6; Clouser Minnow, 1/0-6; Finn's Golden Retriever, 6-10; Forage Fish, 6; Howell's Big Nasty, 6; Kreelex, 2-6; Murray's Lead Eye Hellgrammite, 6; Super Patuxent Special, 6-10,

*For Shad:* Tommy's Torpedo, size 6; Simmons's Shad Fly, 6; various colors Crazy Charlie, 8.

### When to Fish
Fishing the Potomac for shad is great in April, and smallies can be caught from May through October. Fishing below Dam 3 in Harpers Ferry as well as Lock 34 are good in June and July. Swains Lock can also be good during the summer.

Anglers should avoid fishing near Great Falls in Virginia or Maryland altogether for safety reasons. Any angler who wades this river needs to be wearing a personal flotation device. The last time I fished the main stem of the Potomac River, fire and rescue crews from D.C. were

*Bryan Kelly casts a nice line toward excellent holding structure just downstream of Harpers Ferry. Photo by King Montgomery.*

*Continued*

*Dan Davala from the Orvis Company store in Arlington, Virginia, holds a nice shad. Dan is the founder of the Tidal Potomac Fly Rodders, a Federation of Fly Fishers club that promotes fishing on the Potomac. Photo by Beau Beasley.*

CK Baitfish

a week fishing the main stem of the Potomac near Harpers Ferry and leave feeling that they barely scratched the surface of the river. Because it is so large, newbies might consider hiring a guide. Mark Kovach has guided on the Potomac for nearly three decades and knows this river well. Anglers booking a trip with him would get an education as well as a great fishing trip.

Bryan Kelly is also an excellent river guide who spends nearly a hundred days a year fishing the Potomac out of the wooden dory he made by hand. Kelly is owner of The Angler's Inn bed and breakfast in Harpers Ferry. He recently opened Kelly's White Fly Shoppe in Shepherdstown.

Wading anglers can take advantage of the hundreds of yards of riffles and rock clusters near the town. Cast downriver and across. Vary your retrieve and occasionally let the current take your pattern where it will. Controlling your retrieve with a tight line, however, will improve your chances of hooking up. I've had marked success here with Chuck Kraft's Claw-Dad pattern.

The Potomac boasts plenty of water to float and fish, but one of the easiest access sites near D.C. is at Fletcher's Boat House on the east side of the river downstream from Chain Bridge. Anglers can easily enter the river here at Fletcher's Boat House, an angling institution and the home of the annual Congressional Casting Call, which gives fly-fishing professionals an opportunity to fish and talk with legislators about the issues pertinent to the fly-fishing industry and the nation's fisheries. Fly anglers can easily walk upstream from Fletcher's and have easy access to the Potomac. The current is strong here, so wade carefully. There are many access points along this expansive river; I've listed only the sites I feel can be used safely by anglers.

The local Tidal Potomac Fly Rodders club is dedicated to promoting and protecting this fishery—and they're also the resident experts on Potomac River shad. These guys will gladly point you in the right direction if you're in the mood to pursue these hard-fighting fish. Heads up, Washington area anglers: This is your local water. Have you fished it recently?

*"John Brown's Fort" was actually the fire station for the federal armory in Harpers Ferry. It still stands and is within easy walking distance of the river. Photo by Beau Beasley.*

## When to Fish (continued)

searching for an angler who jumped into the water to save a child. They were both lost. No fish is worth your life!

If you decide to fish at Fletcher's Boat House be aware the easiest way to reach this part of the river is off of Canal Road, also known as Clara Barton Parkway. Upstream of Chain Bridge this road runs one-way east in the mornings and one-way west in the afternoon. Heading east, south of Chain Bridge a hairpin turn off of Clara Barton Parkway is required to enter Fletcher's Boat House. Some anglers opt to pull just past the turn off and back down into the park.

## Season & Limits

For up-to-date regulations, check with the fly shop closest to the section of the river you'll be fishing. If you're not sure, always err on the side of buying a Maryland fishing license since this is a Maryland river (www.dnr.state.md.us). To get the latest information on fly fishing the Potomac River near D.C., get hooked up with the Tidal Potomac Fly Rodders (www.tpfr.org).

## Accommodations & Family Activities

There are several places to stay in Harpers Ferry, but I highly recommend The Angler's Inn. I've stayed here before and having Bryan as your guide makes it a wonderful package deal. There are plenty of sights and touristy things to do in Harpers Ferry, most revolving around the Civil War and early American history. I highly recommend going to see some of the old local churches, and I nearly always make time to see John Brown's Wax Museum. There are more things to see and do around Washington, D.C., than one could list—so I won't try.

The Angler's Inn
Harpers Ferry, West Virginia
www.theanglersinn.com
(304) 535-1239

Fletcher's Boat House
Washington, District of Columbia
www.fletchersboathouse.com
(202) 244-0461

Tidal Potomac Fly Rodders
www.tpfr.org

## Fly Shops & Guides

Kelly's White Fly Shoppe
Shepherdstown, West Virginia
www.kellyswhitefly.net
(304) 876-8030

Mark Kovach Fishing Services
Silver Spring, Maryland
www.mkfs.com
(301) 588-8742

### Near Chain Bridge (Virginia)

L.L. Bean
McLean, Virginia
www.llbean.com/tysons
(703) 288-4466

Orvis
Vienna, Virginia
www.orvis.com/tysonscorner
(703) 556-8634

Orvis
Arlington, Virginia
www.orvis.com/arlington
(703) 465-0004

Urban Angler
Arlington, Virginia
www.urbanangler.com
(703) 527-2524

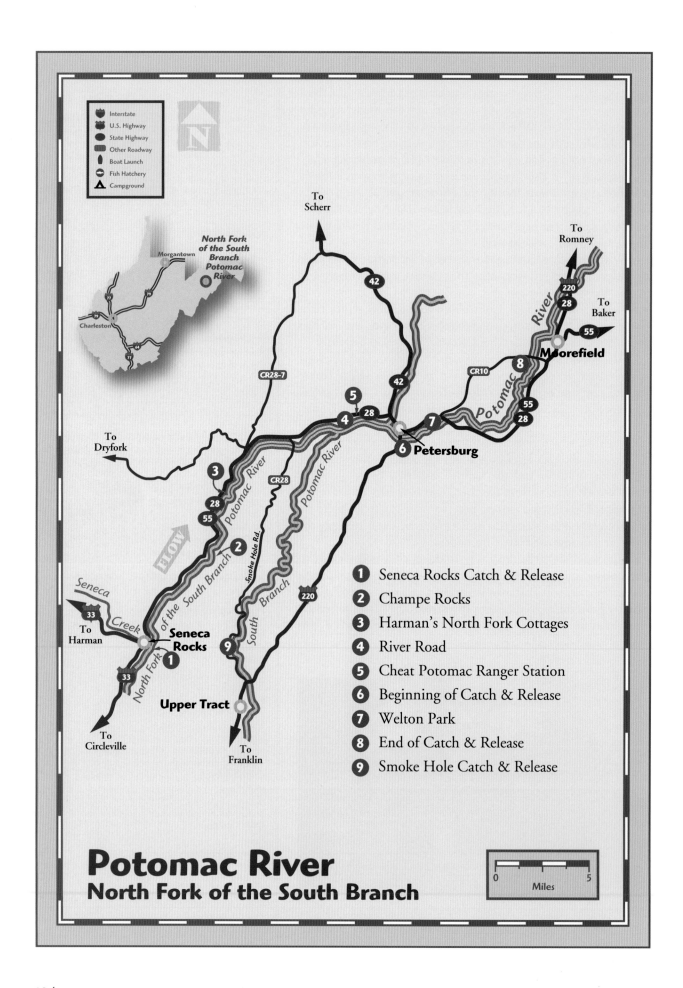

**Legend:**
- Interstate
- U.S. Highway
- State Highway
- Other Roadway
- Boat Launch
- Fish Hatchery
- Campground

N

North Fork of the South Branch Potomac River

Morgantown

Charleston

To Scherr

To Romney

To Baker

42

220

28

55

CR28-7

42

28

Moorefield

5

4

28

CR10

8

Potomac River

7

55

To Dryfork

Potomac River

6 **Petersburg**

3

28

55

CR28

Potomac River

FLOW

2

Smoke Hole Rd.

220

Seneca Creek

33

**Seneca Rocks**

9

South Branch

To Harman

North Fork of the South Branch

1

33

**Upper Tract**

To Circleville

To Franklin

1. Seneca Rocks Catch & Release
2. Champe Rocks
3. Harman's North Fork Cottages
4. River Road
5. Cheat Potomac Ranger Station
6. Beginning of Catch & Release
7. Welton Park
8. End of Catch & Release
9. Smoke Hole Catch & Release

# Potomac River
## North Fork of the South Branch

0 Miles 5

# Potomac River, North Fork of the South Branch

C limbing enthusiasts will no doubt have heard of—or already tackled—West Virginia's popular Seneca Rocks. Beside this climbing mecca, tourists may observe Champe Rocks from Route 28, named after Sergeant Major John Champe, who faked desertion from the Continental Army in an attempt to kidnap the traitor Benedict Arnold. Unfortunately, Arnold had moved his office too far away from the front lines, and Champe returned to his colonial brothers empty-handed—and was promptly treated to a hero's welcome. His reputation only grew when his colleagues discovered that his only reservation about the plan was his feigning desertion. The plan was so secret that Champe was nearly shot to death by pickets who hadn't been informed of the covert op.

Yes, some head to West Virginia to climb rocks. I go to catch trout. Though many anglers float the Potomac in Maryland and Virginia, there is excellent access for wading anglers, primarily off Route 28/55 in West Virginia. You'll find a healthy mix of trout here: mostly browns and rainbows with the occasional brood-stock brookie because it's so easy to stock this river. That sudden jolt

## Types of Fish
Most fly anglers come here looking for rainbow trout, but browns and brookies are also stocked. Don't be surprised if you reel in a nice smallie.

## Known Hatches
Ants, beetles, crayfish, crickets, and hoppers, as well as several baitfish.

## Equipment to Use
*Rods:* 4- to 6-weight, 8 to 9 feet in length.
*Reels:* Standard trout reel.
*Lines:* Primarily weight-forward floating lines work just fine.
*Leaders:* 3X to 6X, 9 feet in length.
*Wading:* Be forewarned: The Potomac can be dangerous, if you wade take a staff and consider cleats.

## Flies to Use
*Drys:* Adams, sizes 14-20; Blue-winged Olive, 14-20; Black Flying Ant, 14-18; Elk-Hair Caddis, 14-20; Flying Ant, 10-18; Gelso's Little Black Stonefly, 16-20; Light Cahill, 14-20; March Brown, 10-14; Murray's Mr. Rapidan, 14-20; Quill Gordon, 12-22; Stimulator, 12-20.

*Nymphs & Streamers:* BH Goldilox, sizes 6-10; BH Hare's Ear, 14-20; BH Prince Nymph, 14-20; Coburn's Inchworm, 12-14; Scotts Golden Retriever, 6-10; Matuka, 4-10; Muddler Minnow, 6-10; Pheasant Tail Nymph, 14-20; Sculpin, 4-8; Woolly Bugger, 6-10; Zonker, 4-6.

*Continued*

*West Virginia is blessed with excellent trout water in many parts of the state. Few places rival the fishing opportunities along the South Branch. Photo by Beau Beasley.*

*The North Fork of the South Branch of the Potomac is very popular and is easily accessible from Route 55/28. Photo by King Montgomery.*

Kraft's Claw-Dad

on your line, however, may come from a smallmouth bass: The state's record smallie, which weighed in at a whopping 9.75 pounds, was caught in the Potomac.

Anglers, know that as you head south on Route 28/55, you'll lose all cell-phone service once you leave the town of Petersburg. In exchange, however, you'll gain excellent wading water along the North Fork. All along the road, you'll find numerous pull-outs that are easy to spot and parking is abundant. If you prefer to float the river in a canoe or kayak, one of the first places you can put in is Welton Park in Grant County. The U.S. Park Service also designates several points at which boats may be launched. The North Fork is loaded with big rocks, many of which can't be seen when the river is running high. I highly recommend going with a guide or contacting an outfitter. For metropolitan visitors the closest outfitter that offers shuttle service on the North Fork is Eagles Nest Outfitters just outside Petersburg.

You can gain access to an easy-wading location from River Road, just a few hundred yards south of Cheat/Potomac Ranger Station. This is a hard-surface road that eventually becomes a gravel road as you head toward the river. The area is popular with campers, but anglers seem to overlook it, probably because one can't see the river from the road at this point. Most anglers unknowingly drive right past this good river access despite the road's telling name. You'll find a defunct dam approximately 1.5 miles from Route 28/55.

One section of the river that seems to hold water—and therefore fish—all year long is on the property owned by Harman's North Fork Cottages. I was lucky enough to land a 20-inch rainbow during my last visit, and I can honestly say that my wife and kids love the place as much as I do because of the scenery and the solitude—and the hot tub on the deck of our cottage. Harman's place is also a great base of operations for anglers who wish to sample other nearby fisheries. They carry a limited selection of local patterns as well.

## When to Fish

Like most trout rivers the spring and fall are best, but this of course depends on yearly rainfall.

## Season & Limits

There is a catch-and-release only section that stretches from Fisher down to Petersburg. For a complete list of regulations contact the West Virginia Division of Natural Resources (www.wvdnr.gov) or call (304) 558-2758.

## Nearby Fly Fishing

Other options include Seneca Creek. If you're up for a bit of a ride you could visit the Elk River, Second Creek, or the Cherry River.

## Accommodations & Family Activities

If you fish here you really should stay at Harman's. This family-run business rents comfortable cottages by the week, and they're right on the river. Todd Harman, a devoted outdoorsman whose family has owned the property for generations, stocks the river occasionally and seeks to keep his operation geared toward families seeking solitude as well as good fishing. The only problem is once you get here there isn't much to do other than hiking, birding, golfing, rock climbing, caving, or taking a train excursion or wilderness tour. Visitors can also visit Dolly Sods, a natural high-plain meadow with a spectacular view.

Harman's North Fork Cottages
Cabins, West Virginia
www.wvlogcabins.com
1-800-436-6254

Eagles Nest Outfitters
Petersburg, West Virginia
www.eaglesnestoutfitters.com
(304) 257-2393

## Fly Shops and Guides

There are no fly shops close by, so plan accordingly. Harman's does have a small supply of local patterns.

Cabela's
Triadelphia, West Virginia
www.cabelas.com
(304) 238-0120

Evergreen Fly Fishing Company
Clarksburg, West Virginia
www.evergreenflyshop.com
(304) 556-7361

Gander Mountain
Charleston, West Virginia
www.gandermountain.com
(304) 746-6130

*Harman's North Fork Cottages make a great base of operations for fishing in West Virginia. The author started writing this book in cabin #3. Photo by Beau Beasley.*

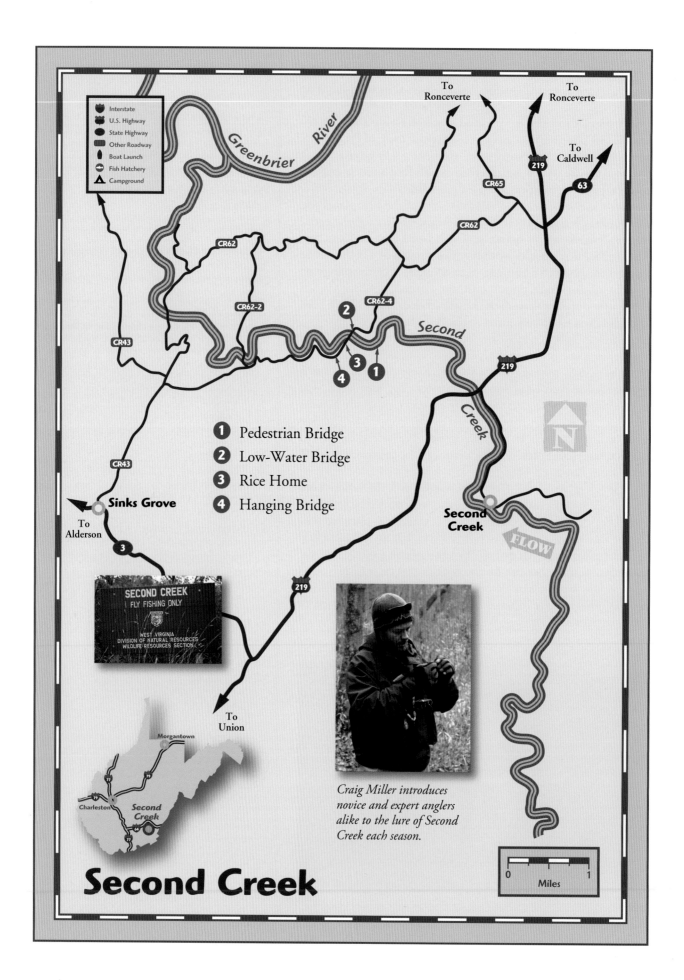

**Legend:**
- Interstate
- U.S. Highway
- State Highway
- Other Roadway
- Boat Launch
- Fish Hatchery
- Campground

Greenbrier River

To Ronceverte

To Ronceverte

To Caldwell

CR65

219

63

CR62

CR62

CR62-4

Second

CR62-2

CR43

2

3

1

4

219

Creek

**1** Pedestrian Bridge
**2** Low-Water Bridge
**3** Rice Home
**4** Hanging Bridge

N

CR43

Sinks Grove

To Alderson

3

Second Creek

FLOW

SECOND CREEK
FLY FISHING ONLY

WEST VIRGINIA
DIVISION OF NATURAL RESOURCES
WILDLIFE RESOURCES SECTION

219

To Union

Morgantown

77

79

64

Charleston

Second Creek

77

*Craig Miller introduces
novice and expert anglers
alike to the lure of Second
Creek each season.*

0     Miles     1

# Second Creek

# Second Creek

S econd Creek, a lovely freestone water near historic Lewisburg, West Virginia, is one of the best-known trout streams in the state. It's also one of only six spots in the Mountain State to offer a fly-fishing-only catch-and-release-only section. Craig Miller of Lewisburg's Serenity Now Outfitters introduced me to Second Creek, and he is generally considered the resident expert. "Most people hear about Second Creek from a friend and just brush it off as another run-of-the-mill mountain trout stream—and so they never fish it. Those who actually take the time to fish here usually fall in love with the place." Let me state for the record that I officially fall into the latter category and plan on returning to fish here as many times as my wife will let me.

The river can be broken into two sections above and below the low-water bridge, which anglers can easily drive across. Directly adjacent to the bridge is the Rice family home. Anglers may fish directly in front of the house, which overlooks the river, but the Rice family requests that you respect their privacy and park only in designated spaces. If you fish below the low-water bridge, you

*While brown trout are the most dominant species on Second Creek, anglers can also catch rainbows and smallies. Photo by King Montgomery.*

*Keeping a low profile often gives anglers an edge against wary trout. Photo by Craig Miller.*

*Craig Miller, owner of Serenity Now Outfitters, guides on Second Creek year-round. The gin-clear water often requires a careful approach and delicate casts. Photo by Beau Beasley.*

Mann's Inchworm

may expect long deep pools and a large oxbow just prior to a second elevated bridge. This bridge is not open to public traffic but can be used by anglers. If you're careful, you can also use this higher vantage point to prospect for trout upstream and downstream.

The river is easy to wade and at some places is only ten yards wide—and yet there's plenty of cover for fish and lots for the local trout to eat. On my last visit, Craig reached down and picked up a handful of leaves from the shoreline that was packed with scuds and other nymphs. I personally like beginning a trip to this river by fishing above an old hanging bridge. In its heyday the bridge no doubt provided a great observation point for those spying out the river's wary trout. It has, however, long since fallen into disrepair and seems to be held together primarily by moss, lichen, and a few strands of rope. So obviously the bridge is no longer in service—it remains, however, a good reference point.

At first blush, Second Creek may not impress. This is where the old adage, "Don't judge a book by its cover," comes into play. Anglers can easily spend the entire day on Second Creek and not come close to covering all the water. You can wade here, but eventually you'll find yourself roll casting. Whatever you do, take your time: Second Creek affords you the opportunity to prospect nearly all of its water because wading is quite easy; a wading staff is not required, except by those who feel that they just aren't wading without one.

Spring and fall are prime times, but something's always biting on Second Creek. Water levels are so low in summer and winter that it's best not to use split shot or even an indicator because the fish are easily spooked in the gin-clear shallow water. The creek has a solid reputation for browns—Craig Miller has landed some that pushed 22 inches—but rainbows and the occasional beefy smallies also call the stream home. My only quibble with Second Creek is its name: It's a first-rate trout water, and from where I stand, it's second to none.

*Second Creek is one of the few fly-fishing-only streams in West Virginia and is a real treasure. Photo by Beau Beasley.*

## Types of Fish
This is big brown-trout water, however, rainbows and brookies are sprinkled through here as well. Smallmouth bass sometimes sneak in here from downstream.

## Known Hatches
Different fly hatches occur throughout the year on Second Creek. These hatches include but are not limited to winter stoneflies, blue quills, blue-winged olives, Hendricksons, March browns, little yellow stoneflies, midges, caddisflies, Cahills, inchworms, and terrestrials.

## Equipment to Use
*Rods:* 3- to 6-weight, 6½-9 feet in length.
*Reels:* Standard trout reel.
*Lines:* Weight-forward floating, matched to rod.
*Leaders:* 2X to 7X leaders, 7½ to 12 feet in length.
*Wading:* Chest waders needed in the spring.

## Flies to Use
*Drys:* Adams, sizes 14-20; Blue-winged Olive, 14-26; Elk-Hair Caddis, 10-20; Flying Ant, 10-18; Gelso's Little Black Stonefly, 16-20; Light Cahill, 14-20; Little Yellow Sally, 14-20; March Brown, 10-14; Quill Gordon, 12-22; Stimulator, 12-20.

*Nymphs & Streamers:* BH Goldilox, sizes 6-10; BH Hare's Ear, 14-20; BH Prince Nymph, 14-20; Mann's Inchworm, 12-14; Matuka, 4-10; Muddler Minnow, 6-10; Pheasant Tail Nymph, 14-20; Scud, 10-18; Sculpin, 4-8; Woolly Bugger, 2-12; Zonker, 2-10.

## When to Fish
Second Creek is fishable almost year-round. To access Second Creek from Route 219 heading southward from Ronceverte, make a right on County Road 65 and then a quick left onto County Road 62 to the low-water bridge. There are 1.5 miles of fly-fishing-only water here, but if you don't mind sharing the river with a few others, it runs for miles before emptying into the Greenbrier, a noted smallmouth river.

## Season & Limits
You can fish Second Creek year-round. For a complete listing of regulations go to www.wvdnr.gov.

## Accommodations & Family Activities
Lewisburg is a great place to spend an entire weekend. There are plenty of historical sites to see and most of the town is easily walkable. If you get the chance, you really owe it to yourself to stay at the General Lewisburg Inn. Jim Morgan, the innkeeper, will be sure to make your stay comfortable. Its accommodations are first-rate and the food is outstanding. I particularly enjoy sitting in their great room and reading by the fire in the fall. The only problem is you won't want to leave.

General Lewis Inn
Lewisburg, West Virginia
www.generallewisinn.com
1-800-628-4454

## Fly Shops & Guides
Serenity Now Outfitters
Lewisburg, West Virginia
www.serenitynowoutfitters.com
(304) 647-9779

# Trout Unlimited Tri-State Conservation & Fishing Camp

Between texting and tweeting and earbuds, young people have little time for nature anymore. All the more reason, then, that anglers should strive to introduce children to nature and expose them to the quiet sport of fly fishing. Teach a young person to fish, and you plant a seed that could grow into a lifelong passion and reward them in ways they never imagined.

Summer camp is a time-honored rite of passage and can be great fun for kids. At the top of the list is the Trout Unlimited Tri-State Conservation & Fishing Camp held at Graves Mountain Lodge in Virginia each June near the Shenandoah National Park. Young folks at least age 13 in 8th, 9th, 10th, or 11th grades learn fly tying, fly casting, hydrology, entomology, fish biology, and much, much more. Campers go home with a new understanding of the importance of proper stewardship of natural resources—and their own fly rod and reel so that they can continue to improve their fly-fishing skills.

Camp staff members include current and former medical doctors, nurses, biologists, entomologists, professional guides, and even a retired battalion chief from the Austin (Texas) Fire Department. I'm usually there as well, snapping pictures, and my daughter Maggie attends, as I've dragged her along to camp since she was 4. And until she is old enough to actually be a camper, she is the unofficial camp mascot. Major sponsors of the camp include Orvis, L.L. Bean, and Dominion. Children from across the Mid-Atlantic attend this camp, and needs-based scholarships are available. Please contact George Gaines (202) 904-3547, or visit www.tucamp.org for more information.

*Students at the Trout Unlimited camp learn about conservation as well as fishing during their week's stay at Graves Mountain Lodge in Syria, Virginia. Photo by Beau Beasley.*

# Virginia Fly Fishing & Wine Festival

Each April the city of Waynesboro, Virginia, invites fly anglers of all ages and abilities to experience the fun of fly fishing along the banks of the South River, which runs through the middle of town. The Virginia Fly Fishing Festival (VFFF) is the largest outdoor fly-fishing event in the Mid-Atlantic and draws thousands of fly-fishing enthusiasts and would-be anglers to Waynesboro to learn how to tie flies, cast Spey rods, and fly fish local and regional waters for everything from native brook trout in the Shenandoah National Park to stripers in the Chesapeake Bay.

Attendees also enjoy streamside bluegrass music, and people over age 21 have the opportunity to sample wines from some of Virginia's best vintners. Children 16 and under are free with a paying adult. Major sponsors of the Virginia Fly Fishing & Wine Festival include the city of Waynesboro, Orvis, Temple Fork Outfitters, Dominion, and Waynesboro Downtown Development Inc. Half of all net proceeds go directly to fund conservation efforts on the South River. For more information on this one-of-a-kind event, please visit www.vaflyfishingfestival.org.

# Project Healing Waters

For many years now American servicemen and women have been fighting "the long war" on two fronts that, to most of us, represent exotic names on a map. We don't know much more about these cities, villages, and mountainous regions than what we glean from sound bites on the news or articles in the newspapers. In fact, Afghanistan and Iraq are the places where many of our veterans have left behind legs and arms and comrades—and in many cases have laid down their lives—in defense of our freedoms and for the cause of furthering democracy around the world.

Wars are costly, in big and small ways. They cost a lot of money, and they often cost soldiers their lives, their limbs, their mobility, and sometimes their sanity. Many veterans return home with wounds that we can't see. Each and every veteran who serves under arms deserves our respect for their sacrifices.

Project Healing Waters helps wounded veterans nationwide to reconnect to civilian life and adjust to their injuries through fly fishing. To find out more about this worthwhile organization, please visit www.projecthealingwaters.org.

*Above: A veteran sets the hook on a nice rainbow trout at the Annual 2-Fly Competition at Rose River Farm in Syria, Virginia. Photo by Beau Beasley.*

*Top right: John Bass is an avid fly angler who travels and fishes widely in the Mid-Atlantic. He's very active with Project Healing Waters and was selected as the 2008 Virginia Fly Angler of the Year. Photo by Beau Beasley.*

# The Future of Menhaden in the Chesapeake Bay

The Chesapeake Bay faces many challenges, including industrial runoff, decimated oyster and crab populations, and a dead zone that stretches from Virginia's York River to Pennsylvania's Susquehanna River. Among the gravest threats to the health of the Bay, however, is that posed by a scarcity of the humblest of baitfish: menhaden. These lowly baitfish are the meal of choice of most of the Bay's favorite game fish, and they are filter feeders that help keep the Bay clean. And as Mid-Atlantic sportsmen know only too well, as the menhaden go, so go the stripers and other game fish as well.

A recent stock assessment by the Atlantic States Marine Fisheries Commission (ASMFC) found that the menhaden population is at an all-time low, down as much as 86 percent from only three decades ago. The Virginia General Assembly oversees menhaden management from the state's coast, including the Chesapeake Bay, to three miles offshore, where the feds take control. While legislators debate the exact percentage of menhaden decline, conservationists of all stripes have turned on the General Assembly to decry its lack of meaningful management of this most precious resource.

As of this printing, Virginia allows 240 million pounds of menhaden to be removed annually from state waters by Omega Protein, a Texas-based commercial operation that harvests menhaden for use in products such as lipstick, pet food, and vitamin supplements—and, ironically, fish food—in its plant in Reedville, Virginia. More than half of the total Atlantic menhaden harvest comes from the Chesapeake, which is the most important nursery for juvenile menhaden on the East Coast. Beyond the three-mile boundary, there is no limit on the amount of menhaden that can be captured in federal waters.

The question that anglers and citizens must ask is this: Why do we allow the Virginia General Assembly to pretend to manage menhaden? Omega Protein and other commercial fishing businesses are not the enemy. They are simply operating in a system that unconcerned citizens and anglers allow. Some stakeholders argue that Virginia politicians should turn over menhaden management to the Virginia Marine Resources Commission, which now manages every other saltwater species in Virginia waters *except* menhaden. If you're concerned about the health of the Bay, the health of menhaden, and the recreational fishery they help support, then you are a stakeholder.

Anglers and striped bass populations all along the Mid-Atlantic coast are affected by the dwindling numbers of menhaden, so what happens in Virginia's waters affects the entire coast. Anglers need to voice their opinions to ASMFC, contact your legislators and legislators in Virginia, or attend ASMFC meetings and see just where you can lend a hand.

The Coastal Conservation Association of Virginia (www.ccavirginia.org) and the Chesapeake Bay Foundation (www.cbf.org) are working diligently to bring the plight of the menhaden to light and to preserve this precious resource for the sake of the region's stripers, false albacore, drum, other sea life, and marine waterfowl. For more information on this important issue, please visit www.savemenhaden.com.

# Conservation

No Nonsense Fly Fishing Guidebooks believes that, in addition to local information and gear, fly fishers need clean water and healthy fish. We encourage preservation, improvement, conservation, enjoyment, and understanding of our waters and their inhabitants. While fly fishing, take care of the place, practice catch and release, and try to avoid spawning fish.

When you aren't fly fishing, a good way to help all things wild and aquatic is to support organizations dedicated to these ideas. We encourage you to get involved, learn more, and to join such organizations.

American Rivers.................................................................................(202) 347-7550
Blackfoot Challenge............................................................................(406) 793-9300
California Trout.................................................................................(415) 392-8887
Camo Coalition.................................................................................(770) 787-7887
Chattahoochee Coldwater Fishery Foundation .............................................(770) 650-8630
Chesapeake Bay Foundation ..................................................................(410) 268-8816
Coastal Conservation Association Virginia...................................................(804) 966-5654
Deschutes Basin Land Trust...................................................................(541) 330-0017
Federation of Fly Fishers ......................................................................(406) 585-7592
Georgia Department of Natural Resources (Fisheries).....................................(770) 918-6406
Georgia Outdoor Network ...................................................................1-800-866-5516
International Game Fish Association...........................................................(954) 927-2628
International Women Fly Fishers .............................................................(925) 934-2461
New Mexico Trout.............................................................................(505) 884-5262
Oregon Trout...................................................................................(503) 222-9091
Outdoor Writers Association of America.....................................................(406) 728-7434
Recreational Fishing Alliance .................................................................1-888-564-6732
Rails-to-Trails Conservancy....................................................................(202) 331-9696
Theodore Roosevelt Conservation Partnership ..............................................(877) 770-8722
Trout Unlimited ...............................................................................1-800-834-2419

# Find Your Way with These No Nonsense Guides

**Fly Fishing Arizona**
ISBN 978-1-892469-02-1
$18.95

**Fishing Central California**
ISBN 978-1-892469-18-2
$24.95

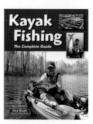

**Kayak Fishing 2nd Edition**
ISBN 978-1-892469-25-0
$24.95

**Fly Fishing New Mexico**
ISBN 978-1-892469-04-5
$18.95

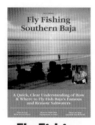

**Fly Fishing Southern Baja**
ISBN 978-1-892469-00-7
$18.95

**Fly Fishing Colorado**
ISBN 978-1-892469-13-7
$19.95

**Fly Fishing Lees Ferry**
ISBN 978-1-892469-15-1
$18.95

**Fly Fishing Central & Southeastern Oregon**
ISBN 978-1-892469-09-0
$19.95

**Fly Fishing California**
ISBN 978-1-892469-10-6
$28.95

**Fly Fishing Georgia**
ISBN 978-1-892469-20-5
$28.95

**Fly Fishing Montana**
ISBN 978-1-892469-14-4
$28.95

**Fly Fishing Utah**
ISBN 978-0-9637256-8-4
$19.95

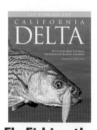

**Fly Fishing the California Delta**
ISBN 978-1-892469-23-6
$49.95

**Fly Fishing Idaho**
ISBN 978-1-892469-17-5
$18.95

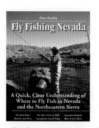

**Fly Fishing Nevada**
ISBN 978-0-9637256-2-2
$18.95

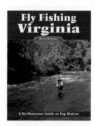

**Fly Fishing Virginia**
ISBN 978-1-892469-16-8
$28.95

**Business Traveler's Guide To Fly Fishing in the Western States** • ISBN 978-1-892469-01-4 • $18.95

**Fly Fishing Pyramid Lake** • ISBN 978-0-9637256-3-9 • $15.95

**Seasons of the Metolius** • ISBN 978-1-892469-11-3 • $20.95

**Fly Fishing Magdalena Bay** • ISBN 978-1-892469-08-3 • $24.95

**A Woman's Guide To Fly Fishing Favorite Waters** • ISBN 978-1-892469-03-8 • $19.95

# Fly-Fishing Knots

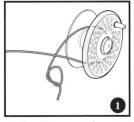 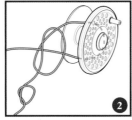 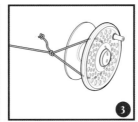

**Arbor Knot:** *(Above) Use this knot to attach backing to your fly reel.*

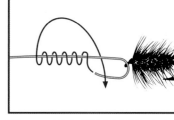

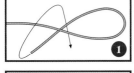

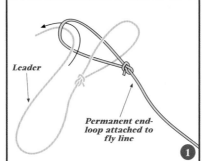

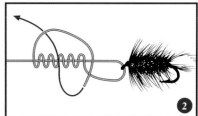

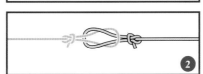

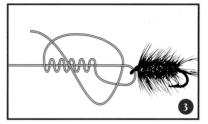

**Blood Knot:** *(Above)*
*Use this knot to connect sections of leader tippet material. Hard to tie, but worth the effort.*

**Loop-to-Loop:** *(Above)*
*Easy connection of leader to a permanent monofilament end loop added to the tip of the fly line.*

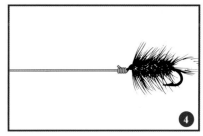

**Improved Clinch Knot:** *(Above)*
*Use this knot to attach the fly to the end of the tippet. Remember to moisten the knot before pulling it up tight.*

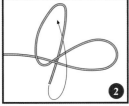

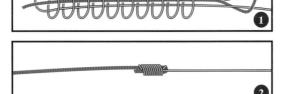

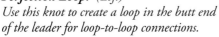

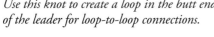

**Albright Knot:** *(Above)*
*Use this knot to attach backing to your fly line.*

**Perfection Loop:** *(Left)*
*Use this knot to create a loop in the butt end of the leader for loop-to-loop connections.*

**Nail Knot:** *(Right)*
*Use a nail, needle or a tube to tie this knot, which connects the forward end of the fly line to the butt end of the leader. Follow with a Perfection Loop and you've got a permanent end loop that allows easy leader changes.*

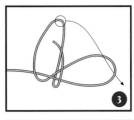

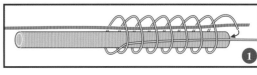

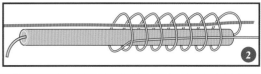

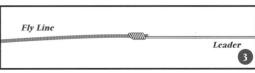

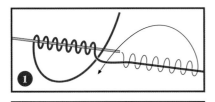

*Fly-fishing icon Lefty Kreh releases a smallmouth back into the Susquehanna. He and other sportsmen such as Bob Clouser have raised concerns about declining smallmouth bass populations on this river. Photo by King Montgomery.*